Genders and Sexualities in the Social Sciences

Series Editors: **Victoria Robinson**, University of Sheffield, UK, and **Diane Richardson**, Newcastle University, UK

Editorial Board: **Raewyn Connell**, University of Sydney, Australia, **Kathy Davis**, Utrecht University, The Netherlands, **Stevi Jackson**, University of York, UK, **Michael Kimmel**, State University of New York, Stony Brook, USA, **Kimiko Kimoto**, Hitotsubashi University, Japan, **Jasbir Puar**, Rutgers University, USA, **Steven Seidman**, State University of New York, Albany, USA, **Carol Smart**, University of Manchester, UK, **Liz Stanley**, University of Edinburgh, UK, **Gill Valentine**, University of Leeds, UK, **Jeffrey Weeks**, South Bank University, UK, **Kath Woodward**, The Open University, UK

Titles include:

Jyothsna Belliappa
GENDER, CLASS AND REFLEXIVE MODERNITY IN INDIA

Edmund Coleman-Fountain
UNDERSTANDING NARRATIVE IDENTITY THROUGH LESBIAN AND GAY YOUTH

Niall Hanlon
MASCULINITIES, CARE AND EQUALITY
Identity and Nurture in Men's Lives

Brian Heaphy, Carol Smart and Anna Einarsdottir (*editors*)
SAME SEX MARRIAGES
New Generations, New Relationships

Sally Hines and Yvette Taylor (*editors*)
SEXUALITIES
Past Reflections, Future Directions

Surya Monro
BISEXUALITY
Identities, Politics, and Theories

Meredith Nash
MAKING 'POSTMODERN' MOTHERS
Pregnant Embodiment, Baby Bumps and Body Image

Meredith Nash
REFRAMING REPRODUCTION
Conceiving Gendered Experiences

Lucy Nicholas
QUEER POST-GENDER ETHICS
The Shape of Selves to Come

Barbara Pini and Bob Pease (*editors*)
MEN, MASCULINITIES AND METHODOLOGIES

Victoria Robinson and Jenny Hockey
MASCULINITIES IN TRANSITION

Francesca Stella
LESBIAN LIVES IN SOVIET AND POST-SOVIET RUSSIA
Post/Socialism and Gendered Sexualities

Shirley Tate
BLACK WOMEN'S BODIES AND THE NATION
Race, Gender and Culture

Yvette Taylor, Sally Hines and Mark E. Casey (*editors*)
THEORIZING INTERSECTIONALITY AND SEXUALITY

Thomas Thurnell-Read and Mark Casey (*editors*)
MEN, MASCULINITIES, TRAVEL AND TOURISM

S. Hines and Y. Taylor (*editors*)
SEXUALITIES: PAST REFLECTIONS, FUTURE DIRECTIONS

Yvette Taylor and Michelle Addison (*editors*)
QUEER PRESENCES AND ABSENCES

Kath Woodward
SEX POWER AND THE GAMES

Genders and Sexualities in the Social Sciences
Series Standing Order ISBN 978–0–230–27254–5 hardback
978–0–230–27255–2 paperback
(*outside North America only*)

You can receive future titles in this series as they are published by placing a standing order. Please contact your bookseller or, in case of difficulty, write to us at the address below with your name and address, the title of the series and the ISBN quoted above.

Customer Services Department, Macmillan Distribution Ltd, Houndmills, Basingstoke, Hampshire RG21 6XS, England

Bisexuality
Identities, Politics, and Theories

Surya Monro
Professor of Sociology and Social Policy, University of Huddersfield, UK

© Surya Monro 2015

All rights reserved. No reproduction, copy or transmission of this publication may be made without written permission.

No portion of this publication may be reproduced, copied or transmitted save with written permission or in accordance with the provisions of the Copyright, Designs and Patents Act 1988, or under the terms of any licence permitting limited copying issued by the Copyright Licensing Agency, Saffron House, 6–10 Kirby Street, London EC1N 8TS.

Any person who does any unauthorized act in relation to this publication may be liable to criminal prosecution and civil claims for damages.

The author has asserted her right to be identified as the author of this work in accordance with the Copyright, Designs and Patents Act 1988.

First published 2015 by
PALGRAVE MACMILLAN

Palgrave Macmillan in the UK is an imprint of Macmillan Publishers Limited, registered in England, company number 785998, of Houndmills, Basingstoke, Hampshire RG21 6XS.

Palgrave Macmillan in the US is a division of St Martin's Press LLC,
175 Fifth Avenue, New York, NY 10010.

Palgrave Macmillan is the global academic imprint of the above companies and has companies and representatives throughout the world.

Palgrave® and Macmillan® are registered trademarks in the United States, the United Kingdom, Europe and other countries.

ISBN 978–1–137–00730–8

This book is printed on paper suitable for recycling and made from fully managed and sustained forest sources. Logging, pulping and manufacturing processes are expected to conform to the environmental regulations of the country of origin.

A catalogue record for this book is available from the British Library.

A catalog record for this book is available from the Library of Congress.

To everyone who is working to make the world a better place for bisexual people

Contents

List of Tables viii

Acknowledgements ix

1 Introduction 1
2 Bisexuality and Social Theory 31
3 Intersectionality 57
4 Sex, Relationships, Kinship, and Community 84
5 Bisexuality, Organisations, and Capitalism 109
6 Bisexuality and Citizenship 133
7 Bisexuality, Activism, Democracy, and the State 155

Bibliography 180

Index 197

Tables

1.1 Characteristics of the UK participants 7
1.2 Characteristics of the Colombian participants 8

Acknowledgements

I would like to thank the University of Huddersfield, UK, for the generous support that has been provided to me in writing this book. Particular thanks are due to Jim McAuley and John Playle. I also wish to thank all the participants in the empirical research, in the UK and in Colombia, for their crucial contributions. I would like in particular to thank Lawrence Brewer, a UK-based bisexual activist who sadly died in 2013.

A number of other people have helped me directly with this project. These include Camilo Tamayo Gómez, who conducted the review of Colombian literature and the fieldwork with Colombian bisexual people, and Ahonaa Roy, who did the web and literature searches on Indian bisexualities and non-heterosexualities as well as providing me with insights about the Indian situation. Antony Osborne assisted me with literature searching and Anna Fry supplied feedback on Chapter 3. Sue Hanson proofed the book and helped with the referencing. I would like to express my heartfelt thanks to all of you.

I am very fortunate in being part of a network of friends, activists, and academics; too many to mention here. People who have helped particularly in inspiring, encouraging, or informing me while I was working on this book include Diane Richardson, Sally Hines, Meg John Barker, Christian Klesse, Gemma Locke, Shiri Eisner, Christina Richardson, Chiara Addis, and Chris Roscoe. Thanks to you, and everyone else who has supported this project. Thanks also to my family, especially my wonderful son Tom, who has had to put up with me spending so much time working.

1
Introduction

Recent years have seen increased support for the equality of same-sex couples in a range of Western countries. There has been a push to include bisexuals together with lesbians and gay men by activists and by state and civil society actors. However, the patterns of stigmatisation and erasure concerning bisexuality also exist. These patterns contrast with the processes of normalisation that have taken place concerning lesbians and gay men in equalities-positive countries such as the UK (see Richardson and Monro, 2012).

The pro-equalities shift that has taken place in some Western nations also contrasts with the huge international challenges concerning basic rights for people who wish to express themselves sexually with others of the same sex. Homosexuality is illegal in 78 countries and is punishable by death in Mauritania, Sudan, Iran, Saudi Arabia, Yemen, and parts of Nigeria and Somalia (Itaborahy and Zhu, 2014). In countries where state-sponsored persecution of people who engage in same-sex sexual acts takes place, it is the same-sex expression that is the key issue, not the individual's identification as bisexual, gay, or lesbian. Same-sex sexualities may be termed 'homosexual' in these countries, but they can be engaged in by people who are only attracted to those of the same sex, or by those who are attracted to people of different sexes. However, it is same-sex sexualities that engender punitive sanctions, not an individual having both same-sex and opposite-sex desires or behaviours, so that focusing only on 'bisexuals' or 'bisexuality' in an international context is a flawed approach. At the same time, internationally, bisexuals are affected by punitive laws against homosexuality, and so the term 'bisexual' has some purchase.

Within an international context, there is another analytical trajectory that requires exploration. Overall, the categories of lesbian, gay, bisexual, and transgender (LGBT) can be seen as limited in scope and imagination, erasing as they do the many and varied forms of sexual and gender identities that have existed – and do exist – internationally. As Evelyn Blackwood argues:

> From a Western viewpoint, sexuality constitutes an essential or core attribute of identity; individuals are said to have fixed sexual identities or orientations. Sexuality as it is understood in the United States and Europe, however, often bears little resemblance to sexual relationships and practices across cultures.
>
> (2000, p.223)

Building on Blackwood's ideas, it can be argued that a Western attachment to 'fixing and naming' sexual orientations and identities can marginalise or erase other ways of doing things. Marking and claiming behaviours as constituting particular sexual identities can be problematic; it may render indigenous sexualities visible and open to interrogation, sanctions, and persecution. At the same time, the Western-originated categories of 'LGBT' form a common parlance, the importance of which cannot be denied when it comes to effecting political and social change and tackling human rights abuses against people whose desires are not limited to people of the opposite sex. The book therefore begins with the premise that the term 'bisexuality', like 'gay', 'lesbian', 'transgender', and 'heterosexual', may be useful at this particular time in anglophone countries, and perhaps in others as well, depending on the politics of those particular countries. Some actors in Southern countries both engage with and develop notions of bisexuality and discourses (sets of ideas) of bisexual rights (see, for example, the Colombian situation (Serrano, 2003, 2010)). This trend will be explored further in the chapters on intersectionality (Chapter 3) and on activism, democracy, and the state (Chapter 7).

This book takes bisexuality as its focus because of the academic marginalisation of bisexuality (see below), which has created a substantial gap in contemporary sexualities literature. The book is needed because bisexuality plays out differently to lesbian and gay identities in relation to a number of key processes. These concern, for instance, the relationship between hegemonic heterosexualities and non-heterosexualities, sexuality-related prejudices and their material impacts, and the interfaces between individuals and state institutions. Bisexuality raises important issues concerning identity construction and its social and political ramifications. This is partly due to the complex and fluid nature of bisexual identities, which are different from the more bounded and static identities assumed by lesbians, gay men and heterosexuals, and partly because of the fragmented and partially submerged nature of the bisexual population.

This book develops theory regarding bisexuality, grounded in analysis of key aspects of bisexual peoples' lives, such as identity construction, relationships and community, experience of workplace organisations, and political activism. In its engagement with key bodies of theory associated with sociology and political science, it will begin to map out territory which is largely uncharted. The text does not attempt to provide a comprehensive analysis of any areas; it summarises progress to date, develops theory using empirical research data, and indicates trajectories which may be of interest for future scholarly activities. In so doing, it attempts also to foreground the lived experiences of people who are bisexual, and those who identify as other than heterosexual, lesbian or gay. The book is largely situated within the trajectory of critical bisexuality studies, encouraging readers to 'interrogate the concept of bisexuality: to think critically about where it has come from and how its origins continue to shape it in contemporary debates' (Storr, 1999, p.1). I build on the work of authors such as Michael Du Plessis (1996), Clare Hemmings (2007), Merl Storr (1999a), and Stephen Angelides (2001), and I contribute to debates raised by contemporary critical bisexuality scholars, such as Shiri Eisner (2014).

There are some areas of possible conceptual development of the field of bisexuality studies (and indeed sexuality and gender studies more broadly) that I wish to flag up in this Introduction because they might prove important for future research. The first of these concerns temporality as discussed by social scientists such as Pierre Bourdieu (cited in Jenkins, 1992):

> Temporality, the inexorable passage of time, is an axiomatic feature of practice: time is both a constraint and a resource for social interaction... Time, and the sense of it, is, of course, socially constructed; it is, however, socially constructed out of natural cycles – days and nights.
>
> (Jenkins, 1992, p.69)

Temporality is important for understanding bisexuality, because if the entire lifecycle of an individual is considered, rather than a particular point in that lifecycle, then the likelihood of behavioural bisexuality (sexual desires or behaviours towards other people of more than one gender) is much greater. If a temporal approach to theorising sexuality is taken, it could be that heterosexual, lesbian, and gay identifications become understood as 'phases' for many people, in a larger pattern of behavioural bisexuality across the life span.

The notion of temporal sexualities can be taken further by using the notion of reincarnation drawn from Buddhism and Hinduism (see, for example, Peter Bishop, 1993). In an approach to bisexuality that seeks to avoid Western-centrism, it is arguably important to consider approaches that look at reincarnation philosophies and other ways of conceptualising subjectivity and consciousness. In Monro (2010a), I mention reincarnation in relation to Indian genders and sexualities and indicate some of the parallels between early Indian philosophies and post-structural approaches, as discussed by, for example, Ruth Vanita and Saleem Kidwai (2001). If reincarnation was to be 'real', then temporalised identities would extend not over the course of one lifetime but many. The 'soul' that incarnates could have different gender identities, physical sexes, and sexual identities, shaped by the social context into which it was born as well as internal predilections.

If an ontological position that reflects the ideas of temporality and reincarnation was taken, then varied gendered/sexual identities might become seen as the usual pattern across lifetimes, even if an individual experiences themselves as having a very fixed gender and sexual identity in a particular incarnation. There could therefore be another axis for understanding gender and sexual identities: fixed or essentialised identities on the one hand (for example, people experiencing themselves as having essentialised gay identities, set within a particular socio-material context) and fluid, mutable, and sometimes liminal (beyond categories) identities on the other. In such a context, conflicts between different identity-based groups (as discussed later in the book) could be interpreted as primarily about access to material resources distributed according to particular socio-political structures (based around, for example, heterosexual couplehood), rather than the 'validity' of any particular identities over others.

A materialist critique of the systems of categorisation that have emerged concerning gender and sexuality is certainly pertinent to understanding bisexuality, and unlike the two themes noted above (temporality and reincarnation), this will be pursued later in the book. Victorian society played a major role in the construction of contemporary, internationally used systems of gender and sexual categorisation. Colonialism and imperialism lent weight, internationally, to the European systems of gender and sexual categorisation which underpin the modern heterosexual/homosexual/bisexual forms of categorisation (see MacDowell, 2009). This had a material basis in colonial efforts to secure and maintain hierarchical systems and access to material privileges – those of white, European, heterosexual people. Thus, there has been a materialist demarcation and essentialisation of sexual identities, which has arguably cramped potentials for fluidity and liminality.

The structure of this chapter

The chapter begins by outlining the methods used for the research that is presented in this book. It then provides a brief historical and cross-cultural contextualisation of non-heterosexual sexualities, charts the development of the notion of 'bisexuality', and situates the text within bisexuality studies and gender/sexuality scholarship more broadly. Definitions of bisexuality and key related terms are discussed. The chapter then looks at prejudice against bisexuality. An outline of the subsequent chapters is then provided. The chapter uses, perhaps unusually, some empirical material in its sections on definitions of bisexuality and biphobia. This is because the evolution of these terms is ongoing, and I wish to highlight their complex and contingent nature at the beginning of the book.

Methods

This book uses research materials that stem from four countries: India, USA, Colombia, and the UK. The choice of countries was made in order to represent both the global South and the global North/West. The majority of the empirical material comes from the UK, and it would be useful for further research to address bisexualities and non-heterosexualities in other countries – especially Southern and Eastern countries – in more depth, given the historical dominance of anglophone scholarship in this area.

The book draws on 40 semi-structured interviews with individuals in the UK and Colombia. The core interviews were conducted with a range of people who identify as bisexual, queer, or non-heterosexual, in the UK (24 interviewees) and Colombia (six interviewees). A further ten interviews were conducted with people involved in the UK fetish and bondage, domination, submission, and masochism (BDSM) communities in 2006 (more details about these projects are provided below). This book also used analysis of web material and research literature, specifically from India, the USA, and the UK. The UK and Colombian empirical research was conducted in 2012, as was the web analysis of Indian sexualities. It should be noted that the UK-based qualitative interviews were supplemented by my participant observation, as a bisexual person, in the UK bisexual communities in the 1998–2014 period; this is drawn on mostly in Chapter 7 and I have made it clear where it is used.

For the UK research, qualitative interviews were conducted with 22 individuals, and a further two individuals filled in the extensive semi-structured interview schedule (due to their personal preferences to contribute in written form). Snowball or purposive sampling was conducted using the following criteria: age, gender, sexual orientation, ethnic heritage, ability/disability, class background and current identification, links with alternative communities (other than bisexuality-related), and location in the UK. Using snowball approaches and existing networks, the sampling strategy enabled recruitment of people who were somewhat representative across these different criteria. Both monosexual and non-monosexual people were included in the study. In addition, efforts were made to include people who were not part of the organised bisexual communities, as well as those who were, and parents, as well as non-parents. The sampling strategy was broadly successful, but there is over-representation of some groups, notably people from Northern England, 30–50-year-olds, and those involved in the organised bisexual communities. The term 'organised bisexual communities' is used in the book to mean those networks and groupings of people who identify as bisexual and who have established groups, events, and organisations. It is recognised that the term is problematic; not everyone linked to these communities is bisexual, and other groupings of people who are bisexual may exist outside of these 'organised bisexual communities'.

It is not possible to identify each participant by their social characteristics in the analysis of findings provided in the book, as this could lead to the identification of individuals. However, a table is provided in order to demonstrate the key characteristics (Table 1.1).

Findings were anonymised, or if preferred the individual's first name only was used, with the following exceptions who wished to be fully named: Meg John Barker, Lawrence Brewer, Grant Denkinson, and Christian Klesse.

The UK bisexuality research took an *a priori* approach (see Gibbs, 2007), in which research themes were identified in advance. The key themes around which the questions were developed were as follows: bisexual identities and their construction; bisexual and other communities; biphobia; intersectionality; sexuality, kinship, and relationships;

Table 1.1 Characteristics of the UK participants

Age	21–30 (2), 31–40 (13), 41–50 (6), 51–60 (2), not answered (1)
Gender identity	Female (11), male (7), male/genderqueer (1), transman (1), genderqueer (2), questioning/unsure (diagnosis of intersex condition at puberty) (1), not answered (1)
Ethnic heritage	British Asian (1), mixed heritage (3), white English/British (10), white/Caucasian (1), white European (2), black British (1), Chinese (2), white other (3), non-white European (1)
Sexual orientation	Bisexual (18), queer/bisexual (2), queer (2), undecided – probably bisexual (1), not answered (1)
Disabled	Yes (7), No (16), not answered (1)
Class background	Working class (6), mixed working class/middle class (2), lower middle class (1), middle class (4), upper middle class (2), mixed working class and upper class (1), don't know (2), not answered (5), don't identify with class (1)
Current class identification	Working class (5), lower middle class (1), middle class (11), mixed working class/middle class (1), middle class with some working class experience (1), don't know (2), don't identify with class (1), not answered (1)
Active links with bisexual communities/networks	Yes (16), no (8)
Links with alternative communities (e.g. kink, swingers, goths)	Yes (16: queer, LGBT, trans, black/BME/people of colour, kink, BDSM, sexual freedom, anti-censorship, civil libertarians, secularists, humanist, vegetarians, vegans, fannish/fandom, folk, indie and goth/rock music scenes, boating community, deaf community, cross dressing, swinger, poly, asexuality, outsider art/music, mad pride, ex squatter, anarchist); no (4); not answered (4)
Location	Southern England (3), Midlands (3), Northern England (17), Scotland (1)

employment; the commodification of bisexuality; activism; and democracy and the state. The interview data and the data from the two semi-structured interviews that were completed in written form were then analysed using a thematic approach (Braun and Clarke, 2006).

Table 1.2 Characteristics of the Colombian participants

Age	21–30 (2), 31–40 (2); 41–50 (2)
Gender identity	Female (2), male (2), transgender male (1), transgender female (1)
Sexual orientation	Bisexual (1), not given (5)
Current class position (inferred from occupation)	Working class (2), middle class (3), unclear (1)
Active links with bisexual communities/networks	Yes (1), links with sexuality/gender activism but not specified if bisexual-specific (1), no (4)
Location	Bogotá (2), Cali (1), Medellín (1), Barranquilla (1), Pasto (1)

The Colombian research followed a similar approach to that of the UK. A qualitative interview schedule was developed which addressed the themes above and purposive/opportunity sampling was undertaken by a Colombian colleague, Camilo Tamayo Gómez, who conducted the interviews in Spanish and then transcribed key quotes and translated them into English. First names were used, as the participants expressed no preferences about anonymisation/non-anonymisation. Some of the characteristics of the participants were recorded; see Table 1.2.

For the Indian research, a framework with the key themes for the research was developed drawing on the UK and Colombian research instruments, and an Indian colleague, Dr Ahonaa Roy, conducted web searches and blog and literature analysis in order to generate materials which could be used in providing an Indian perspective. Both Indian and US case studies drew on existing autobiographical and activist contributions, such as Robyn Ochs and Sarah E. Rowley's (2009) *Getting Bi: Voices of Bisexuals Around the World*. There was extremely limited funding for the project and a decision was made to use what resources there were to fund two emerging scholars (Roy and Gómez) to conduct research in the global South in order to begin to counter the anglophone bias in the literature. For the US case study, existing literature formed the main source of material.

Chapter 4, 'Sex, Relationships, Kinship, and Community', draws on empirical material from a further qualitative project conducted by Monro in order to enable analysis of the overlaps and divergences between the bisexual and BDSM communities. The original aim of the research was to address the identities of people taking part in the 'scenes' (communities/spaces) associated with BDSM (also known as 'kink') and the norms and institutional practices found in these scenes. The research was conducted in 2006 with five BDSM and fetish club organisers and five participants in BDSM clubs and activities. The sample included people with a mixture of sexual orientations and genders (all identifying as either male or female; nine cisgender (born as the sex they continue to identify with) and one trans male). Nine of the participants were white and one was British Asian. The sample was obtained using a snowball technique and was accessed via known gatekeepers. In-depth interviews were conducted; questions included the sexual and gender roles that people took within the BDSM scene, power dynamics, the self-regulation of the 'scenes', and intersectional issues. The findings were anonymised and analysed in relation to the themes pertinent to the book on bisexuality.

Bisexuality: A brief historical and cross-cultural contextualisation

This section of the chapter provides an overview of key themes concerning the historical and cross-cultural construction of non-heterosexualities, including bisexualities. It is difficult to discuss bisexualities without also discussing same-sex sexualities, as bisexuality encompasses both heterosexual (opposite-sex) and homosexual (defined here as same-sex) desires and sexual activities, as well as those between people of gender identifications that are other than male or female.

Authors such as Ron Fox (1998) provide evidence that sexual attractions and/or sexual behaviours towards people of different genders have existed throughout history and across many cultures. For example, a growing body of literature disputes the notion of exclusive heterosexuality across Africa (see Epprecht, 2006). Mark Blasius and Shane Phelan argue that 'Same-sex love is a phenomenon common to almost every culture, one occurring throughout recorded history' (1997, p.2).

It can be difficult to trace the existence of bisexualities, historically and cross-culturally. As Fox (1998) notes, the notion of 'bisexuality' is often erased from anthropological and historical discussions about sexualities (see also Epprecht, 2006). However, the literatures about pre-modern and cross-cultural sexualities do provide a means of beginning to explore different forms of sexuality, gender identity, and intimate relationships. These can be mapped out in the following way (following Fox, 1998):

Gender role variance: This is where individuals take the role traditionally associated with the other sex, including sexual identity and expressions. Variations are present amongst some Native American two-spirit people and Indian hijras, but also, for instance, in Madagascar, Samoa, and several African and Latin American countries (see, for example, Murray and Roscoe, 1998). Gender role variance may be linked with a formulation of sexual difference based around an active/passive dichotomy (amongst cisgender males); the active partner (penetrator) may have sex with both men and women but is considered to be heterosexual, whilst the passive partner (male recipient) is seen as homosexual. For example, the male-bodied *homosexuals* of Dakar in Senegal form two groups: the *oubis* who are effeminate and who are penetrated during sex and the *yauss* who penetrate the *oubis* during sex (see Teunis, 2001).

Egalitarian same-sex relationships: These may involve sexual and/or emotional relationships and sexual activities which are not necessarily linked to particular identities, as well as those that are identity-oriented. They include people who engage in homosexual and heterosexual behaviours in tandem, for example, the *motsoalle* – an intimate female partner who often coexisted with a woman's husband, as found amongst earlier generations in Lesotho (Blackwood, 2000; see also Epprecht, 2008). As Fox (1998) indicates, contemporary lesbian, gay, and bisexual (LGB) relationships also fall within the 'egalitarian' category. Of course, all of these types of relations may not actually be egalitarian, but they would usually have a more equal power distribution than some of the initiatory relationships discussed next.

Initiatory relationships: These take place when individuals of different ages form temporary relationships or engage in sexual practices for a certain period of time. For instance, Joseph Boone (2010) discusses the ways in which same-sex male erotic practices in the Middle East (that would now be identified as child abuse if minors were involved) were institutionalised for hundreds of years. In another, more contemporary set of examples, Evelyn Blackwood (2000) discusses *intimate friendships*, such as culturally sanctioned 'mummy-baby' relationships in Lesotho, where older and younger females have close, sometimes sexual, relationships, sometimes in tandem with having boyfriends; *erotic ritual practices* such as the sexual initiation ceremonies found amongst Australian aboriginal women and girls, and *adolescent sex play* found amongst the !Kung of Southern Africa.

These different types of identity and behaviour indicate the widespread nature of what could be termed 'bisexuality'. However, it would be a dangerous generalisation to claim that bisexuality is universal, historically and cross-culturally. It may be that the expression of bisexuality is largely contingent on social and historical specificities.

Following Gilbert Herdt (1984), societies vary in their social norms concerning sexuality due to factors such as economic structure and sexual stratification. For example, some Melanesian societies had sexual norms that steered young males towards same-sex sexualities for a few years; these norms were congruent with 'harsh taboos associated with premarital heterosexuality, virginity in women, and adultery' (1984, p.163 in Storr, 1999a). These young males might be interpreted as behavioural bisexuals but the reasons for their behaviours, and the identities that these behaviours are connected to, were very different to those associated with Western bisexualities. Such variations point away from any kind of 'universal' bisexuality, even if sexual behaviours and desires towards persons of different genders are fairly ubiquitous.

The origins of the term 'bisexuality' and the formation of homosexual, heterosexual, and bisexual categories

The term 'bisexuality' stemmed initially from Middle Eastern and Southern European cultures, and then from Western science. This section of the chapter outlines historical definitions of bisexuality, and the ways in which they evolved, set within the context of Western imperialism. It provides further evidence supporting Herdt's (1984) argument above, that sexual and gender categories are historically and socially contingent.

The early, mostly theological use of the terms 'bisexed' or 'bisexous' in Europe related to ideas of primordial androgyny, drawing on Ancient Greek and Near Eastern mythology. These were superseded in 1859 in the West by the introduction of the term 'bisexuality' by anatomist Robert Bentley Todd, who was writing at the same time as Charles Darwin. Therefore:

> From the middle of the nineteenth century, the term *bisexuality* is used in the fields of anatomy and physiology to refer to forms of life that are sexually undifferentiated or thought to exhibit characteristics of both sexes. By the early years of the 20th century, bisexuality is used to describe a combination of masculinity and femininity in an individual – psychical rather than physical traits – and had also come to signify a sexual attraction to individuals of both sexes... although the three meanings of bisexuality – a combination of male/female, masculine/feminine, or heterosexual/homosexual – have different histories, they are far from distinct.
>
> (MacDowell, 2009, p.4)

These three uses of the term 'bisexuality' were forged via, and in relation to, socio-political developments. The Western social construction of contemporary bisexualities revolved around three main, interlinked, axes. The first axis concerned structural dynamics associated with industrialisation and the development of capitalism. As Donald Hall suggests, 'Capitalism demands specialization and categorisation for most efficient operation and is inextricably intertwined with patterns of social organisation beyond the realm of the strictly economic' (1996a, p.101). Following Michel Foucault (for example, 1977), Hall argued that the development of binary notions of heterosexuality and homosexuality in Victorian times reordered the mechanisms with which people constructed their identities; only two rigidly and mutually exclusive sexual identities (heterosexuality and homosexuality) were seen as possible and 'Activities once encompassed within an overall notion of an ecstatic, perverse, libertine sexuality were dichotomised into notions of oppositional sexualities' (1996a, p.102). In other words, society became increasingly rigidly structured; for example, individuals took more specific and more heavily gendered domestic and employment roles when communities moved from agrarian and craft-based work to factory and white-collar work. This was combined with a shift away from female-centric emotional (and sometimes sexual) relations amongst women (see Rust, 2000, 2000a), and more fluid erotic possibilities generally, so that 'the same nineteenth century beliefs in the mutual exclusivity of womanhood and manhood and in the inescapable importance of gender that produced concepts of gendered eroticism also produced the belief that sexual attraction must be directed towards *either* men or women' (Rust, 2000a, p.206). For some theorists (for example, Angelides, 2001), the dominant modern categories of sexuality (heterosexual, homosexual) are dependent for their existence on the absence of bisexuality.

The second set of dynamics within which contemporary LGB and heterosexual categories have been forged concern those of imperialism, colonialism, and racial inequality. Merl Storr (1999a) suggests that the development of the modern categories of 'male', 'female', 'homosexual', and 'heterosexual' was intertwined with the development of other categories, including that of 'race', as part of the colonial project of mapping and imperial conquest. In other words, people in colonising countries (such as England) sought to map out, and regulate, not only land but also peoples' identities. Mark Epprecht, following Michel Foucault, contends that the rising class of bourgeoisie (middle classes) in industrialising Western countries 'promoted ideas that served their material interests' (2006, p.189). These included the idea that certain groups (sexual and racial 'others') were less suited to govern others and to enjoy economic and social privileges. Non-heterosexual and non-white 'others' formed groups against which the Western, white middle classes could construct themselves as 'superior' (see Williams and Chrisman *et al.*, 1993). Overall, different forms of hierarchical categorisation (such as gender, sexuality, ethnicity, and socio-economic class) were consolidated and then used by those with the most social power to subordinate others.

Science provided the third main axis around which the homosexual/heterosexual and bisexual systems of categorisation developed in the 19th century and subsequently. The imperialist project was linked with the development of scientific knowledge, including the hierarchical ordering of categories. The psychomedical discourses which developed between the mid-1800s and the 1960s were linked with a patriarchal and race-based assertion of power: women and non-white people were framed as 'less evolved' than men and white people (patriarchal is defined here as the domination of females by males). Discourses of sexual science developed to establish supposed scientific evidence for innate differences between different sexes, races, and classes, so that the dominance of white men could be justified and bolstered (Angelides, 2001). It was in this context that the hugely influential sexologists developed their systems of homosexual, heterosexual, and bisexual classification.

Before looking at the work of the sexologists, there is a need for some clarification and contextualisation of the above discussion. The 19th century evolution of sex/gender categories appears to stem from a basis in material power struggles. The influence of these systems of identity categorisation, as tied to the colonial project, has been enormous. The homophobic, and by default biphobic, legacy left by Western legal and normative systems is highly influential today; homophobia, which is present in many Southern countries, can be traced to the laws and religious norms imposed by Western colonisers, for example, in India (Thomas *et al.*, 2011). However, the modern colonial and industrial era is not the only one in which systems of sex/gender categorisation have been imposed on individual subjects as part of materially grounded social structuring processes. For example, ancient Roman societies were heavily structured in ways that we can now interpret as highly problematic. In Rome, relations between males took place mostly between adult men and their male slaves (or in some cases male prostitutes). These subordinate males took a passive role and the freemen used aggressive, violent sexual acts to bolster their social position (Cantarella, 1992). Eve Cantarella (1992) notes that from the Augustan period onwards, there are accounts of what appear to be romantic, consensual sexual relationships between free men (although the pederastic model continued). It is around that time that laws emerged with penalties against both active and passive same-sex male sexualities. This could indicate that romantic, consensual sex between male adults was disrupting the hierarchical structures of Roman society, provoking a need for governors to contain and prevent love-based same-sex expressions. Therefore, when analysing the evolution of modern sexualities, it is important to be mindful that dynamics concerning the interplay of power, social control, and the hierarchical distribution of material resources based on the classification of people into categories is not just a modern Western phenomenon.

Sexologists and the evolution of 'bisexuality'

During the 19th century, medicine became increasingly dominant as a framework within which sex and gender identities were constituted in the West (see Weeks, 1977). Sexologists such as Richard von Krafft-Ebing and Henry Havelock Ellis were highly influential in the formation of sexual categories, including bisexuality (see Storr, 1999a). They initially termed sexual attraction to both men and women as 'psychosexual hermaphroditism' (see above and Ellis, 1897). However, by 1915 Havelock Ellis had begun to use the term 'bisexual' for people who were attracted to both sexes, and he categorised people into three types: heterosexual, homosexual, and bisexual. This appears to have been a key point in the development of contemporary notions of bisexuality.

Another important strand of early theorising about bisexuality came from Sigmund Freud and his contemporaries, such as Wilhelm Fleiss (Storr, 1999a). Freud's ideas about bisexuality were ambiguous and contradictory (Strachey, 1953; see also Angelides, 2001). Overall, he rejected the essentialism of the early sexologists (who saw sexual identities as having an innate, organic cause) and instead argued in some parts of his work that bisexuality was the original form of sexuality, found amongst children and the so-called 'primitive races'. As Storr (1999a) indicates, this very problematic, racialised and hierarchical framing of bisexuality mirrors broader patterns of imperialism and inequality, in which some ethnic groups and some people with sexual identities were framed as less 'advanced' than others. Angelides (2001) describes the ways in which, post 1900s, heterosexual and homosexual oppositional categories were consolidated in an ongoing way via psychomedical discourses, excluding bisexuality.

However, other developments were also taking place, which ran counter to the hegemonic project of 'fixing and freezing' bisexuality as an inferior category, or excluding it from consideration altogether. Of the sexological and psychological approaches, there were some early attempts to depathologise and indeed celebrate bisexuality, notably in the work of Wilhelm Stekel (1950 [1922]) who 'boldly asserts that everyone is innately bisexual and that monosexuality – exclusive heterosexuality or homosexuality – is unnatural' (Storr, 1999a, p.28). Later that century, the research conducted by US-based Alfred Kinsey and colleagues (1948, 1953) became hugely influential. It differed from much previous scholarship because of its basis in large-scale empirical research, although as Storr (1999a) says, there are questions about the reliability and validity of the data. Kinsey and his colleagues developed a scale of sexual identities (or orientations), from exclusively heterosexual (a Kinsey '0') to exclusively homosexual (a Kinsey '6'). Kinsey and his colleagues suggested that a considerable proportion of the population had sexual activities, experiences or sexual responses with (or towards) people of both sexes at some time.

Fritz Klein (1978) followed Kinsey's work by developing a more nuanced approach to categorising sexuality, known as the Klein Sexual Orientation Grid (KSOG). This addresses individual sexual identities in the past, present, and possible future, using a seven point scale (ranging from same-sex only to opposite-sex only). It includes factors such as sexual attraction, behaviour, and fantasies; emotional, social, and lifestyle preferences; and self-identification. This seminal work spawned, in turn, a range of other approaches. For example, James Weinrich and Fritz Klein (2002), using results from a large online survey, modelled three subgroups within the bisexual population: 'Bi-Gay', 'Bi-Straight', and 'Bi-Bi'. As well as the work of Klein and colleagues, a number of other important books about bisexuality were published in the 1970s, including Margaret Mead's *Bisexuality: What's It All About?* (1975) and Charlotte Wolff's (1979) *Bisexuality: A Study* (see Storr, 1999a).

The second half of the 20th century, therefore, saw the development of typographies and systems of categorisation that are supportive of a range of sexual identities, and that do not necessarily either erase or marginalise bisexuality. There was, to a degree, a movement away from medicalising approaches, towards nuanced models such as the KSOG which provide a means of challenging sedimented, hierarchical structures of heterosexism, and notions that only discrete heterosexual and homosexual identities exist. This trend was set within the context of the burgeoning movement for the rights of sexual minorities in the USA and the UK (see Richardson and Monro, 2012). Fox (1996) suggests that a more affirmative approach to bisexuality developed due to changes in the conceptualisation of bisexuality itself, in particular more acknowledgement of bisexuality as a valid identity category. He discusses the beginnings of a critical interrogation of the binary model of sexual orientation (sexual orientation is defined here as 'an individual's physical, emotional, and erotic attractions to others' by Patrick Mulick and Lester Wright 2002, p.47). Overall, therefore, the pathologising models of bisexuality that developed during the late 19th century and early 20th century were to some extent supplanted by the work of later sexologists, as well as the social movements associated with gay, lesbian, bisexual, and trans emancipation (see Chapter 7).

Key literatures

Whilst a small glut of anglophone bisexuality-related scholarship was produced in the 1970s, little bisexual scholarship emerged in the USA and the UK between the late 1970s and the 1990s (George, 2002). During the 1990s and the early 2000s, there was a mushrooming of reparative bisexual studies in the USA and the UK (see Rose et al., 1996; MacDowall, 2009). In other words, a body of literature developed which addresses the stigmatisation of bisexuality and/or its erasure of bisexuality from psychological, political, and sociological discussions. This literature includes interdisciplinary collections (for instance, Firestein, 1996; Rust, 2000; Atkins, 2002); collections drawing on – and contributing to – cultural theory (Garber, 1995; Bi Academic Intervention, 1997); psychology (Barker, 2004, 2007; Barker and Langdridge, 2008; Bowes-Catton et al., 2011); education (Jones and Hillier, 2014; Robinson, 2014); anthropology (Herdt, 1984; Blackwood, 2000); sexology (Cerny and Janssen, 2011); cultural geography (Hemmings, 2002); cultural studies more broadly (for example, Bryant, 1997; Braziel, 2004), feminism (Weise, 1992) and theology (Hutchins, 2002). Those contributions specifically relevant to sociologies include Paula Rust's work on bisexual identities (1996, 2000) and Martin Weinberg et al.'s (1994) study of bisexuality in the San Francisco area (see also Highleyman, 1995; Steinman, 2011; Anderson et al., 2014; McCormack, 2014). Some interdisciplinary contributions are also available, notably Fox's (2004) comprehensive annotated bibliography of literatures of relevance to bisexuality as well as the many contributions contained in the *Journal of Bisexuality*.

Whilst these studies about bisexuality have largely stemmed from people affiliated with the bisexual communities, another very substantial strand of studies has come from the medical communities as a reaction to the HIV/AIDS crisis (for example, Doll and Beeker, 1996; Morrow and Allsworth, 2000; Sandfort and Dodge, 2008; Reddy *et al.*, 2012). Concern about HIV/AIDS transmission has been a major force behind research about bisexuality amongst males since the 1980s (Storr, 1999a); this concern is reflected in the literature internationally, for example there are a large number of studies relating to Men who have Sex with Men (MSM) and HIV in China (see Yun *et al.*, 2012).

There is also some scholarship that takes a political science approach, for example, Mark McLelland and Katsushiko Suganama's (2010) scholarship on sexual minorities and human rights in Japan, which documents the emergence of politicised discourses of lesbian and gay rights but notes an absence of a bisexual movement in that country to date. A substantial body of literature is emerging in Latin America relating to LGBT politics generally (see, for example, Corrales and Pecheney, 2010). Little Western scholarship about bisexuality speaks directly to political science. However, Surya Monro (2005), Diane Richardson and Monro (2012), Matthew Waites (2009, 2009a), and Waites and Kelly Kollman (2011) have begun to integrate analysis of bisexuality with broader political science discussion of sexualities (see Chapter 7 for a fuller literature review). There are substantial, largely anecdotal contributions concerning identity politics in the reparative bisexual literature discussed above, for example, Kevin Lano (1996) (identity politics is defined here as 'political organizing based on membership of a group or class' following Liz A. Highleyman, 1995).

This text is situated within the social sciences branch of the bisexualities literature (specifically, sociology, and political science), but also within sexuality studies more broadly. As such, it straddles (and begins to integrate) two largely disparate bodies of literature: the fairly small, largely bisexual-originated bisexualities literature discussed above, and the much larger literatures centred on sexualities and feminisms (Jackson and Scott, 1996; Richardson, 2008); queer theory (Sedgewick, 1991; Warner, 1993; Seidman, 1997); sociology (Weeks, 1968, 1977, 1985, 2009; Altman, 1993; Plummer, 1995; Richardson, 2000), and political science (Riggle and Tadlock, 1999; Dugan, 2005; Smith, 2008). There is some scholarship addressing other areas of sexualities that are also relevant to understanding some bisexualities, for example, Robin Bauer's (2014) study of BDSM. In addition, some of the broader sexualities literature does include bisexuality (for instance, Beemyn and Eliason, 1996) as does some scholarship concerning queer identities (for example, Klesse's, 2007 UK-based study). However, much of the 'LGBT' literature either overlooks or marginalises bisexualities, or subsumes bisexualities into other identities.

Academic scholarship is, of course, specific to the social context from which it stems, and since the 1970s, the anglophone bisexual communities have developed largely separately from the lesbian and gay communities. This may be due to a number of reasons, including exclusion and stigmatisation by lesbians and gay men, as well as a focus on different relationship and social norms (see Chapter 4). Perhaps this is why, during the 1970s and subsequently, there was a silence concerning bisexuality (especially identity-based bisexuality as opposed to behavioural bisexuality) within sexuality studies, as demonstrated in the work of influential scholars, for example, Ken Plummer (1975), Lillian Faderman (1981), and others (for example, Cooper, 1994). For instance, Plummer discusses married men having sex with other men in public places, but does not mention bisexuality, and his typology of homosexuality (1975, p.98) incorporates men who are having sex with men and women as 'homosexual', thereby rendering bisexuality invisible. It appears that erasure of bisexuality in the sexualities scholarship of this period may have be carried through into subsequent social and political science scholarship (for instance, many of the contributions in Tremblay *et al.*, 2011). The sociological and political science silences regarding bisexuality seem to have been compounded by the influence of queer theory (see Warner, 1993), so that the queer deconstruction of identity categories on the one hand and the reassertion of the more dominant lesbian and gay identities on the other has rendered bisexuality largely absent from the field of lesbian and gay (LG), LGBT, and queer studies, despite the inclusion of the word 'bisexual' in the 'LGBT' acronym (see Chapter 2). Overall, therefore, this book addresses a large gap in the literature.

The definition of bisexuality and related terms

This section of the chapter provides contemporary definitions of bisexuality and examines these critically in relation to some other terms. It draws on the empirical material from the UK bisexuality project in order to demonstrate variations in definitions of bisexuality, as well as diversities concerning peoples' identification as bisexual (or not). The chapter does not provide general definitions regarding gender and sexuality, as these are well-rehearsed elsewhere (see, for example, Richardson and Robinson, 2008).

The three historically grounded interpretations of bisexuality outlined above (biological, gender identity, or sexual identity) have continued to influence developments concerning sexuality. However, the 'bisexuality as relating to sexual identities and acts' interpretation is the most common in contemporary anglophone society. It is worth pointing out that the term 'bi' is sometimes used as shorthand for bisexuality and bisexual people. Since the 1980s, two distinct (if overlapping) forms of bisexuality have also been documented: bisexuality as a sexual identity, and bisexuality as sexual practices with people of different genders, which is often known as 'behavioural bisexuality' or 'situational bisexuality' (see Rust, 2000; MacDowall, 2009).

Overall, in anglophone contexts, the term 'bisexual' is widely used both as an adjective to refer to sex acts and attractions to both same-sex and other-sex persons (see, for example, Rust, 2000), and as a noun to refer to bisexual people. This usage was reflected in some of the narratives provided by bisexual people in the UK research. For example, when I asked Anne how she defined bisexuality, she said, 'wanting to have emotional and sexual relationships with both men and women'. It is also reflected in some of the UK equalities legislation, which refers to attraction to same and other-sex people (see Mitchell *et al.*, 2008).

The notion of 'bisexuality' is itself flawed for a number of reasons. As Rust contends, 'the term *bisexual* itself is problematic because it incorporates a dualistic understanding of sexuality, in which bisexuality is composed of parts of heterosexuality and homosexuality, which many bisexuals reject (Rust, 2000, p.xvi). For Storr (1999b), there are also difficulties with the notion of behavioural bisexuality. Like notions of identity-based bisexuality, it is dualistic and it can also involve a reductive notion of human sexuality, excluding aspects such as fantasy. The KSOG is broader, but as Storr argues, even this excludes aspects of sexuality such as personal body image and understanding of erogenous zones. Critiques of the notion of bisexuality also come from other sources, as indicated earlier in the chapter. As Epprecht (2006) argues, it is questionable as to whether the same/other sex sexualities found in some parts of Africa, for example, should be termed 'bisexual'. Internationally, there is a plethora of locality and community or ethnicity based terms for what could be seen as behavioural bisexuality, for instance the 'Down Low' (DL) lifestyle in the USA (see Pettaway *et al.*, 2014). Being 'on the Down Low' involves publically identifying as heterosexual but being behaviourally bisexual. The term is associated with African American men (Heath and Goggin, 2009) although according to the San Francisco Human Rights Commission LGBT Advisory Committee (undated) it is not specific to African American men. 'Down Low' is also a problematic term, as it has become freighted with racialised stigma (see Sandfort and Dodge, 2008; Ward, 2008).

It is important to point out that there are also difficulties with other terms relating to sexuality, such as 'heterosexual', 'lesbian', 'gay', and 'sexual orientation'. For instance, in a UK review of research about sexual orientation, Mitchell *et al.* (2008) state that the term 'sexual orientation' has been criticised for being deterministic because it forces people into a particular category which might not fit their overall experience or reflect the potentially mutable nature of sexuality. All of these labels may sediment particular sexual identities in a way that invites subjects (individuals) to erase, hide, or reject some of their desires. One common thread is that all of them, except 'behavioural bisexual', assume a connection between identities and sexual attractions and desires. One alternative term is 'Men who have Sex with Men' (MSM).

The label 'MSM' has been taken up in international development since 2000 as 'the preferred descriptor for myriad expressions of same-sex desire by men' (Gosine, 2006, p.1). According to Gosine, the term 'MSM' has been used to challenge Western frameworks of sexuality (including the LGBT system), given the ways in which terms such as 'bisexual' and 'queer' 'were produced in particular social and economic conditions that primarily referenced metropolitan white cultural expressions of sexuality' (2006, p.3). However, the term 'MSM' is also problematic, because it has:

> collapsed cultural differences between non-western (and non-white) people and marked them as 'Others'. *Kothis* in Bangladesh, *Ibbi* in Senegal, *Yan dauda* in Nigeria, *African-American men 'on the down low'* in the USA, and *hijra* in India are collectively tagged 'MSM' despite speaking different languages, holding different religious beliefs, occupying different social positions in various environmental spaces, and being engaged in different kinds of sexual practices and emotional relationships.
>
> (Gosine, 2006, p.3)

Discussions about sexuality internationally also appear to be biased towards male sexualities, perhaps because of the focus on HIV/AIDS transmission that funds and fuels much of the work, but the term Women who have Sex with Women (WSW) is also used. The notion of 'MSM' has now been followed by the development of the terms 'Men who have Sex with Men and Women' (MSMW), and 'Women who have Sex with Men and Women' (WSMW) which are used to cover what could also be interpreted as behavioural bisexuality (see San Francisco Human Rights Commission LGBT Advisory Committee undated). There are other, related, terms, for example, 'Married Men who have Sex with Men' (MMSM) (Hudson, 2013).

There are other alternatives to the terms 'bisexual' and 'bisexuality'. In anglophone societies, these include 'metrosexual', which is used to denote liberal tolerance (see Balding, 2013). This term is problematic because it uses notions of urban living and culture as markers of sexual diversity. More useful terms include 'pansexual' and 'omnisexual' (both mean being attracted to people of all genders, see Barker et al., 2012). Alternative terms were discussed by some of the research contributors, for example, Lena said, 'I like the idea of polymorphous perversity and all that; it's all old fashioned sixties...life lived as the erotic in sensibly non-erotic settings, that could be a really political [thing]'.

Some of the contributors to the UK bisexuality research used other identities instead of, or as well as, bisexual, including 'pansexual' and 'queer'. The organised UK bisexual community has been strongly influenced by the increase in visibility of transgender and gender-diverse people (see Chapter 4), so that overall there has been a shift within the community to modelling bisexuality as being about attraction to people of all genders rather than just men and women. Being transgender or gender-diverse and also bisexual may lend a further layer of complexity to understanding sexuality. This is demonstrated in a quote from Dave, who is transgender:

> I also feel my own sexuality is nuanced; I have emotional attraction generally to women, and sexual attraction to men. And when I put people in those categories I'm talking about their identity rather than their physical body type. It is quite complex because I'm talking about a range of different types of people, gender identities, physical features, that sort of thing...there is something about the process of [gender] transitioning and what it actually means in terms of who you are attracted to...sometimes transition is a game-changer.

For Dave, and some other research contributors, then, there was a more expanded and fluid use of the term 'bisexual' taking place than the binary definition outlined at the start of this section. There are further approaches, where bisexuality is associated with the rejection of sexual identity categories (somewhat paradoxically), or sometimes associated with queer identities (see Chapter 2). The rejection of categories was fairly common amongst the UK research contributors. For example, Lena, who is cisgender, remarked that:

> I think of it [bisexuality] as an openness to all experiences and a rejection of binaries... a rejection of binaries in all aspects of my life really. I really abhor all kinds of conventional conformist categories; I really reject categories; I always have done.

A number of other research contributors identified as 'queer' rather than 'bisexual', using the term 'queer' to denote 'non-heterosexual'. It seems that, in the UK, the definitions of the terms 'bisexual' and 'bisexuality' have evolved from a binary focus in response to queer politics and the rise of the transgender and gender-diverse movements. This is evident in the UK in the report by Meg John Barker *et al.* (2012) (quote one) and in the interview material (quote two):

> [bisexuals are] People who experience their sexual identities as fluid and changeable over time... People who see their attraction as 'regardless of gender' (other aspects of people are more important in determining who they are attracted to)... People who dispute the idea that there are only two genders.
>
> (2012, p.11)

> I meet more and more people and I read the testimonies of more and more people who do use bisexuality much more in order to signify a particular ambiguous gender identity or shifting gender identity or a rejection of certain gender identities, a sort of transgender identity... sometimes also in combination with other terms [such as transgender].
>
> (Christian Klesse)

This book uses the following definition of bisexuality: 'attraction to people of more than one gender', and the following definitions of bisexuals: 'people who are attracted to other people who are of more than one gender'. It is acknowledged that this is a strategic move that overlooks the binary composition of the word. A full(er) evolution of terminology would require development of terms for desire between people of different genders (for example, an androgyne and a gender transient person) as well as further destabilisation of heterosexual, lesbian, gay, and bisexual identities as discrete, complete categories – or alternatively, the use of terms such as 'non-heterosexual' and 'queer'. However, there are also difficulties with the latter (see Chapter 2). In addition, given that heterosexuality is an aspect of bisexuality (opposite-sex desires/sexualities are usually an aspect of bisexual people's behaviours and identities); the use of the term 'non-heterosexuals' does not work well when applied to bisexuals.

Biphobia and the erasure of bisexuality

The term 'biphobia' was introduced by Kathleen Bennett to mean 'prejudice against bisexuality' (1992, p.205) and 'the denigration of bisexuality as a life-choice' (1992: 207). 'Biphobia' has subsequently been defined as 'any portrayal or discourse denigrating or criticizing men or women on the sole ground of their belonging to this [bisexual] sociosexual identity, or refusing them the right to claim it' (Welzer-Lang, 2008, p.82; see also Barker and Langdrige, 2008; Barker et al., 2012). It can also be termed 'antibisexual attitudes' (McLean, 2008). 'Biphobia' can be related to other terms, such as 'double discrimination' (Ochs, 1996); the discrimination that bisexual people can face from both heterosexual and lesbian/gay people. Another term that has recently been introduced is 'bisexual burden', which denotes the additional stress that bisexuals may experience, as compared to lesbians and gay men (see Anderson et al., 2014).

Biphobia can be modelled using a typology developed by Daniel Welzer-Lang (2008), who conducted a survey about biphobia with approximately 90 French individuals. Fifty-nine per cent of respondents were neutral, or pro-bisexuality. Welzer-Land categorised the biphobic responses (41 per cent) in the following way:

[i] Strict (or direct) biphobia, which includes seeing bisexuals as indecisive, hypocritical, or promiscuous, or indeed as 'not existing' (10% of the sample);
[ii] Liberal biphobia, which manifests as a concern with boundaries and with positioning bisexuals outside of the community of lesbians and gay men, so that bisexuals have to prove their allegiance to the gay and lesbian communities before being included despite the existence of the LGBT acronym (5%);

[iii] The refusal to recognise bisexuality as a valid social category; this can manifest as outright denial that bisexual people exist (see above), or as the view that categorisation as a bisexual is unnecessary whilst continuing to support 'lesbian' and 'gay' as social categories (12%);

[iv] Pathologisation: Bisexuality is seen as a psychiatric diagnosis and linked to a supposed inability to choose between men and women (4.5%).

This typology provides a useful means of analysing different types of biphobia. Overall, biphobia can be seen as a manifestation of symbolic violence. Symbolic violence means the imposition of systems of meaning on groups of people (see Jenkins, 1992, p.104) which impact on their lives in negative ways, that is, 'The violence which is exercised upon individuals in a symbolic, rather than a physical, way. It may take the form of people being denied resources, treated as inferior or being limited in terms of realistic aspirations' (Webb *et al.*, 2002, p.xvi). There are concerns about whether 'biphobia' can actually be classed as a phobia, in the psychiatric sense, in the same way that there are questions about 'homophobia' (see Mulick and Wright, 2002, 2011). However, the notion of 'homophobia' provides a discursive resource for individuals and collectives to name and respond to their oppression (Bryant and Vidal-Ortiz, 2012, p.387); the term 'biphobia' is similarly deployed in this book.

Biphobia and other forms of discrimination

Bisexual people may experience homophobia, as well as biphobia. The term 'homophobia' has been defined as a fear of homosexuality and homosexuals (Weinberg, 1972). Biphobia is also linked with other forms of prejudice, including erotophobia (fear of eroticism), prejudice against people who have more than one sexual partner (see Klesse, 2005), and AIDS-phobia (Wright *et al.*, 2011; see also Monro, 2005). There are also a range of cross-cutting forms of structural discrimination that intersect with biphobia in diverse ways (see Chapter 3). According to Mulick and Wright (2011), bisexual men appear to experience higher levels of biphobia than do bisexual women and in different ways; the stereotype is that 'bisexual men are dangerous whereas bisexual women are titillating and not to be taken seriously' (Owen, 2011, p.495; see also Klesse, 2005). Patterns of racial discrimination also affect the types of biphobia experienced by individuals. For example, the San Francisco Human Rights Commission LGBT Advisory Committee (undated) analysed medical texts to demonstrate that African American MSMW are more heavily stigmatised than MSMW of other ethnicities whilst Beverly Greene (2000) analyses the complex ways in which racism and sexism shape the lives of African American lesbians and bisexual women.

In the UK research, it was clear that the term 'biphobia' is not in universal use; some contributors to the research did not know the term or rejected it in favour of broader terms such as 'prejudice'. A few individuals felt that they had not experienced any discrimination due to their sexual orientation. In several other cases, people reported facing biphobia from heterosexuals, and lesbians and gay men. For example:

> I have experienced biphobia in quite a few different forms, some from people telling me I shouldn't identify as bi (because I'm in a stable relationship), some from people telling me they were fine with gay people but thought bi people should have to 'make up their minds', and a huge amount of biphobia from my parents, who said I was just 'polymorphously perverse' and clearly this bi thing was just a phase, and then later conveyed to me that they thought I was lying about my sexuality in order to rebel. They reasoned that bi people were diseased and perverted, and I hadn't died of sexually transmitted diseases yet, so clearly I must be lying.
>
> (Elisabeth)

In an international context, prejudice against bisexuals manifests via a plethora of terms and practices. For example, in Colombia, there has been an issue with some lesbians and gay men seeing bisexuals as 'confused' homosexuals or 'disorientated' lesbians that at some point are going to construct their identity based on some of the traditional gay or lesbian dichotomies and turn back to the lesbian, gay, and transgender (LGT) mainstream. Terms such as *Lesboflexible, Homoflexible, Bicurioso* or *Heteroflexibles* are some examples of some terms and words that the LGT community in Colombia have been using. This phenomenon is discussed by Colombian research contributor Carlos as follows:

> I think the people that are more aggressive to bisexuals are the gay community, because they can't understand our sexuality and preferences, and they believe that we are just a couple of undecided people... and this is really, really difficult because the gay community think that bisexual people don't know what they want and just want to have fun.

International aspects of biphobia will be discussed in more depth in some of the subsequent chapters, including Chapters 3 and 7.

Understanding biphobia

Overall, biphobia can be seen to stem from a combination of pathologising socio-medical discourses as discussed above, and the formation of the rigid, discrete identity categories of 'lesbian' and 'gay man' which emerged during the 1960s and 1970s in the West. The notion of 'homosexuality', like 'bisexuality', describes certain types of sexual *acts and desires* rather than sexual *identities*. The terms 'lesbian' and 'gay' were used in the 1970s and 1980s by people with unidirectional sexual desires to depathologise homosexuality. These labels were used to help foster resistance to the oppression of people engaging in same-sex desires and sexual acts. However, in so doing, the lesbian and gay identities that were forged became exclusive and excluding of people who included both heterosexual and homosexual desires/acts within their subjectivities; bisexuals were shut out by people seeking to consolidate discrete lesbian and gay identities (see, for example, Monro, 2005). This meant that there was an ontological erasure of bisexuality, so that 'serving as the contested middle ground between heterosexuality and homosexuality, bisexuality must ultimately disappear in order to prop up theories of hetero/homosexual difference' (James, 1996, p.218).

The erasure of bisexuality is widely apparent, for example, in the UK policy-related literature. For instance, the report *Profiles of Prejudice: The Nature of Prejudice in England: In-Depth Analysis of Findings* is described as having 'sought to address the extent and nature of prejudice against minority groups' (Citizenship 21 undated, p.7), however, whilst it includes lesbians and gay men throughout, it completely ignores bisexuals. Other areas where bisexual erasure is very apparent include the media (Barker and Langdridge, 2008; Barker, 2012), service provision, and political representation (Richardson and Monro, 2012). Biphobia is also present within academic spaces. The erasure or marginalisation of bisexuality by lesbian and gay theorists, as mentioned above, cuts across many areas of scholarship, including queer scholarship. As Clare Hemmings argues, the queer theoretical resistance to bisexuality is dual in nature:

> ...bisexuality has been understood as undermining lesbian or gay claims to legitimacy, bringing opposite-sex relationships very firmly into the frame' (Hemmings, 2007, p.14) and at the same time

bisexuality is seen to 'reproduce the oppositional identity categories that queer theorists wanted to challenge'.

(Hemmings, 2007, p.14).

There are some indications that biphobia may be lessening in the UK; notably, a small qualitative study of bisexual teenage girls in the UK shows a lack of experiences of biphobia, and that any biphobia that girls experienced on coming out dissipated due to bi-positive peer pressures (Anderson *et al.*, 2014), but more research would be needed to explore if this is a wider trend.

Biphobia has material impacts, shaping the lived experiences of bisexual people (see Barker *et al.*, 2012). It also affects wider notions of what is possible in terms of sexual orientation, affecting heterosexuals, lesbians, gay men, and others. The causes of discrimination against bisexuals and bisexuality can be seen to stem from the structural erasure; both heterosexuals and homosexuals have an investment in the maintenance of a binary (heterosexual-homosexual) which, because heterosexuality and homosexuality are constructed against each other and do not allow for any middle ground or porosity, actively elides bisexuality and bisexual subjectivities (MacDowall, 2009; see also James, 1996; Hemmings, 2007). For Collins (2013), the stigmatisation of bisexual identities acts to reinforce heterosexual and homosexual binaries. As noted above, there are other forces behind the erasure and stigmatisation of bisexuality, including those relating to monosexism and mononormativity (see Bennett, 1992; Barker *et al.*, 2012), homophobia, and sexism. In any sociological analysis of a phenomenon, it is crucial to consider the way in which individuals negotiate, resist, and rework structural forces, and subsequent chapters will also pay heed to the ways in which bisexual people forge their social worlds as active agents (see Cashmore and Tuason, 2009).

Overview of the book chapters

Bisexuality and social theory

This chapter explores some theoretical tools in order to develop an understanding of bisexuality. Interactionist theory can be used to analyse the construction of bisexual identities, and how and why bisexuality is stigmatised. Post-structuralist theory provides a way of further interrogating identity construction, and the erasure and 'othering' of the multiple, fluid sexualities associated with bisexuality. Queer and post-structuralist approaches can be used to theorise bisexual resistances to normativity, as well as the overlaps between the bisexual and transgender communities. Sociological analysis of bisexuality would, however, be incomplete without grounding it in materialist analysis, which can be used to explain why bisexuals occupy socially marginal positions in relation to the reproduction of labour, and why bisexuality is commodified and hypersexualised in certain contexts and not in others.

Intersectionality and bisexuality

Intersectionality theory has produced some sophisticated mechanisms for understanding the construction of identities and the social relations in which individuals are embedded. It can be used to understand diversity within groups and the ways in which categories such as 'bisexual' can be used strategically. Intersectionality theory can be used to understand and model the ways in which bisexuality is cross-cut by other social characteristics such as nationality, ethnicity, ability, gender, and age. These intersections are extremely relevant to the bisexual community, where diversity concerning health, ability, and age is noticeable, but ethnicity less so. The chapter provides an analysis of the ways in which Indian bisexualities can be analysed using intersectionality approaches. It also includes a UK-specific analysis of the intersections concerning race, faith, and bisexuality.

Sex, relationships, kinship, and community

This chapter maps out the UK bisexual community and provides some insight into the communities with which it overlaps. These communities have different, sometimes highly divergent, sets of underpinning norms and values. Some, including the 'out' bisexual community and the kink community, have strongly developed forms of habitus, and kinship-type links, and in this context it is possible to examine not only sexuality-related practices of intimacy, but also those associated with care for the ill and disabled, children, and older people. These communities and their practices can be viewed as a form of social capital, and they contribute to civil society. From a materialist perspective, many of their practices fall outside of the remit of organised capitalism, placing these communities in a marginal position as compared to the heterosexual, lesbian, and gay communities.

Bisexuality, organisations, and capitalism

This chapter examines the lived experiences of bisexuals within workplace organisations, drawing on material from the UK and the USA.

It addresses the issues which bisexuals face concerning 'outness', given the high levels of stigma associated with the identity and the complex ways in which bisexuals can manage prejudice. The chapter also explores, by way of contrast, the sectors in which bisexuality and related forms of sexuality are commodified. These include the use of expressly bisexual imagery/action (female–female sex performed for a male consumer) in pornography and sex work, and the use of female-female eroticism within the music industry. The chapter explicates the ways in which the commodification of certain types of bisexuality is highly gendered. This commodification fuels notions of the hypersexualisation of bisexuality and impacts negatively on some groups of bisexuals. It also addresses the ambivalences that some research contributors expressed towards the commodification of bisexuality.

Citizenship

This chapter adopts, in a critical fashion, concepts from mainstream, feminist, and sexual citizenships and applies them to bisexuality. In so doing it aims to provide insight into some of the issues facing bisexuals, and also to inform the development of citizenship studies, particularly in relation to sexual and intimate citizenships. Citizenship rights are important for bisexual people, given the ways in which bisexuals are marginalised and stigmatised. However, there are tensions between reformist or assimilationist trends within bisexual politics (in which bisexuals seek to become part of the 'mainstream') and the queer and highly diverse identities and strategies found in the bisexual communities, which cannot easily be assimilated into heteronormative citizenship frameworks. Another issue concerns the tensions between particularist, or bisexual-specific, activist aims and policy interventions, and more universalist approaches, which include bisexuals within citizenship discourse alongside other populations. The chapter addresses these issues via an analysis of the citizenship agendas of bisexual people in the UK.

Bisexuality, activism, democracy, and the state

This chapter provides a contribution to an empirically based political science of bisexuality. It addresses the ways in which bisexual activism has developed, and the ways in which rights claims are made – and in some cases rejected – by bisexual people. It looks at activism, participative democracy, and the state in two contrasting countries: Colombia and the UK. For each of these countries, the trajectory of bisexual activism is traced, and bisexual activist relationships with the LGBT movement (in Colombia) and the lesbian and gay movement (in the UK) are examined. The chapter addresses activist strategies and actions in each of these countries, including the ways in which bisexuals have engaged with the state via participative democratic mechanisms. The chapter finishes by exploring some themes that emerge from comparative analysis of bisexual activism in both countries.

2
Bisexuality and Social Theory

Chapter 1 to this book provided a route into theorising bisexuality from sociological and political science perspectives. It analysed the ways in which bisexualities, and indeed sexualities and genders more broadly, have been historically and culturally constructed. It addressed the role of sexologists and academics both in forging pathological notions of bisexuality and in developing broader, more bisexuality-positive approaches. Chapter 1 also provided a constructionist analysis of prejudice concerning bisexualities. In mapping out these issues, Chapter 1 complemented existing sociological and critical approaches to bisexuality, locating the book within critical bisexuality studies.

This chapter builds on Chapter 1 by exploring the application of four strands of social theory to the topic of bisexuality. The first of these approaches, social constructionism (specifically, interactionism), is used because it provides a means of understanding the construction of bisexuality at a micro level, the level of everyday interactions between people. Different strands of interactionist thought are drawn on while explicating the following themes: the interpersonal construction of identities; sexuality and desire; intrapsychic processes; the issue of bisexuality as unintelligible, and interactionism in relation to biphobia. The chapter then moves on to discuss queer theory, which is pertinent to bisexuality not just because some bisexual people identify as queer but also because many of the issues that are relevant to bisexual people (such as the tension between people using identity categories and rejecting identity categories) can be debated via the prism of queer theory. Trans theories are then examined, again partly because of the trans/bisexuality overlaps but also because of shared concerns with identity categorisation, fluidity, and liminality. Lastly, a materialist approach is explored. The chapter aims both to map out some of the theoretical territory and to demonstrate the utility of social theory in understanding bisexuality. It uses material from the UK bisexuality study because 'drilling down' into a particular dataset can provide useful insights. However, it is of course acknowledged that identity formation varies considerably across different countries (see Chapter 1).

There is a great deal of territory which is yet to be mapped regarding bisexuality and social theory. For each of the bodies of theory used in this chapter, there are lines of thinking that could be pursued which are not included here. For example, other strands of interactionist theory, particularly theories of deviance and labelling (see, for example, Gagnon and Simon, 1967; Plummer, 1975) could be further developed in relation to bisexuality (Callis (2013) has begun this work based on the US situation). In addition, other bodies of theory entirely could be applied to bisexuality. For example, whilst I have previously used post-structuralism in relation to trans (Monro, 2005), a post-structuralist route is not taken in this book, although it informs the development of queer and trans theories. This is because interactionism arguably provides more nuanced tools for addressing processes such as the non-verbal communication of sexual desires. Some aspects of post-structural analysis are clearly pertinent to bisexuality (see, for example, Callis, 2009) but are not addressed in this chapter. For example, post-structuralist feminist Judith Butler's notion of performativity is highly relevant to certain types of bisexuality such as the phenomenon of girls kissing in front of their boyfriends. For Butler, sex, as well as gender, is constructed via performativity; 'identity is seen as performatively constituted by the very "expressions" that are said to be its results' (Butler, 1990, p.25). As noted above, the chapter begins by looking at interactionism in relation to the UK bisexuality research findings, and then moves on to address queer theory, trans theory, and materialist approaches.

Interactionism

Social constructionist theory comprises a 'matrix of overlapping perspectives that converge with and diverge from each other in various ways' (Brickell, 2006, p.87–88). Stevi Jackson and Sue Scott (2010) note that social constructionist approaches stem from two traditions: North American pragmatism as developed by authors such as George Herbert Mead (1934) and Herbert Blumer (1969) into symbolic interactionism, and social phenomenology (Schutz, 1972, cited in Jackson and Scott,

2010). There are many varieties of interactionist thought, but Herbert Blumer has captured the core ideas:

> human beings act towards things on the basis of the meanings that things have for them; the meaning of such things is derived from, or arises out of, the social interaction that one has with one's fellows...these meanings are handled in and modified through an interpretive process by the person dealing with the things he [sic] encounters.
> (Blumer, 1962, p.2 cited by Plummer, 1975, p.10)

This focus on the interpretive construction of 'reality' and the related destabilisation of notions of biological essentialism (ideas that peoples' gender identity and sexuality are determined by the sex they were born as) has underpinned a range of critical thinking about gender and sexuality in the USA and UK from the 1960s onwards. For example, ethnomethodologist Harold Garfinkel (1967) took a critical position regarding 'gender rules' and this was followed by other constructionist gender scholarship (notably Kessler and McKenna, 1978). Social constructionism drove much of the work of progressive and radical gender and sexuality writers during the 1970s and 1980s, including that of Mary McIntosh (1998, [1968]), Ken Plummer (1975), and Jeffrey Weeks (1968, 1977, 1985). It also informed the work of key theorists John Gagnon and William Simon (1967, 1969, 1973) with respect to sexuality.

Gagnon and Simon used concepts drawn from symbolic interactionism to reject the idea that sexuality is simply the result of 'natural drives' and contend that 'sexuality is an aspect of social life like any other and that the meanings granted to it constitute its most important characteristic' (Brickell, 2006, p.95; see also Plummer, 2002). Gagnon and Simon also analysed the ways in which social norms constrain and shape an actor's behaviour, viewing the process as dynamic, changing over time (Gagnon and Simon, 1967). They focused specifically on people's ability to use symbols, defined here as systems of making and conveying meaning in the course of everyday interactions (Brickell, 2006), so that these interactions together form the social 'realities' that we take for granted.

Simon and Gagnon (see Brickell, 2006) provided a seminal contribution to understanding human sexuality via their analysis of sexual behaviours as social scripts. The term 'script' is used broadly, to denote the sets of symbolic meanings that affect how individuals develop sexual identities and the sexual actions they may or may not take part in. Initially Simon and Gagnon provided two dimensions of scripting: interpersonal (which was about interactions between people) and intrapsychic (which concerned internal, reflexive processes and internalisation of wider sexual meanings, and the development of sexual careers (see Brickell, 2006)), but in response to criticism they then added the cultural dimension, which concerned cultural narratives.

Unlike many sociologists working in the 1970s and subsequently, Gagnon discussed different types of bisexuality, including sex where people are aroused and taking part in sex within a group context, and he noted:

> There are people whom ideological bisexuals prefer to call 'true bisexuals'. These are people emotionally and sexually attracted to both men and women, and who have relations with them accompanied by all the 'correct' emotions... affectionately caring and desiring.
> (1977, p.272)

However, he also stated that 'people who have sexual partners of the same and opposite gender during their lives seem to represent a serious intellectual and scientific problem for those trying to understand human sexual conduct' (1977, p.259). For Gagnon, this was partly because of the gender-binary basis of sexual orientation categories, and partly because different types of sexual conduct use different sexual scripts. This contradictory, ambivalent position towards bisexuality will be discussed below, in the section on bisexuality as unintelligible.

Overall, Gagnon (1977), and other interactionists, contend that our social world is constructed via our interactions with each other, which are mediated via our perceptions of each social situation. This is basically an anti-essentialist position. However, the UK bisexuality research data raised some questions about purely anti-essentialist, constructionist conceptual frameworks. Because of this, the chapter will briefly look at essentialism and constructionism, before pursuing different interactionist trajectories.

Essentialism and constructionism

As we have seen above, interactionists, and constructionists more widely, argue that identities are socially constructed, as opposed to being driven by biological factors such as physiology and hormones. Whilst the findings from the research with UK-based bisexual and other non-lesbian, gay and heterosexual (LGH) people indicated that many social factors are at play in the formation of bisexual identities, they also revealed the extent to which individuals experience themselves as having essential identities, which they may interpret as bisexual. This finding 'speaks to' the arguments that I have presented elsewhere with respect to gender identities (Monro, 2005) about the importance of, firstly, accepting individual's reports of their lived experience as valid (as opposed to false consciousness) and secondly, the pertinence of material, specifically biological, factors in the development of sexed and gendered identities.

The UK bisexuality research participants were asked whether they saw their sexual identity as being innate or constructed. Typically, they discussed sexual identities as resulting from a combination of essential and constructed factors. In some cases people experienced limitations concerning agency (choice) about their bisexuality, for instance contributor Dave said that 'I don't think it's something I can help, it's not freely chosen, but the way I interpret it is freely chosen'. Some level of essentialism is also implied in the following quote:

> I realised [I was bisexual] when I was 15 or 16 years old, and I gave myself a very hard time, I was quite narrow minded and being anything other than straight never crossed my mind until then, although I had clues, I hadn't put them together...I was very narrow minded, it did not go with my plans, and also I think I was still influenced by my religious background. My parents had a very religious...religion is everywhere in Spain. (Pia)

Some contributors felt that their bisexual identity was constant, whereas others experienced considerable variation in the types and level of sexual feelings and identifications. For example, one of the trans men who contributed to the study reported that 'I've gone back and forth between mostly being attracted to women but being attracted to the occasional man, to mostly being attracted to men and being attracted to the occasional woman'. Hormonal changes were seen as relevant by some contributors. For example, Elizabeth reported:

> At a certain time during the month, I am just much more likely to be physically attracted to men. The rest of the time, I'm mostly indifferent to them, generally. Even my relationship with my husband runs along these lines – there is a time of the month we are much more likely to want to have sex than other times.

These findings imply that some level of biological or other essentialism is at play in the formation of bisexual identities. Interactionists such as Plummer (1975) do not deny the existence of physiological realities such as genitalia, arguing that biological factors can be socially interpreted in different ways. However, the findings from the bisexuality research suggest that biology may play a more formative part in the construction of identity than is perhaps allowed for by interactionists. That important caveat aside, let us proceed with an examination of the role of micro-level interaction in bisexual identity construction.

The interpersonal construction of identities

Analysis of the UK research findings showed that the interpersonal construction of bisexual identities is multi-faceted. Research contributors described a variety of early experiences which they saw as shaping the development of their sexual identity, including family norms and relationships with parents and other family members. Some people grew up in environments which were hostile to sexual diversity, but others felt supported by friends and in some cases family. For example:

> other people maybe had pressure from family and friends but I do not really have that pressure, my friends and family are quite supportive, even my mum. She thought I was a lesbian and then... at some point she said 'OK, Jo, I don't care whether you are homosexual, bisexual or whatever. The most important thing is that you are happy and you enjoy your life'. So, I don't really have pressure to come out. (Jo)

In this quote, Jo indicates the supportive role her family background has played in her bisexual identity construction. The research findings also indicated that having access to bisexuality-related information and resources is important in the formation of bisexual identities. Contributors who had been involved in the organised bisexual community talked at some length about the importance of this community in providing identity validation and support (see also Chapter 4). For example:

> I discovered that there is a bi community... When I first went [to BiCon (an annual convention of bisexual people and their allies)] it was incredibly exciting, incredibly liberating... I thought I had got as far as I could get with being out and happy as a bi person. But being in that space... the friend I went with, hand holding... the plan was I would go to stay at his, and go for the day, and what ended up

happening was I went all day and ended up crashing with people and I stayed all weekend. And it was incredible – it *was* life-changing. It was life-changing to be in a space where the assumptions of straight and gay didn't exist. (Camel)

Other types of communities were also discussed by a number of people, including internet communities which were seen an important resource for individuals seeking an understanding of sexual identities and wanting to connect with others. Some contributors described being influenced by the media, and one contributor discussed the importance of bisexual role models coming out in the media ('coming out' is defined, following Heidi Green *et al.* (2011) as willingness to have one's sexual orientation known by others). For some individuals it was not information specifically about bisexuality that provided a means of identity formation but other types of material. For example, research contributor Elizabeth discussed fandom/fanfiction community materials as being crucial to her developing her own sexuality.

There are also other forms of community and organisation that are important in forging bisexual identities, such as activism (see Chapter 7). Taking part in activism or capacity building concerning bisexuality involves challenging biphobia in interaction with others, and it can lead to stronger bisexual identity development and validation of a bisexual identity. This is extremely evident in the literature, for example Shiri Eisner's (2012) account of bisexual activism in Israel/Palestine. It is also reflected in some of the research findings. For example, contributor Kay reported:

if it [bisexuality] comes up I will quite happily discuss it, and one time I would have shied away...I didn't like to talk about it. Obviously if I am an advisor and a lead as someone who is involved in LGBT groups I can't hide it...it was a massive step to take on those two roles...this might be really strange but I took on that role, I got off on the fact they looked at me and think 'bisexual lead'.

For a few contributors, identifying as bisexual was partly about a rejection of cultural norms associated with gay or heterosexual culture. For instance, Pablo described how he had spent time on the gay scene and disliked its music and commercial nature; identifying as bisexual was a means of widening out his cultural field and he continued to identify as bisexual despite being single and having limited sexual engagements. Identifying as bisexual was sometimes actively chosen as a means of building an identity that is 'other' than heterosexual or gay/lesbian. For instance, Camel described how prior to his gender transition he 'latched onto bisexual as a way of saying "I am not either of those" [lesbian or heterosexual]'. For quite a few people, identifying as bisexual went along with identifying as queer, and rejecting gender-binarisms, and in some cases embracing other lifestyles such as polyamory (which is defined here as openly negotiated intimate relationships with more than one partner). Understanding the formation of bisexual identities requires an analysis of sexuality and desire, as well other aspects of identity, and this forms the basis for the next section of the chapter.

Sexuality and desire

A few of the contributors to the UK bisexuality research did not see sexuality as being particularly important to them in terms of their bisexual identity. For example, Reggie said that 'on Friday I play bridge and I don't know how many of those people are gay or bisexual or whatever, they are more interested in talking about the ace of clubs...rather than anybody's sexuality'. However, many of the contributors described their sexuality as being central to their identity as bisexual or queer.

Sexual desire and sexual practice both formed a key part in the formation of identities for some individuals. This included experiences of desire for people of different genders. Some of the research contributors experienced different sorts of attraction for different types of people, for example, Dave talked about the way he has 'emotional attraction generally to women, and sexual attraction to men. And when I put people in those categories I'm talking about their identity rather than their physical body type'. Other key aspects of bisexual identity development included sexual activities with other people, the use of pornography (in a minority of cases), and cultural expressions of sexuality. For example, for contributor Jacqui, writing erotic literature which foregrounds black working class queer people was important on a personal level.

With respect to sexual interactions, some people forged bisexual identities via one-to-one relationships, others added in new partners to existing relationship formats, and in one case a contributor had experienced taking part in sex parties which were behaviourally bisexual and not categorised in any particular way. The non-categorisation of sex acts was a theme for some of the other contributors too. This is particularly relevant to behavioural bisexuals, for whom having an identity as bisexual, constructed through interacting with other people, is not a main aim. The non-categorised nature of behavioural bisexualities fits well with Simon and Gagnon's (see Brickell, 2006) notion of sexual scripts; each of these social contexts has particular scripts or 'rules' whereby people can engage in sexual experiences which are outside of the social norm, whilst still remaining within some normative frameworks. For example, contributor Andy described how:

> with male saunas, it's all done with eye contact or just a touch, people don't speak, with the [pornographic cinema] screen it's usually the back row where stuff happens, and if you are sat next to someone and they touch your leg with their leg or your hand with their hand that's a signal and if you let that happen that's a signal that you want to do something, or else you might go to one of the private rooms to be with somebody as well... there is a coffee area but the people who sit there don't talk about it, they tend to talk about anything else, they'll talk about football or whatever.

For those people for whom actual sex, rather than sexual identity formation, is important, the idea of alternative sexual scripts may be particularly useful, as it enables negotiated interactions that support sexual expression.

Intrapsychic processes

The processes of identity construction, whereby people reflect on their experience and develop specific bisexual sexual careers, have been indicated in the sections above. As noted in Chapter 1, there is a substantial body of bisexual literature which is either autobiographical or which integrates some autobiographical with some academic work in a reflexive way (for example, Hutchins and Kaahumanu, 1991; Atkins, 2002).

Various reflexive processes were apparent in the UK bisexuality research findings, depending on the individual's life circumstances and personality. Most of the research participants had made considerable efforts to think about their identities, and in some cases to research bisexuality. Their intrapsychic processes included in one case the consideration of desires followed by attempts to access community resources and the formation of bisexual relationships (Kate), and in another case, longstanding emotional conflict and soul searching involving recourse to therapy (Pia).

The following vignette provides a sense of one particular sexual career, following in the interactionist tradition of authors such as Plummer (1995). Yaz is a natal female of mixed ethnic heritage. She has never been a member of the organised bisexual community and is monogamously partnered with a man:

> When I was about 13–14 I specifically remember looking through a Sunday magazine and seeing a topless model, it wasn't page three, it was a very lovely picture, something to do with putting on sun cream or not, it was my mum's magazine, and I immediately felt an attraction. And it wasn't to do with 'oh she's really pretty, I'd like my hair like hers' or something, it was like 'wow I'm physically attracted to her' and it scared me, because coming from a Muslim background, I didn't really understand it... my parents were quite liberal about Islam, but according to the Islam we were brought up with lesbianism and gay or bisexuality was completely wrong... There were lots of women who had a big influence on me, there was this Asian girl and she had a girlfriend who had lots of piercings, I was so scared of her girlfriend but I was so attracted to this woman, she used to cycle, she would cycle down the road and I used to go, 'Oh My God, you are so gorgeous...' It wasn't that I woke up one day deciding to be bisexual, I think it was that those feelings were able to come out, I was away from my culture and my family [at university] and I was able to discover who I was and what I was feeling... I was in various bands and they all pretty much knew about my sexuality and they were all fine about it... there wasn't any judgement, for example. I went to a club with my male friend and we were drinking and there was a girl there, we said let's go and talk to her, we had a snog, got her number, we had a date... doing that in [city where lives] now, obviously because I am a Mum, have kids and all that... it wouldn't occur to me to do that now because there would be so much controversy around it.

This vignette demonstrates a number of processes that took place as part of Yaz's intrapsychic reflexivity; her interpretation, mediation and expression of desire, the negotiation of different social norms (see Chapter 3) and the operation of biphobia as a structuring force, particularly in Yaz's early life and then later, as a married mother. It also shows how, in her early life, Yaz struggled to understand bisexuality. The unintelligibility of bisexuality forms the topic for the next section of the chapter.

Bisexuality as unintelligible

One marked finding from the UK bisexuality research concerned the levels to which bisexual identities are socially unintelligible, as experienced in the course of day-to-day interactions that the UK bisexuality research contributors described. For example, I asked Jo if she had experienced prejudice because of her sexual identity, and she said that 'lay people, it's really difficult... people just don't understand [bisexuality]'.

Unintelligibility was connected, in the interviews, with social awkwardness. Some people experienced social discomfort or prejudice from other people when they 'came out' as bisexual. Arguably, social discomfort about bisexuality is not just due to biphobia, it is also about the ways in which bisexuality scrambles established sexual scripts. As noted above, this was discussed by Gagnon (1977) but little has been written about it from an interactionist standpoint since then. It is demonstrated in the quote below, from Pablo:

> If I think re my heterosexual friends I think the majority of time, if you say to them 'I'm gay' they don't necessarily empathise but they can understand and respect it and they know there is no point talking about pornography or sending you a certain sort of email... they know they can be friends with a gay person without it being sexual, and there are established society rules... precedents for how you behave with a gay friend. But with a bisexual friend people are a bit less sure about how they should behave and they are not quite sure whether they empathise with you or not.

The research contributors described a variety of strategies for managing social awkwardness, ranging from closeting (being secretive), to being selectively out, to taking on an educational role regarding bisexuality. Contributor Rosie avoided the term 'bisexual' altogether in order to avoid the interactive work associated with having a stigmatised identity:

> I'm sorry but the word [bisexual] has got stigma attached to it and although I am happy to sit and discuss what bi means to me... I find... I am bored of sitting for twenty minutes and explaining to straights in all sense of the word – whether they are straight-gay people, or straight-gay people – why I should call myself 'bisexual', what the word 'bisexual' means, and if I just say 'queer' it means I don't have to talk for so long.

The difficulties faced by bisexual people are not just about the cultural unintelligibility of bisexuality as attraction to two or more differently gendered sets of people, or about the challenges to mononormativity that bisexuality can pose (mononormativity is defined here as social norms that enforce the idea that people should be monogamous). The challenges faced by bisexuals are also about the nature of bisexuality, which was discussed by some of the contributors as 'floating', or 'fluid'. The rejection of clear-cut gender-binarisms and LGH categories causes difficulties in sexual scripting, given the deeply categorised nature of Western society. This can play out socially as an erasure of bisexuality and as patterns of biphobia.

Erasure and biphobia

An academic analysis of biphobia was provided in Chapter 1; here, some further material will be provided, focusing on lived experiences of the social construction of bisexuality. The social erasure of bisexuality was discussed by a number of contributors to the UK bisexuality research. For example:

> for many people, you don't exist. It's the complete invisibility and erasure of bisexuality [pause] you need to be stronger, to say all the time 'I am bisexual; I identify as bisexual' when other people tell you 'you don't exist' or, if they recognise that you exist, then you are 'greedy', you 'can't decide', you are 'not able to decide', you don't have the, you 'lack the mental skills' to decide... but now I really feel that I have to say all the time, that *I am bisexual*. It's this constant battle. (Merina)

In interactionist terms, if someone's bisexuality is socially erased or denied, then the construction of a bisexual identity can be very difficult on a personal level. For other research contributors, it was the social construction of bisexuality in particular ways that was problematic. Biphobia was apparent in the exoticisation or hypersexualisation of bisexuality, for example Yaz discussed couples contacting her via an internet dating site wanting to have sex in threesomes because she said she was bisexual, even though she had made it clear she wanted a dyadic (couple) relationship. Hypersexualised and stigmatising views of bisexuality were described as having negative social effects in various social settings (for example, healthcare providers), and also affected bisexual people's access to social spaces. For example:

Lena: It's the feeling of not being gay enough, or not performing to particular standards... [experiences of] going out, late teens, having a boyfriend but going out to spaces which I knew were women-only and being rejected on those grounds, because you have a boyfriend.
Interviewer: You were actually shut out from the space?
Lena: Yes, completely. The very same thing happened to me last year [short laugh] and I am 37 years old now.

In this interview snippet, the construction of particular spaces as 'gay' can lead to self-exclusion by bisexuals. However, the data also demonstrates the ways in which particular norms and processes of stigmatisation have real, material effects (the active exclusion of the bisexual woman Lena from spaces where she might meet a female partner). One of the critiques of interactionism is that it can lack analysis of such power dynamics. It can be argued that symbolic interactionism does in fact address power relations in its 'demonstration of the often routine ways in which the formal processes of institutions ensure the *authoritative* categorisation of individuals, or whole groups, as subordinate or morally unacceptable in some way' (Dennis and Martin, 2005, p.200). However, to complement this, there is a need for materialist analysis, as discussed later in the chapter. The next section of the chapter turns to queer theory as a means of conceptualising bisexuality.

Queer theory

Queer theory, and queer politics, emerged during the late 1980s and the 1990s, at the intersections between (mostly) gay and lesbian cultural studies and AIDS activism (see Hall, 2003). Queer theory draws on poststructuralism, with a focus on denaturalising and deconstructing gender and sexual identities and binaries (see Butler, 1990, 1991; Sedgewick, 1990; Seidman, 1996, 1997; Halberstam, 2002; Hines and Sanger, 2010), and on identity multiplicity and complexity (Hall, 2003).

Initially queer theory and politics concerned the reclamation of the stigmatised term 'queer'. 'Queer' became used to mean mutable, amorphous sexual desire which threatened systems of sexual classification. Queer politics was developed to mean 'resistance to the regimes of the normal' (Warner, 1993, p.xxvi), with 'normal' being interpreted as 'mainstream society', including government and the academy (Hall, 2003). It therefore became associated with a transgressive, radical politics that challenged heteronormative and mononormative institutions and cultural practices (Angelides, 2001; Jeppesen, 2010).

The term 'queer' has many uses and interpretations, and some more recent authors and activists, especially in an international context, use the term 'queer' as a catch-all for non-heterosexual people (see, for example, Downing and Gillett, 2011). Also, 'queer' activism can encompass activities associated with various networks and groups. For example, some people who are involved in the bisexual communities are also members of anarchist counterpublics as described by authors such as Jeppesen (2010), and as reflected in the UK bisexual research findings:

> someone I didn't know well told me about Queeruption 1, which was in London, 1999 I think... there was a lot of space and possibility within how those things were set up, there wasn't an assumed version of what queer was, and so that was very exciting. And there was a connection to wider politics which is important – to politics about race, disability, and feminism. (Camel)

Queer theory has largely overlooked bisexuality (Angelides, 2001; Callis, 2009). Authors such as Eve Sedgewick (1991) have not made bisexuality central to the deconstruction of the opposing categories of heterosexual and homosexual, and 'in spite of occupying an epistemic position *within* this very opposition, the category of bisexuality has been curiously marginalised and erased from the deconstructive field of queer theory (Angelides, 2001, p.7). For Angelides, this is partially because 'contrary to stated aims, one of the tendencies of many queer theorists has been to think the two axes of gender vertically or hierarchically rather than relationally and obliquely' (2001, p.162). This ties in with the more general criticism provided by Ken Plummer observed in 1995: 'The newly emerging 'Queer Theory' is an attempt to get beyond the gendered and sexual practices of the social world, yet it continually harks back to those categories which is seeks to undo; male, female, straight, bisexual' (p.xvi). It also relates to broader tensions between identity categorisation and the deconstruction of categories.

Bisexual theorists have responded to queer theory in a number of ways. Some take queer approaches in rejecting a 'progressive' and 'marketable' model of a bisexual continuum (Hall, 1996a, p.12). Others have developed queer bisexual perspectives. For example, Erich Steinman (2011) traces a trajectory within bisexuality research which foregrounds the queer transgressive, liberatory, and abject aspects of bisexuality. Other strands of bisexual scholarship address epistemologies 'of the fence' (see Pramaggiore, 1996), or 'interstitial' (in-between spaces)

(Horncastle, 2008); in other words developing knowledge about having an identity at the borders between homosexuality and heterosexuality.

Other authors have engaged critically with queer theory. For example, Angelides contends that queer theory has problematically subordinated systems of gender categorisation to systems of sexual categorisation. He argues that there is an analytical need to disarticulate these two systems in order to open up space for considering sexuality differently, because 'some routes of identification, desires and pleasure have little if anything to do with gender' (2001, p.189). Bisexuality as a 'polymorphic analytic category' has, Angelides argues, much to offer feminism and queer theory (2001, p.189). This approach is relevant to understanding contemporary bisexual communities in countries such as the UK, where some bisexual people define bisexuality in terms of desire that is not focused primarily on the gender of the desired person(s) (see Chapter 4). The term 'queer' was also discussed critically by a few contributors to the UK bisexuality research, notably scholar and research contributor Christian Klesse, who noted the multiple usages of the term 'queer' and suggested:

> an alternative, of course, would be a more ambiguous identity which referred, which could accommodate multiple desires and multiple sexual engagements and also the struggle for same-sex desire could be queer...I feel that queer works best if it is not appropriated as an identity category...A lot of more abstract queer theoretical work tried to understand exclusive practices through the act of identification and claiming identities, on that level you could argue that claiming queer as an identity is counter-intuitive.

To summarise, then, for those theorising bisexuality, 'queer' can mean an epistemology in which sexual identity categories are deconstructed; a political practice in which categories are disputed and heteronormativity and mononormativity are actively challenged; a description of interstitial or 'in-between' spaces; where desires and sexualities can be fluid, multiple, and complex; or an umbrella term for LGBT. These definitions were picked up by a number of the UK bisexuality research contributors, some of whom identified as queer rather than bisexual, or as both queer and bisexual. For example:

> bisexual people tend to think I may like men or I may like women, and so I think it's really different...queer [and] bisexuality...for me if people identify as bisexual people tend to think of two directions,

but for me queer is something [pause] the focus is not as much on gender, for me, I just like that person...the gender is not that important. (Jo)

Attitudes towards the term 'queer' varied quite widely, from people who embraced and used it, to those who rejected it because they saw it as stigmatising. For example, Yaz said, 'I wouldn't call myself queer. I can understand why people do want to take [back] that word in the way taking back the word 'nigger', taking back the word 'paki' – taking away the negativity'.

Some of the difficulties with the use of queer theory for theorising bisexuality are indicated above. Other difficulties include the following: [i] The 'vanguard' nature of queer theory sets particular subjects in opposition to a perceived mainstream and this may either override people's desires to be part of the mainstream and/or create new social hierarchies. It can also result in a lack of sensitivity to bisexual people's lives (see Steinman, 2011), for example the way in which strategic closeting is used as a survival mechanism. [ii] The origins of the term 'queer', which developed amongst an elite group of white, Western academics, may mean that it has little purchase amongst other groups (see Monro, 2005). [iii] Queer theory and politics can overlook material inequalities and processes (Whittle, 2006). In terms of the UK bisexuality research findings, the use of the term 'queer' was strongly shaped by class, education, and ethnic origin, with educated British people using it more than others, some of whom demonstrated a lack of affinity with the term:

> it's too abstract for me, and I don't have the cultural baggage of all the people here, I never knew anything about queer theory until it was too late...it doesn't mean anything really to me and I can't identify with it. (Pia)
>
> I must be queer as I am not straight, but sometimes queer theory feels heady and quite extreme and I can't relate to it. (Andy)

[iv] Queer theory can be seen as politically dangerous because it dissolves the basis for identity politics. Because queer theory destabilises identity categories, it can involve the erasure of identities such as bisexuality. As I have demonstrated above, one of the difficulties for bisexuals in countries like the UK is social marginalisation and invisibility. From an interactionist perspective this difficulty is entirely understandable; externally plausible social labels are required to negotiate the social

world. However, using a queer lens, bisexuality swiftly disappears in a multiplicity of sexed and gendered positions, subsumed within 'queer' deconstructionism. The specificities of bisexual queer experience – indeed, the term 'bisexual' itself – can be lost, leaving space where the more socially intelligible gay and lesbian identities can take precedence. The way in which queer can erase the specificities of bisexual experience was discussed by some contributors to the UK bisexuality research. For example, Merina remarked that it can involve the invisibility of bisexuality, and Kate said:

> I understand that queer is trying to bring everything together but I feel like I've become a bit cynical about the degree to which I'm being brought into broader based numbers, without actually being considered. The more I learn about research that is carried out about queer identities, I realise how much bis are being sidelined – either discounted because they don't fit, or grouped in; their voices are lost in the data.

Is queer theory useful, then, for theorising bisexuality? The analysis of the literature and research findings indicates that it has a place, particularly in allowing for analysis of transgressive identities, and multiple, fluid desires. The critiques of the approach are clearly pertinent to bisexuality, in particular the vanguardist, elitist, and classed tendencies associated with it, and the tendency for bisexual experiences to be erased or marginalised within a broader 'queer' set of identities. However, the use of the term 'queer' by non-heterosexual people internationally to denote multiple, non-categorised, or non-normative sexual and gender identities runs counter to some of these critiques. Also, (in an overlapping argument), some people who are behaviourally bisexual prefer to identify as 'queer', making the inclusion of queer theory important within an analysis of bisexuality that centres bisexual people's experiences.

Transgender theory

Transgender (trans) theory is relevant to understanding bisexuality for two reasons: firstly, because many bisexual people are also trans or gender-diverse, and secondly, because the transgender destabilisation of gender binaries and the movement towards other models, such as seeing gender as a spectrum rather than as discrete male/female categories, opens up space for thinking about non-binary models of sexuality. However, it appears that bisexuality has been rather absent from trans studies to date, for instance Angie Fee's (2010) useful analysis of the heterosexual matrix and trans addresses only gay men, lesbians, transvestites, and transsexuals. It seems that the shift in trans theorising towards gender diversity (drawing on both post-structuralism and materialism) has bypassed a consideration of bisexuality as a valid social category. This is problematic in that it erases the voices of trans people who identify as bisexual, and renders 'bisexual' a defunct category (in a similar way to the erasures of queer theory) and in doing so it may foreground LGH categories.

This section of the chapter maps out some mechanisms for thinking about gender diversity in relation to sexual identities. The type of trans theory that is drawn on developed initially via interactionism (for example, Ekins, 1997), and then subsequently it took post-structuralist and materialist trajectories (Monro, 2005, 2010; Hines and Sanger, 2010). Post-structuralist analysis (Monro, 2005) was important in destabilising the idea that 'male' and 'female' are the only sex and gender categories that are possible, and similarly challenges notions of lesbian, gay, and heterosexual as unitary categories. It led to three broad approaches to conceptualising trans and gender diversity: the expansion of binary categories; moving beyond sex and gender; and gender pluralism.

The expansion of 'male' and 'female' categories 'stretches' the existing gender binary system to include various non-normative gender expressions, such as butch lesbians, or intersex people who identify as male, as well as trans people who identify as either male or female. This approach is important in a number of ways; in particular, it allows gender-diverse bisexual people to be socially intelligible, which, as demonstrated in the section on interactionism above, is important in terms of daily liveability. However, there was little evidence of the UK bisexuality study participants consciously taking such a position. In fact, in the counter-normative space of the organised bisexual community, genderqueer and other non-binary gendered identities are common.

The second approach involves moving beyond sex and gender (see, for example, Lorber, 1994), so that society is degendered as far as possible, and people are able to identify as non-male and non-female. The difficulty with this approach lies in the entrenched nature of sex and gender binaries in contemporary society; however, it does potentially render sex, sexuality, and gender categories and accompanying unequal social structures less powerful. The desire to move beyond gender was reflected in some of the research findings from the UK bisexuality research, for example Jo said that 'I would rather not name myself as a gender' and Elizabeth reported:

> I still struggle with identity on a general level – it sometimes feels like bisexuality is the one thing I'm totally sure about. I often speak of myself as inhabiting liminal spaces – somewhere in between gay and straight, somewhere in between Scottish and American, somewhere in between woman and neuter, a polyamorous person in a monogamous relationship.

The third approach is gender pluralism, where sex and gender are conceptualised as a spectrum, or continuum, or set of spectra/continua. This follows a 'call for new and self-conscious affirmations of different gender taxonomies' (Halberstam, 2002, p.360). It includes the development of new terms (such as the pronoun 'hir') as well as a recognition that LGB and heterosexual categories are insufficient in describing the plethora of different desires that people may experience.

During the last 25 years, there has been a social shift in the UK and in some other countries towards support for gender diversity, conceptualised here as gender pluralism, and increasing visibility (to a degree) for a multiplicity of identities such as genderqueer, third gender, multiple gender, bigender, and androgyne. This is evidenced in several online communities and resources, such as http://genderfork.com/ and http://freelgbtqpia.tumblr.com/. As noted above, gender diversity is apparent in the organised bisexual 'scene', where gender variations are common, and social spaces are constructed which are relatively supportive of trans people. Gender pluralism is evident in the narratives supplied by some of the research contributors. For example, Lee says:

> I came out as a gay woman and I thought 'ah this is why, this makes sense' but it was still not quite right, felt much more comfortable but not quite right. The person I was with at the time was also looking at transitioning and we found out together we are both men. So I thought about my sexual orientation and I thought well, I am still attracted to him whether he is male or female, and that opened up a lot of doors for me. If my gender is more fluid maybe my sexuality is too.

Gender pluralism, in particular, incorporates acknowledgement of physiological sex diversity (as per Anne Fausto-Sterling's (2000) typology of sex variations), moving away from purely constructionist or indeed queer approaches. Gender-pluralist type theories may prove a fruitful direction for future theorisation of bisexuality (and other sexual identities), given that they allow for conceptualising physiological sex, gender, and sexual identity in finely grained, fluid, and complex ways without some of the transgressive baggage that limits queer theory. People of all types of social and political aspiration (those who want to assimilate into mainstream society and those who wish to live outside of, or in opposition to it) can identify as gender/sexually pluralist or diverse, arguably providing a far more useful tool in gaining basic rights for sexual/gender minorities than approaches that focus on transgression (see Chapters 6 and 7). Gender pluralist type approaches also allow for binary gender identifications, so long as these are not framed as the 'only way to be', or as 'better' than multiple-gender, third/other gender or gender-fluid positions. This is important because, as research contributor Meg John Barker argued, some bisexual and trans people are very identified with binary ways of thinking about the self, and there is a need to be cautious not to marginalise them.

Gender pluralist theory calls for material analysis of the gender binary system and the attendant homosexual/heterosexual binary, because of the need to understand the structures that perpetuate rigid gender binaries and LGH systems of categorisation. If sex and gender are seen as existing along a spectrum or set of spectra, especially if thinking along intersectional lines (see Chapter 3), then why are certain types of gender diversity so heavily penalised in mainstream society in terms of access to civil rights, personal safety, employment, healthcare, and housing (see for instance Whittle *et al.*, 2007)? What does structural transphobia mean for the stigmatisation of bisexuals, who also disrupt norms concerning gender via their non-traditional sexual identities? How are bisexuals affected by these structural, material forces of inequality, and how do they engage with them? The next section of the chapter begins to build a materialist analysis of bisexuality.

Materialism

I have argued elsewhere that 'there is a need for a "materialist turn" in thought concerning gender diversity, grounding post-structuralist gender analysis in the "realities" of social structures, material forces, and embodied subjectivities' (Monro, 2010, p.254). A materialist turn is important in theorising bisexuality, and it will include a concern with lived and socially situated experience, power dynamics and inequalities, economic factors, and biological diversities. The latter might appear contentious, given the historical meaning of feminist materialism as pertaining to anti-essentialist thinking (Brickell, 2006). However, this chapter follows Myra Hird's (2006) discussion of a 'new materialism' which foregrounds biological sex/gender variance. In other words, the material forces that shape people's lives include not only economic forces, and gender, race, ability-related, age-related inequalities and the social structures and institutions that support these, but also bodily 'realities', including aging, bodily limitations, and mortality. It is important to point out that a materialist analysis of bisexuality cannot be complete without considering international inequalities (see Hemmings, 2007; Ahmed, 2011); however these shall be addressed in Chapter 3 rather than here. This section provides an overview of the development of materialist concepts of gender and sexuality, and then looks briefly at how these might apply to bisexuality.

As Hines (2010) contends, the materialist analysis of sexuality has a historical precedent in the work of a range of authors (including Seidman, 1996; Richardson, McLaughlin and Casey, 2006; Taylor, 2007; see also Evans, 1993). Materialist approaches to gender have a substantial pedigree, in Marxist and Socialist feminisms (for example, Delphy, 1984), and Black feminisms (for example, Hooks, 2000). These approaches to studying gender inequalities have at their core a concern with structural inequalities concerning the distribution of wealth and resources, with axes of inequality stemming from the social institutions (for example, the law, the family, organised religion, and employment) and with the structuring forces that work through these (such as racism and sexism). Materialist approaches may have tended to reinforce gender binaries at the same time as challenging them, with transgender theorists (Wilchins, 1997; Monro, 2005; Whittle, 2006; Hines, 2010) bringing in a (far less developed) materialist analysis of gender diversity substantially later.

There is a glaring absence of bisexual-specific materialist scholarship within the sexualities literature which takes empirical, materialist approaches. For example, M.V. Lee Badgett and Jefferson Frank's (2007) collection on the economic aspects of sexual orientation discrimination includes some discussion of bisexuals together with lesbians and gay men, but does not address bisexuality-related prejudice and its material impacts. The materialist analysis of bisexuality has not emerged as a cohesive body of scholarship to date, but there is some literature which heads in this direction. For instance, Erich Steinman's analysis of bisexuality research leads him to suggest 'that more empirical attention to material relations, social structures, and everyday social interactions is needed to complement the symbolic emphasis of queer theory and cultural studies' (2011, p.399). Steinman argues that what is required is critical examination of the 'multiple social processes that generate bisexual "absences"' (2011, p.399).

This book does begin to trace some of these absences, but also, in its centring of bisexual people's stories, renders the lived experiences and material forces affecting this population evident. Whilst interactionist approaches are useful in understanding the micro-level construction of bisexual identities, a more structural approach which addresses institutions, the regulation of gender and sexuality, and the operation of heterosexism, mononormativity, and other forces, is required. Using materialist approaches, forces such as biphobia can be understood as foundational (fundamentally life-shaping) in themselves, with material effects on people's lives (for example, their ability to secure and maintain employment). Some theoretical tools can be taken from the sociological literature. For instance, prejudice against bisexuals overlaps with heterosexism, and:

> Heterosexism may be defined as a *diverse set of social practices* – from the linguistic to the physical, in the public sphere and the private sphere – *in an array of social arenas... in which the homo/hetero binary distinction is at work whereby heterosexuality is privileged.*
> (Plummer, 1992, p.19, his italics)

The findings from the UK bisexuality research indicated a need for the materialist conceptualisation of bisexuality in a number of ways; in particular there is a requirement to highlight the lived experience of bisexual people as an antidote to the widespread erasure and/or hypersexualisation of bisexuality, and a requirement for analysis of the ways in which mononormativity, heterosexism, biphobia, and a range of other forces (economic, social, and physical) shape bisexual people's lives. It is important to point out that other forms of prejudice impacting on bisexual people are also relevant, for example one contributor discussed lesbophobia as also impacting on bisexual women.

Research demonstrates that bisexual people do experience a number of different forms of structural discrimination (discrimination that is embedded in cultural and institutional norms, processes, and practices). For example, a European-wide survey of 6,424 bisexual women and 7,200 bisexual men conducted in 2012 (FRA, 2013) showed that bisexual people experience a whole range of forms of discrimination. For instance:

- 28 per cent of the women, and 25 per cent of the men, had been physically or sexually attacked or threatened with violence in the five years preceding the survey.
- 9 per cent of both women and men had felt discriminated against on the grounds of their sexual identity in finding housing in the 12 months preceding the survey.
- 18 per cent of bisexual women, and 14 per cent of bisexual men, felt that they had been discriminated against by an educational institution in the 12 months preceding the survey, due to their sexual identity.
- 47 per cent of the women and 36 per cent of the men felt that they had been discriminated against or harassed on the grounds of their sexual orientation in the last 12 months.

There was a link between LGBT persons being open about their identity with healthcare providers and experiencing negativity. This was especially true of bisexual men and women and transgender respondents. Those who were out to medical staff and healthcare providers were at least 50 per cent more likely to have ever experienced such problems than those who were not out.

The UK bisexuality study added to the picture concerning bisexuality and structural discriminatory forces. It was apparent from the data that bisexual people sometimes experience the social erasure of non-heterosexual, fluid, and multiple sexualities sharply (see also the section on biphobia, above and in Chapter 1). For example, Pia remarked:

> it feels like we are in a nowhere land, obviously most of the world is for straight people, they are there in the media and everywhere... then there are certain spaces for lesbians and gays, but there isn't as much for bisexuals.

This sense of social exclusion, which has its roots in the practices of the heterosexual mainstream and lesbian and gay organisations, impacted on Pia's subjectivity and the options that were available to her socially and culturally. These exclusions then manifested in material terms in a number of ways, for example a lack of helplines and support services for bisexual people, insufficient and inappropriate sexual health services, discrimination or erasure in healthcare provision (see above), and marginalisation and/or exoticisation in mainstream culture. Meg John, for example, explained:

> you just don't fit in the same way, it's similar to L and G in the sense the heterosexuality is certainly privileged in our culture, so to say you are L or G is to say yes you are in the dichotomous framework but on the less privileged side, it's still quite a step because you are assumed to be heterosexual unless you say otherwise, and I think bisexuality is like an extra step, because people don't really think – even though government policy is starting to use 'you can be attracted to both' it's still thought that bisexuality doesn't exist, or is a phase, a way to a mature sexuality – all those prejudices remain, so it's an extra hurdle you face.

Whilst structural biphobia, and other forces such as homophobia, have real impacts on bisexual people's lives, they do have some means of resistance or survival (depending on their social context). Contributors to the UK bisexuality project demonstrated a wide range of agentic responses (they showed that they had agency, or choice) when faced with social marginalisation. Dominant norms or scripts were used strategically by people to stay hidden in some cases, for example the middle class participant Reggie described the way in which he hid his bisexuality-related literature when his cleaner visited, so that she assumed that he is heterosexual. For other contributors, it was primarily a case of developing a lifestyle that fitted their desires, for example Kate, who was also middle class, negotiated an open relationship with her husband and started a new relationship with a women who was also married. For others, a political bisexual identity was strategically adopted as a means of countering prejudice, as the following quote shows:

> I think the reason I identify with bisexual – not necessarily *as*, because I don't necessarily think of identity as something that is solid, that I *am*, that include other identities – queer, and black, and disabled – and I think it's important – the specific identity as bisexual is important because the world as I've experienced it, the world we seem to live in – specific to now, Western Europe, 21st century, British or Anglo world – it's that the world is structured for people who are straight, who are heterosexual, who know that they are one gender or the other and fancy people of the opposite gender. (Camel)

The UK is relatively pro-equalities internationally (see Itaborahy and Zhu, 2014), and the UK bisexuality research data need to be seen in that context. It would be unthinkable to come out as a bisexual equalities representative in a workplace, for example, unless legal and policy initiatives were in place to support this. Therefore, international perspectives on the material construction of bisexualities are required. This book begins to indicate some of these in the subsequent chapters.

This chapter has used four strands of theory to understand bisexualities, using material from the UK bisexuality project. Starting with interactionism, the chapter explored the micro-level construction of bisexual identities, looking at the ways in which individual bisexual people's identities have developed. Interactionism is also used to analyse the social erasure of bisexuality, and the way in which biphobia is constructed at the micro-level. The chapter then uses two bodies of theory to understand other dynamics associated with bisexuality, such as the construction of bisexuality as transgressive, and as multiple, fluid or ambiguous. These theories are queer theory and trans theory; one strand of trans theory, gender pluralism, is potentially of particular use in building bisexuality-related theory because it encompasses a wide range of gendered, sexed, and sexual identity positions. The chapter is then grounded in materialist theory, given the need to centre bisexual people's lived experiences, and the processes of structural discrimination that affect them. These bodies of theory are not mutually exclusive (although there are tensions between, for example, deconstructionist queer theories and theories that take a more materialist stance), and they are used here to provide different ways of understanding bisexuality.

Summary

- Interactionist theories form a useful means of looking at processes of bisexual identity construction at the micro level. A number of the concepts provided by interactionist theorists are highly applicable, including sexual scripts.
- Interactionism can be used to illuminate biphobia, and also to explain why the social erasure of bisexuality is so problematic for bisexual people. If people create realities on the basis of shared understandings and there is no socially viable understanding of bisexuality, then it is very difficult for a bisexual person to build their identity.
- Queer theory and politics are discussed positively by some bisexuals, some of whom also identify as queer. There is a small amount of queer bisexual literature.

- Queer theory is problematic when applied to bisexuality for a number of reasons, in particular because the queer deconstruction of identities can, in practice, lead to a deconstructionist void where more socially viable identities, such as 'gay', then predominate.
- Some forms of trans theory can be useful for theorising bisexuality, partly because some bisexual people are also trans, and partly because there is shared territory in terms of identity multiplicity and complexity and challenges to gender-binary heteronormativity.
- Interactionist, queer, and trans theory approaches to conceptualising bisexuality would not in themselves be sufficient in interrogating the structural inequalities that bisexual people face. Therefore, some materialist analysis that explains the structures that render bisexual people marginal is brought into the chapter towards the end.

In the following chapter I use another, related body of theory, intersectionality theory, in conceptualising bisexuality in the UK and in India.

3
Intersectionality

This chapter utilises intersectionality theory in relation to bisexualities. Intersectionality theory draws on a number of the theoretical frameworks that have previously been discussed in this book, in particular materialism. However, by undertaking a materially grounded synthesis of feminisms, critical race theories, and other theories that address social forces and structures, intersectionality theory provides a particularly flexible and nuanced mechanism for understanding the ways in which bisexualities, and other non-normative sexualities, are forged.

The chapter begins with a brief overview of the development of intersectionality theory followed by a discussion of the work of Leslie McCall, which will inform subsequent analysis. The chapter then provides an exploration of bisexualities in India, focusing on macro-level dynamics. I explicate some of the ways in which Indian sexualities are cross-cut by structures and dynamics relating to gender, socio-economic class and caste, religion, and spatial location. The chapter then moves on to provide a micro-level analysis of intersectionality in the UK organised bisexual communities, focusing overall on issues of race and ethnicity. The section on Indian bisexualities is preceded by a discussion of colonialism and Southern sexualities, enabling it to be historically and politically situated. A complementary discussion of UK bisexualities was provided in Chapter 1.

It is impossible to include all diversities in one chapter if the aim is to provide some depth of understanding. Intersectional analysis in the following areas would contribute substantially to our knowledge of bisexuality: ability/disability (Shakespeare *et al.*, 1996; Cook, 2000; Davies, 2000; Lofgren-Martenson, 2009; Caldwell, 2010; Rembis, 2010), class (Bell and Binnie, 2000; Taylor, 2007), gender (Klesse, 2005), spatial factors (Wilson, 2000; Browne *et al.*, 2007), corporeality (Monro,

2005), and age (Nilan and Feixa, 2006; Cronin and King, 2010; Binnie and Klesse, 2013; McCormack *et al.*, 2014). There are other dimensions of intersectional analysis concerning bisexuality that require attention and that are not included here. For instance, it would be useful to build on the work of Wim Peumans (2014) regarding queer Muslim migrants; how are bisexualities relevant (or not) to migrants, and how do those migrants who identify as bisexual negotiate their sexualities in the context of both countries of origin and destination?

An introduction to intersectionality theory

Intersectionality theory was forged by feminists of colour and critical race theorists, drawing on insights provided by poststructuralism/postmodernism (McCall, 2005). US scholar Kimberlé Crenshaw (1989, 1991) introduced the term 'intersectionality' to mean a crossroads where different identities (in her case, race and gender) intersect. Other theorists have subsequently explored intersectionality as an axis of difference (Yuval-Davis, 2006), a dynamic process (Staunaes, 2003, cited in Davis 2009, p.68), or as relationships along multiple dimensions and modalities of social relations (McCall, 2005).

There has been a blossoming of interest in intersectionality theory and methodologies in recent years across a number of disciplines, including political science and sociology (see, for example, Cho *et al.*, 2013), but there has been a tendency for intersectionality studies to have focused mostly on gender, class, and race (see Crenshaw, 1997; Hurtado and Sinha, 2008). Intersectional sexuality studies is an emerging field, and there are only a few studies which address bisexuality, for example, K. Caldwell's (2010) research about intersectionality, bisexuality, and disability, and James Egan *et al.*'s (2011) study concerning urban environments and MSM. Other relevant scholarship includes Melita J. Noel's (2006) intersectional analysis of the lack of understanding of diversity within the US poly communities.

As noted above, intersectionality theory stemmed from the work of authors such as Crenshaw (1991, 1997) and Avtar Brah and Ann Phoenix (2004), who wished to challenge the exclusion of black women from feminist thought and research. There have, recently, been concerns voiced about the transposition of intersectionality theory from its roots in critical race and black feminist thinking to other loci of analysis. For example, Devon Carbado (2013) discusses the issue of colour blind intersectionality; this is intersectional analysis in which the whiteness which helps produce particular social categories is invisible or unarticulated. For white people, it is easy to overlook whiteness; because white people occupy a hegemonic position in Western societies (and carry the traces of colonial privilege in some postcolonial countries, as well). One of the privileges assumed by those in racially hegemonic positions is a lack of awareness of the discrimination and subordination of subaltern (non-hegemonic) subjects. This invisibility removes (from white people) the emotional labour associated with facing social inequalities, and the guilt that can accompany visible, acknowledged privilege; the injustices of racism are displaced elsewhere, playing out in the lives of black and minority ethnic (BME) people. The interrogation of whiteness is therefore important in moving discussions away from a focus on people of colour, and towards the underpinnings of structures of racial inequality (see, for example, Teppo, 2009). This chapter uses intersectionality approaches which address whiteness and racism in its examination of dynamics in the UK bisexual communities.

Intersectionality theory has a great deal to offer to those concerned with gender and sexuality, including bisexuality and unnamed sexual identities. This is evident in some recent work provided by bisexual theorists concerning intersections (even where intersectionality theory is not itself used), notably Eisner's (2014) discussion of race, nationality, and bisexuality. In basic terms, intersectionality approaches can be used to examine the way in which we are not just defined by sexuality, or gender, or ethnicity, or social class, or ability; we are each a unique mixture of different social characteristics. Because society is structured by many forms of inequality, some people – and groups of people – have identities that combine two or more marginalised or stigmatised characteristics. Importantly, these marginalised identities do not just add onto each other, but rather intersect in particular ways. In addition, characteristics such as race and sexuality are seen as being routed through each other, or mutually constitutive, so that it is not possible to think of 'race' and 'sexuality' as discrete social forces. The term 'social forces' is used to mean patterns of social opportunity and access to resources. Social forces also concern barriers to accessing opportunities and resources (for example, being denied access to reproductive technology) and the violence that people may endure (for instance being the victim of hate crime) when they are a member of a particular social group or groups.

It is important to note that there are differences between marked and unmarked social characteristics, which affect intersectional analysis. For instance, bisexual people may have the option of staying closeted about their sexual identity, which means that the structuring of their experience will be more subtle, including, for example, self-censorship and the mental health difficulties that may result from being socially erased (see Barker *et al.*, 2012). In contrast, people with visible ethnic characteristics that differ from those of the dominant social group (for example, Asian people in the white-dominated UK) may face prejudice in more overt ways, for instance being discriminated against in the labour market or being the victim of police harassment. Therefore, not all of the social forces that can be addressed using intersectional theory will play out in similar ways, and there may be situations where visible ethnic differences may, for example, override issues of sexual identity in terms of subjects' lived experience.

Intersectionality theory provides, overall, a way of addressing complexity and the different ways in which social characteristics work in interaction so that, for example, at one point discrimination on the grounds of sexuality and gender might shape someone's life chances, but this person might simultaneously use class privilege to resist or circumnavigate this. Each socio-cultural context provides a different site for the intersectional construction of sexuality. This is demonstrated in the following quote, provided by Mario (one of the contributors to the Colombian bisexuality research), who is a sociologist. The quote exposes the way in which several intersections operate for white and African heritage Colombians, particularly in terms of ethnicity, space, and gender.

> I think that in order to talk about the relationship between bisexualism [sic] and the Afro-Descendent population in Colombia, it is important to understand that there are a lot of different social structures, dynamics and conditions for white people, and different social structures for black people in Colombia that affect the issue of being a bisexual or not, and they are related with the geographical context as well... if you live in the centre of the country or if you live in the coast, being a bisexual could be a totally different experience... a good example is the case of some Afro-Descendent communities from Cartagena [Colombian Caribbean Cost] or from Chocó [Colombian Pacific Cost] where polygamy and bisexuality are culturally accepted... but you can find a really interesting thing at the same time: bisexuality is only accepted for men and not for women, reproducing some rules of the Colombian patriarchal society.

To summarise, intersectionality theory is used in this chapter because it accomplishes some crucial conceptual and political tasks, including the following:

- It moves beyond the debate about whether sexual (and other) categories are necessary by developing the notion of strategic essentialism; where, for example, someone identifies as bisexual in order to raise the political profile of the non-LGH population.
- It provides a means to address within-group differences and inequalities without destroying the basis for group identification; this is important politically as well as conceptually for communities grappling with diversity issues.
- It reveals areas of privilege as well as marginalisation, providing a more nuanced picture of groups such as bisexuals; again, this is crucial politically in enabling inequalities to be tackled and in increasing agentic possibilities (for example, enabling bisexual or queer individuals to identify issues which they can take a stand on from positions of relative privilege).
- The notion of intersectionality has entered political realms and may provide a useful means of effecting positive change (see Chapter 7).

Anticategorical, intercategorical, and intracategorical approaches to intersectionality theory

This section of the chapter provides a way into the work of one particular theorist, Leslie McCall (2005), so that some of her key ideas can be applied to bisexualities and other non-normative sexualities later in the chapter. It is of course acknowledged that other approaches could be used, and that there is a need to work further around intersectionality theory and bisexualities.

According to McCall (2005), there are different methodological approaches to intersectionality studies. The first of her three approaches, *anticategorical complexity*, deconstructs identity categories. This deconstructive approach builds on post-structuralism, but is complementary to the interactionist and queer theories, and some aspects of the trans theories, as discussed in Chapter 2. Anticategorical approaches can be used to dismantle, for instance, the assumption that people have fixed, discrete sexual identities, and the assumption that monosexuality is normal. Both of these assumptions are institutionally embedded (for example, in legal frameworks), self-replicating, and tied in with the unequal distribution of material and social resources in such a way as to marginalise individuals and groups who do not conform to them. Anticategorical approaches speak well to those people who reject identity categories such as 'bisexual'.

Whilst anticategorical approaches to gender and sexuality are useful, there are difficulties with approaches which dismantle categories without then addressing the ways in which new categories form, power dynamics remerge, and power structures cut across particular identities or communities in unacknowledged, unmarked ways. For example, later in the chapter it will be demonstrated that the most established UK bisexual communities, whilst effectively providing space for deconstructed sexual identities, are very much structured by unmarked (unacknowledged and invisible) white privilege. Overall, the difficulties with anticategorical intersectionality theories mirror the problems associated with the 'degendering' approach outlined in the trans theory section and the queer theory sections of Chapter 2.

McCall termed her second approach to intersectionality *'intercategorical'*. For McCall, *'intercategorical complexity*... [which] requires that scholars provisionally adopt existing analytical categories to document relationships of inequality among social groups and changing configurations of inequality along multiple and conflicting dimensions' (2005, p.1771). Intercategorical intersectional theories are more akin to the materialist theories discussed in Chapter 2, than to post-structural, queer, or interactionist approaches. They enable interrogation of the ways in which power and access to resources are unequally distributed, along (for example) gendered, sexual, or socio-economic class lines. This is relevant to understanding inequalities within bisexual populations. With the intercategorical approach, there is also an understanding that categories can be used strategically, in an agentic way. For bisexual people, this is important because there is widespread acknowledgement within the community that the term 'bisexual' is fictitious (socially constructed) and incomplete (see Chapter 1), however, given the widespread social erasure of bisexuality and the social marginalisation and inequality that may accompany this, the term 'bisexual' remains strategically important.

McCall discusses a third approach to intersectionality, termed *intracategorical*. For McCall:

> *intracategorical complexity* inaugurated the study of intersectionality... it falls conceptually in the middle of the continuum between the first approach [anticategorical], which rejects categories, and the third approach [intercategorical], which uses them strategically. Like the first approach, it interrogates the boundary-making and boundary-defining process itself, though that is not its raison d'être. Like the third approach, it acknowledges the stable and even durable relationships that social categories represent at any given point in time, though it also maintains a critical stance toward categories. This

approach is called *intracategorical complexity* because authors working in this vein tend to focus on particular social groups at neglected points of intersection.

(McCall, 2005, p.1771)

Intracategorical theory therefore allows for analysis of individual-level subjectivities and experiences, as forged in relation to diverse social structures. Intracategorical theory is very useful in considering bisexuality, because it can be used to address the ways in which bisexual people can face multiple discrimination; as bisexual *and* (for example) poor, disabled, female, working class, or from BME groups. It also enables an exploration of particular gendered/classed/sexed identities which do not fit with Western definitions of sexuality/gender, making it crucial for understanding some forms of Southern sexualities. An example of the way in which intercategorical theory could be used regards the sexual abuse and exploitation of thousands of young boys by adult males, some of whom are behaviourally bisexual, in Pakistan's public spaces such as bus stations (Anon, 2014; see also UNICEF, 2009). These boys are socially marginalised (for example, runaways from domestic abuse or orphans); their sexual identities as victims of abuse are shaped by spatial and socio-economic class factors. Gender is also relevant, specifically because the men who abuse boys claim that rigid gender norms (sex segregation) 'force' them to engage in abuse. Religion provides a further dynamic; the prohibition of homosexuality in the Islamic faith means that child abuse, also prohibited by the Islamic faith, may be seen as inconsequential. This chapter, like the rest of the book, does not focus on abusive bisexualities, but further research on this area is required.

Having outlined McCall's three approaches to intersectionality theory, the chapter now moves on to bring in some postcolonial insights which are relevant to understanding bisexuality and other non-LGH sexualities.

Postcolonial analysis of Southern sexualities

Why is postcolonial analysis relevant to a discussion of bisexualities and intersectionality? As indicated in Chapter 1, contemporary internationally dominant sex, sexuality, and gender systems of categorisation, and the social inequalities with which they are intrinsically linked, stem at least partially from a Western colonial past. This colonial past was the locus of the formation of not only modern Western sex/gender/sexuality categories, but also homophobia, biphobia, and heterosexism. These sets of categorisation and hierarchies developed together, as part of the systems of racialised, sexualised, and gendered inequalities that underpin many contemporary societies. It is unsurprising that critiques of LGBT identities categories have emerged from postcolonial sites (and in the West; see Waites, 2009, 2009a), although postcolonial critiques of colonial prejudices and persecutions regarding sexual diversity have been comparatively subdued.

A number of writers, politicians, and activists from Southern countries, many of which have experienced colonial rule or invasion by Western countries such as the UK and the USA, have interpreted the categories of LGBT as being a Western phenomenon (see Rouhani, 2007). For some people in these countries, same-sex sexualities and gender variance have become associated with Western economic and political dominance. Resistance to Western dominance appears to have become discursively linked with (sometimes state-sponsored) hate crimes and discrimination against people who engage in same-sex sexualities and/or who are gender variant, sometimes with a faith-related spin (typically, fundamentalist Christian or Islamic). The Southern framing of same-sex sexualities as 'Western' and in some cases 'diseased' has developed despite widespread evidence for early Southern same-sex indigenous sexualities and forms of gender variance (see, for example, Fox, 1998; Safra, 2003). Southern homophobias and biphobias are, to date, a largely unacknowledged legacy of colonialism.

Postcolonial countries appear to have been mostly reluctant to 'decolonise' in relation to sexual norms. There are some exceptions; critiques of colonial legal legacies, for example, have been used strategically to challenge homophobic and biphobic laws in India (see Waites, 2010). This may be because homophobia, and by default biphobia, have become woven into nationalist discourses. The linkage between homophobia (and biphobia) and nationalism is also present in Western countries, for instance in Ireland (Richardson and Monro, 2012). It appears to stem from the relationship between patriarchy, heterosexuality, and nationalism, in which dominant groups in society seek to control reproduction by regulating relationship forms, in order to strengthen ethnic power bases and control of land and resources (see, for example, Feinberg, 1996). Crucially, the notion of same-sex sexualities and gender diverse identities as being 'Western' is countered by the wide range of Southern LGBT and related activisms (see, for example, Salazar, 2009), some of which will be discussed in Chapter 7. There is also a growing body of international literature about non-white LGBT people of faith (Yip, 2010; Peumans, 2014).

An important trend that reflects (and perhaps reinforces) the Southern notion of LGBT identities as being a 'Western import' has emerged in (mostly) Western countries in recent years. Some national identities have become bound up with the LGBT rights agenda, with progressive attitudes towards LGBT people being used by politicians as an indicator of democracy and 'modern' society, which may (or may not) translate into a better human rights record. This 'homonationalism' (Puar, 2007) can then become linked with anti-immigrant, ethnocentric discourses, where people of colour and Southern peoples are framed as homophobic (see, for example, Jivraj and de Jong, 2011). It can also be used cynically by nations to present themselves as progressive, despite their human rights abuses, as in the case of Israel (Puar, 2011).

The issue of homonationalism plays out differently in relation to homosexuality and bisexuality. Because bisexuals are still socially marginalised and stigmatised generally within Western countries and amongst some 'lesbian and gay' organisations, 'bi-nationalism' has not emerged. Sexualised forms of nationalism are only likely to develop where the subjects (individuals) in question are seen as domesticized, 'respectable' citizens who uphold dominant norms (such as monogamy) within particular countries. There are domesticized, monogamous bisexuals who support normative citizenship frameworks (see Chapter 6), but they are not very apparent in homonationalist narratives.

Although specifically 'bi-nationalist' discourses have not developed, homonationalist discourses that emphasise sexual diversity and tolerance over ethnic inclusion may act to consolidate various problematic, racist ideas, such as the notion that BME people in a Western country cannot be bisexual. Such ideas can have disastrous effects on bisexual individuals, in the context of transnational migration. For example, participant observation at the BiCon Bisexual conference in 2014 showed that a bisexual asylum seeker in the UK (male, of Jamaican origin) was being denied asylum despite being at risk of murder, should he be forced to return to Jamaica (see UK Bisexual Community Outraged by Deportation, 2014).

Overall, broader conflicts concerning cultural, economic, and territorial dominance frame the ways in which sexual identities are constructed and play out in different countries. It is important to note that there are wide variations both within and between countries. In addition, local people may have traditional sexualities which could be interpreted as bisexual, regardless of whether this is reflected in national rhetoric and structures. For example, the quote about Afro-Descendent Colombians earlier in this chapter demonstrates context-specific Southern bisexualities.

The complexities associated with national identities in relation to gender and sexuality indicate a need for context-specific analysis that draws on intersectionality theories. One example of this type of analysis is provided in the next section of the chapter, which concerns Indian bisexualities and Indian non-heterosexual sexualities more broadly. The section starts with a historical overview of gender and sexual variance in India, before looking at the ways in which notions of bisexuality have been developed in India. This section of the chapter uses intercategorical approaches in tracing the forces relating to (for instance) gender, faith, spatiality, and socio-economic class that shape sexualities in India, but it also draws on an intracategorical approach, in that it addresses the multiple forces that act to marginalise Indians who engage in bisexual behaviours.

Indian bi/sexualities

Whilst providing a comprehensive account of the variations in Indian sexualities and genders is beyond the remit of this chapter, it is possible to explore some of the patterns and trends found in India as a means of illustrating the formation of genders and sexualities in a Southern nation of increasing economic, political, and cultural importance. This section of the chapter provides a historical snapshot of Indian sexualities and some insight into the ways in which bisexualities are currently constructed in India, focusing on the key intersectional dimensions of gender, caste, class, and spatiality.

Gender is centrally included for two reasons in the discussion of sexualities in India. Firstly, the deeply patriarchal nature of modern Indian society: heterosexual marriage and procreation is considered a universal 'duty', and India is traditionally sexually repressive, with heterosexual practices as well as same-sex practices being strictly regulated (for example, heterosexual partners have been murdered due to violations of caste boundaries) (see Bouchard, 2007; Mishra and Sharma, 2007; Chakrapani and Ramakrishnan, 2009; Ravikumar and Kumar, 2011). Secondly, India has some socially existent (if heavily stigmatised) gender variant identities for natal males and intersex individuals (Khan, 2004), which means that the binary heterosexual/homosexual system with is predicated on male/female binaries is complexified.

Other key factors structuring the lives of Indian bisexuals, MSM/WSW/MSMW and WSMWs and queers are as follows:

- Class, caste, and spatial dynamics, which are all tied into the hierarchical structuring of Indian society (and indeed the Indian diaspora) with important implications for sexualities.
- High HIV rates, which are disproportionately found amongst MSM/MSMW (Thomas *et al.*, 2011).
- The impact of globalisation on sexual cultures in India (Ramasubban, undated).

The evidence of gender variance in India dates back thousands of years (Thomas *et al.*, 2011) with depictions of *hijras* (individuals who are born as male or intersex and who form a third sex/gender community) and MSM found in ancient temple carvings. Traces of bisexuality – particularly the interpretation of bisexuality as psychological dualism, but also sexual and gender variance in different forms – are apparent in a range of ancient teachings (see Nandi, 1980; PUCL-K, 2003). Although there were specific social roles for gender and sexual variant people (see Chakrapani *et al.*, 2002), a range of authors (such as Seabrook, 1997) suggest that sex/gender roles were more fluid in ancient India than in the modern west:

> The identities of 'Homosexual' or 'Bisexual' did not exist, because a man's [sic] sexual identity was based strictly on actions (what he 'enjoyed'), and not something intrinsic to his personality or – in the case of contemporary scientific jargon – his genetic make-up.
> (Budding Polymath, 2008, via Roy (personal communication, May 2013))

Ancient India, which comprised, over time, a complex and sophisticated set of societies, was colonised by the Mughals (who were Muslim) starting from the 8th century AD (this declined in the 18th century AD) and then for a much shorter period by the British, initially on the basis of trade and then more directly (from the middle of the 18th century AD to 1947). When the British took control of India, they imposed legal penalties for same-sex sexualities. As Thomas *et al.* state, 'Homophobia was formally codified by legal code Section 377 [in 1860] which made sexual relations between men a criminal offense... MSM in India, therefore, experience multiple forms of social and legal discrimination' (2011, p.921). In addition, cultural traditions which had supported sexual and gender diversity were steadily eroded, so that:

> Indian culture came to be reconstructed as unilinear and co-terminus with Hinduism, and Hinduism, in turn, as narrowly 'pure' and norm driven... Widespread 'norms' of universal marriage, monogamy, and procreative heterosexuality involving chaste women and masculine [sic] men and enforced by the triumvirate institutions of patriarchal family, caste, and community, contribute to a consensual societal framework of silence about sexuality'.
> (Ramasubban, undated, p.93–94)

The criminalisation of same-sex sexualities continued post-independence, and as Apphia K contends, 'The common misconception amongst a lot of naïve people, even intelligent ones, is that Westernization brought alternative sexualities to India' (2009, p.206). In 2009, in a landmark victory for struggles for sexual rights, sex between consenting same-sex adults was decriminalised in India (Waites, 2010). However, this ruling was overturned in December 2013 (Shyamantha, 2013). It is against this backdrop that contemporary Indian bi/sexualities are played out.

The number of MSM (and MSMW) in India were estimated to be 3.1 million in number in 2010 (see Thomas et al., 2011). The two main groups that overlap with and make up the umbrella category of 'MSM' are [i] *hijras*, who have many diverse characteristics and sub-identities (Reddy, 2006) and [ii] male-bodied people who self-identify as gay, *kothi* (passive partner), *panthi*, (active partner) *do-partha* (both active and passive), or bisexual (Mishra and Sharma, 2007; see also Chakrapani et al., 2002; Khan, 2004; Phillips et al., 2010). Overall, therefore, the picture concerning sexual and gender diversity is rather more complex than that found in some other countries.

Contemporary Indian bisexualities

The majority of MSM in India are in fact behaviourally bisexual (see Phillips et al., 2010; Zahiruddin et al., 2011) and are married to women. However, whilst behavioural bisexuality may be common, identity-based bisexuality is not. As Venkatesan Chakrapani and L. Ramki Ramakrishnan say:

> Bisexuality is relatively uncommon in India, mainly because here, even people with alternative sexualities do not think in terms of

sexual orientation and identity. Also, even among well-educated persons [sic] the word 'bisexual' is unfamiliar, although this is changing. Doctors often mistakenly apply this term to intersexed individuals.
(2009, p.218)

Identity-based male bisexuality was virtually absent in India in 2002 (Chakrapani *et al.*, 2002). This needs to be seen in the context of wider dynamics. Gay identities in India are also not discretely articulated or represented, and the category of 'male' itself is diverse (Khan, 2004). According to Ahonaa Roy (2012), there is also a pattern of homo-social male-to-male relationships that are culturally blended into the male sociability. Gay visibilities and relationships become blurred due to relationships among men that are physically intimate but not framed as erotic.

There is little literature about cisgender female bisexuals in India, but there are a number of support organisations for lesbians and bisexual women in urban centres (Chakarapani *et al.*, 2002). Chakarapani *et al.* discuss the way in which 'Absence of a self-conscious lesbian identity in most women means their identity will remain "invisible" in society' (2002, p.21); the same appears to be true of bisexual women. Chakarapani *et al.* also describe a 'lack of space for discussion of alternative sexuality (or sexuality, period)' (2002, p.20). Many bisexual and lesbian women marry men because of familial pressures and they are expected to maintain the façade of a marriage, which is reinforced due to their economic dependency.

However, in a trend that illustrates the intersectional effects of financial and class privilege, bisexual identities are emerging alongside gay and lesbian identities amongst the upper and middle classes (Ahonaa Roy, personal communication, May 2013). It is only a few groups of middle and upper class women in metropolitan centres who are able to form lesbian and bisexual communities (Chakrapani *et al.*, 2002). It is important to point out that Indian people who engage in same-sex sexualities, and those who are gender-diverse, face severe risks and abuse, including domestic violence, forced marriage, and abuse by the police (including sexual abuse and extortion) (Ramasubban undated; PUCL-K, 2003; Monro, 2010); these risks may be avoided by some middle and upper class Indians who live in safe localities and have more protected lifestyles.

According to Roy (personal communication, May 2013), socio-economic class also shapes cisgender male Indian sexualities and bisexual behaviours, forging middle and upper class identities of 'bisexual' which contrast with working class behavioural bisexualities. Indian men who identify as gay or bisexual are currently largely upper and middle class are English speaking and urban. For men and, to a lesser degree, women, there are gay groups and scenes in a number of cities. However, within these, bisexuality tends to be framed in terms of marital status (married men and women seeking some same-sex sexual contact) rather than as discrete identities (see Chakrapani and Ramakrishnan, 2009). Urban gay, lesbian, and bisexual identities are shaped by the politics of cosmopolitanism and cultural globalisation, so that some bisexual Indians have a sense of 'global queer identification' (Roy, personal communication, May 2013). However, the term 'bisexual' is also used in some of the medical and activist literature (for example, Khan, 2004).

In contrast to the upper and middle classed metropolitan, globalised identities of 'gay' and to a lesser degree 'bisexual' Indians, the (natal male) identities of 'kothi' and 'panthi' are usually found amongst lower socio-economic groups. '*Kothis* think of themselves in stereotypically feminine terms and identify themselves in opposition to *panthis*, constructed as "real men" or "masculine men" who are predominantly attracted to women' (Chakrapani and Ramakrishnan, 2009, p.218). *Kothis* and *panthis* seek each other out for sex, sometimes establishing relationships which are usually supplemental to their marriages. Also, working class men who are behaviourally bisexual have sex with other men and/or with *hijras* and *kothis* (see Zahiruddin et al., 2011). The literature shows, for example, that truck drivers engage more in same-sex sexualities than members of the general population (Khan, 2004). Intersectional analysis is particularly useful here. This population experiences their sexualities being shaped by the pressures of work and by spatial factors. They are distant from their wives for lengthy periods of time and therefore unable to have sex within marriage; at the same time, this distance creates opportunities for non-heterosexual sex.

Autobiographical material from Indian bisexuals supports some of the arguments presented above, but also challenges some of them. Robyn Ochs and Sarah E. Rowley's (2009) edited collection *Getting Bi: Voices of Bisexuals Around the World* includes writings from more than ten Indian people for whom the term 'bisexual' is personally relevant. It demonstrates a wide variety of Indian bisexualities, with bisexuality being variously defined by the authors. For example, Paramita Banerjee says:

> Bisexuality for me is primarily an attitude, a way of life, a mind set that privileges plurality and dares to tread beyond narrow one-dimensional binds of identity. In sexual terms, bisexuality has taught

me to revere individual sexual autonomy over any specific collective identity. I understand bisexuality to mean an ability to relate to persons as persons – unconstrained by gender roles or norms, allowing such relationships to traverse different spaces, including the sexual.
(2009, p.105)

In terms of intersectional dynamics, the contributors to the edited collection are anglophone, but several people are involved in grassroots and feminist activism (for example, Paramita Banerjee), suggesting that there may be sites in which Indian bisexualities are emerging, that are other than the relatively privileged metropolitan ones discussed above. The narratives also challenge other assertions made in the literature. For example, Rajiv Dua notes, 'I began my journey of explaining my bisexuality to my mom... Identifying as a bi person has not been easy. In the monosexist society of urban India, I was seen as either heterosexual or homosexual' (2009, p.33). For Rajiv Dua, the family appeared to be a place of some acceptance (see also Apphia, 2009), whilst the gay groups that he discussed were problematic.

One of the themes raised in the autobiographical material concerns commonalities between Indian and UK-based bisexualities. Some of the contributions to Och's (2009) collection indicated that Indian bisexuals may experience social marginalisation by both heterosexuals and lesbians and gay men. However, there are also important differences between the Indian and UK situations. These include existence of varied, highly intersectionally striated forms of gender and sexual variance in India, as discussed above, which contrast with the more homogeneous and discrete LGBT categories that dominate in the UK. Another notable difference from the UK situation is the way in which the history of diverse genders and sexualities is drawn on by some contemporary Indian writers. For example, Rami Ramakrishnan notes, 'We have been around as long as homosexuals, and have been part of queer culture whether we have chosen to identify ourselves as bi or not' (2009, p.244). For some authors, faith is drawn on in conceptualising sexualities. For example, Maya Ganesh relates the 'concept of the Omni-erotic and pan-gendered deity Shiva [who] appears through Hindu, Buddhist, and Tantric streams of philosophy and ritual' (2009, p.100) to her own identity development. She rejects the 'three deceptively neat pigeonholes' [heterosexual, homosexual and bisexual] (2009, p.99) and says:

[Shiva] can magically assume the female form to be sexual with another man, or vice versa. The concept here is about being both, living and loving both, so that you distil something that goes beyond both – that is neither? I don't know – I'm still learning – but I think these powerful and sexy ideas are not exploited enough.

(Ganesh, 2009, p.100)

Whilst reference is made to gender binaries in this quote, what is also apparent is a liminal turn which mirrors the 'moving beyond sex and gender' approach to theorising trans diversities (see Chapter 2), grounded in an historical trajectory of identity plurality. There is an emphasis on high levels of individuation in this quote and the one above (from Paramita Banerjee), as opposed to category-based identification. This sort of discourse is absent within public UK bisexual narratives, although there may be discussions of this type taking place amongst bisexuals in the UK.

This section of the chapter has addressed Indian sexualities in relation to bisexuality, drawing on the literature, some personal communications with Ahonaa Roy, and autobiographical material. It illustrates intercategorical intersectionality by exploring the ways in which gender, socio-economic class/caste, and space shape sexualities in India. The final section of the chapter addresses UK bisexualities, using intercategorical and intracategorical approaches.

Intersectionality and bisexuality in the UK

Intersectionality theory can be applied in many different ways to any given social context. This section of the chapter looks at intersectionality theory and bisexuality in the UK in three specific ways: firstly by noting that some UK-based bisexual people are actually using the term; secondly by providing a snapshot of some key social forces in relation to bisexuality; and thirdly, by addressing the ways in which whiteness, ethnicity, and bisexuality intersect. The choice of a focus on ethnicity was made to reflect both the findings from the data, and my own concerns with racialised inequalities.

It is important to avoid developing a hierarchy of oppression when analysing patterns of inequality and privilege (see Richardson and Monro, 2012) because to do so undermines the possibilities of positive collaborations which support diversity and equality. It is also necessary to point out that bisexual people do not necessarily see social forces such as racism or ageism as playing a leading role in shaping their lives. The contributors to the UK research, when asked about different aspects of their identity, included a range of characteristics such as professional role, being a parent, interests such as music, gender identity, feminism, identification as metropolitan, and country of origin.

The notion of intersectionality is known, and used, by some of the people who contributed to the UK bisexuality research project. Their interpretations of the term varied. For example, when asked in the interview, 'Are you familiar with the term "intersectional"?' Meg John said, 'I think probably most of the tensions within bi activism and the bi communities are around intersectionality, I think they do end up being sort of tensions around who is more oppressed or who is more privileged', whilst Elizabeth reported:

> Yes, I use it all the time and think it's a very useful term. It brings the focus back to the individual, which is where it should be. People are not just black, or disabled, or queer – we are not statistics. Strand-focused diversity initiatives lose sight of this sometimes, and intersectionality is a good way of getting them back where they should be.

It appears that, where research contributors were aware of ideas of intersectionality, an intercategorical approach addressing different identity/social characteristic strands was most commonly taken. Such an approach can be used to look at some of the key social forces affecting bisexual people in the UK, notably differences of ability, gender, age, and socio-economic class. It is not possible to do justice to these forces here, but I will look at them very briefly.

The research data, and my participant observation, indicated that there is substantial awareness of diversity concerning disability in the organised bisexual community in the UK, including neurological diversity and mental distress (which is common in the community, see Yockney, 2013). The awareness of diversity manifests as statements regarding, for example, possible triggers for trauma in the descriptions of the workshops that are available at BiCon. There is also awareness about gender inequalities, for example there was a workshop about feminism at the 2012 conference, and there is support for trans and gender-diverse inclusion, for example non-gendered signs were placed on the public convenience doors at the BiCon 2012 conference. The organised bisexual community includes adults of all ages (as well as children at some family-friendly events such as the Big Bi Fun day) but the population is mainly in the 20–40 age bracket, and age discrimination against older bisexual people may be an issue.

The bisexual communities are highly structured in terms of socio-economic class, as the following interview section demonstrates:

> Lawrence: The bi community concentrates on looking at diversity issues which is a great [thing] but in and of itself it is not the highest priority... class is a backward issue that no one wants to look at because they don't know how to look at it. The community that doesn't come to BiCon doesn't come to BiCon because of class issues, do you know what I mean?
> Interviewer: Yes, I do know what you mean. Do you have a sense of those people who do not come to BiCon – who they are, what their interests are?
> Lawrence: I used to be involved in online groups the online communities are just like [pause] cruising, they might be cheating on their wives, the discussions online were about what they were doing, and also about people making sense of their sexual orientation, communicating with other people, discussing the emotional side, that is an equally real side of bisexuality... for example it could be people who go to football matches, working men who would never go to BiCon, it's not on their radar.

The predominantly middle-class composition of the organised bisexual community is compounded by economic factors. Some of the research contributors talked about the high financial cost of BiCon, and geographical accessibility issues, meaning that people without jobs or less well-paid jobs find it harder to access (although there is a sliding scale and a bursary fund).

Overall, ability, gender, age, and class-related forces are all important in addressing bisexuality in the UK and further research addressing these factors would be useful. The remainder of the section, however, turns to issues of race and ethnicity. Faith is included in the discussion because the research findings suggested that faith is often linked to ethnic affiliations and communities, and that racism operates in association with faith-related prejudices in the white bisexual communities. Also, faith is negotiated and reworked by bisexuals as shown, for example, in Alex Toft's (2014) study of bisexual Christians.

Bisexual people and ethnicity/race

This section of the chapter will analyse one set of social forces that structure the lives of people who have bisexual attractions and behaviours; those associated with race and ethnicity and, where relevant, faith.

Ethnicity is defined as a bundle of norms, shared histories, and social practices that are generationally transmitted via families and immediate communities. The terms BME and 'people of colour' are used interchangeably, to reflect different conventions in the UK, USA, and elsewhere. It is recognised that these terms are debated; what is sought here is an approach that will be acceptable to as many people as possible. The complexities within the 'race' categories that are used in the UK are also notable because they can erase differences amongst bisexual BME people. For example, contributor Susan expressed unhappiness about the way in which people see her as Asian; she identifies as Hong Kongese. The UK bisexuality research included people from a range of BME backgrounds, who had diverse relations with their countries and cultures of origin. The research contributors' experiences of ethnicity also varied widely; whilst some people's narratives demonstrated sharp intersectional disadvantage (see below), a minority indicated that minority ethnic status had some advantages. For example, Merina, who is of southern European heritage, said that:

Merina: I feel so lucky to be bisexual, for me, to be an outsider.
Interviewer: Can you explain?
Merina: Because I can see things...cultural or outsider lens... depending on the situation and the people, I am able to see things from other points of view and that is *so* precious...I have got more knowledge, can maybe interact with people and connect because I have a different part of me.

This quote illustrates some of the reasons why it is important, when discussing intersectional dynamics, to consider individual agency, and the complexities of social forces which can both privilege and marginalise people. Overall, these notes about complexity form a way into the rest of this section of the chapter, which addresses faith and ethnicity, and whiteness and racism, in the UK bisexual communities.

Faith and ethnicity

Faith can form an important conjunct to ethnicity, and the following section of the chapter addresses these two social characteristics together. Most of the BME bisexual/queer UK research contributors were of faith and/or had been strongly influenced by faith in terms of their sexual identity development. For a few of the contributors, faith communities formed an important part of their current support network, whether or not they were 'out' about their sexuality. These findings are reflected in the literature about faith and sexuality more broadly, which indicate the reclamation of traditionally homophobic and biphobic faiths (including Christianity and Islam) in some countries by LGBT people. For example, Angelia Wilson (2000) describes the way in which Southern US Christian gays and lesbians are developing their own churches and interpretations of Christianity, whilst Farhang Rouhani (2007) discusses Al-Fatiha, a prominent queer Muslim group in the USA (see also Peumans, 2014; Toft, 2014).

Despite demonstrating a shift towards an LGBTQ reworking of traditionally homophobic faiths in some places, the literature indicates that there is conflict concerning some religious organisations and entrenched prejudices against non-heterosexuals. The intersectional discriminations faced by BME bisexuals (and LGT people) are evidenced in the research in the UK, for example 'the consequences of coming out (or being found out) can be extremely harsh for Muslim LBT women, particularly for those who are entirely dependent on their families' (Safra project, 2003, p.5).

The UK bisexual research, with its limited sample (which will have excluded very socially marginalised bisexual people because I was not able to sample them), demonstrated a wide range of faith/community/sexuality permutations. However, the homophobic, and by default biphobic, element of some religions and cultures did impact on the contributors. It was noticeable that all of the BME research contributors had spent time away from their communities of origin and for some, for example Yaz, this was important in allowing them to acknowledge and accept their same-sex attractions and to construct their sexual identities. Two bisexual contributors had moved to the UK specifically to escape from cultures of prejudice related to Catholicism, and in order to access bisexual communities that were very marginalised, or non-existent, in their countries of origin (Spain and Italy). At the same time, some BME research contributors reported white bisexual people's insensitivity affecting bisexual people of faith, for example, Islamophobic comments being posted on social media by white bisexuals. The lived experiences of BME bisexuals in such cases demonstrates intracategorical intersectional disadvantage; they face prejudice from their communities of origin, plus bigotry from white bisexuals.

There are also nuances in the research findings concerning the impacts that faith and culture in intersection have in shaping sexual identities, which are exemplified in the following quote from Jo who is of Chinese origin:

> I have some friends, Catholics, quite conservative, but they are quite kind to me as well.... I guess it's the Chinese culture in a way. First of all I never openly say that I am whatever, because first of all I don't know how to identify myself and secondly I don't find that I need to *come out*, or whatever, so even for the Christians, say, some of them, they don't really like the idea, they reject homosexuality. But they never say something back to me.

This quote indicates that there may be an anticategorical 'pull' which is connected to the structuring effects of faith, and traditionalism, so that any form of sexuality is kept within the private realm and is likely to be unnamed; the 'pull' is away from discrete and named sexual identities. This leads into a discussion about the ways in which BME people (and others whose lives are strongly structured in particular ways, for example by disability, age, or caring commitments) may have to prioritise other parts of their identity over sexuality. Various authors (for example, Ahmed, 2011) critique 'gay imperialism', the assumption that sexual minority status is the master status; it would be possible to think of critiques, also, of 'bisexual imperialism'. The assertion of bisexuality as a master identity is common in the white UK bisexual community; this overlooks and renders invisible the importance of ethno-racial (and other) identities. Not all the UK bisexual/queer BME contributors did prioritise other characteristics over sexuality, for example Camel remarked, 'at some point I realised I had basically chosen sexuality and gender over race, and that is stark but its true'. However, the BME communities associated with non-mainstream sexualities in the UK appear to have different norms to both dominant white cultures and various non-bisexual minority ethnic communities. Negotiating these different sets of norms may be a challenge that some people simply do not see as a priority because of the need to survive as a parent, partner, or community member within social groups that form their core support.

There is another issue concerning ethnicity and sexual identity categories that emerged from the UK bisexuality research, and that partially mirrors postcolonial critiques of LGBT categories. As Jacqui (who is black British) said:

> the word 'bisexual' is a very European word, and I really like the acronyms 'Men who have Sex with Men' and 'Women who have Sex with Women', just I can think about where I grew up...black men would go to a sauna or a club and have sex with other men but they would never call themselves 'gay' or 'queer'.

A few contributors connected this kind of anticategorical or queer critique of sexual categories with postcolonial theory, or critical race theory. Notably, Lena (who was of mixed heritage) discussed her worries with rigid Westernised identity categories, as well as the way in which 'it is a privileged position that allows us to do so [consider sexual categories]... asylum seekers, from... the global south, and their choice to be gay, or bi, it's a matter of life and death for some people'. Similarly Lawrence, who was white British, noted that the term 'bisexual' is a useful organising term in the West but not necessarily elsewhere. Overall, the difficulties with the term 'bisexual' (and LGH) that were discussed above, in an international context, are also likely to play out within BME communities within the UK. This may form a point of tension with the organised (predominantly white) bisexual communities that seek increased visibility for bisexuals, because identity-based bisexual politics may not be a priority or even be seen as a goal for people (including those of colour) who are outside of these communities.

Whiteness and racism within the organised bisexual communities

In what ways are the organised bisexual communities, for example BiCon, BiFests, and bisexual support groups, racialised? Before addressing racial dynamics within the organised communities, it should be noted that there are some organised BME bisexual groups (see below), but that the focus of this section of the chapter is the predominantly white bisexual communities that have been established for many years. Also, it is worth pointing out a number of the UK BME research contributors had had little or no contact with the organised bisexual community. Some, such as Yaz and Lena, socialised with non-heterosexual people as part of broader networks centred around music, childrearing, the arts, and/or academia, but either did not know about the organised bisexual community or had no interest in it. None of these contributors discussed experiencing racism from other non-heterosexual or bisexual people, in stark contrast to BME contributors' discussions of racism in the organised bisexual community (see below). Another caveat is that, of those BME bisexual people who were involved in the organised bisexual community, there seemed to be agreement that it is important in a number of ways, providing a crucial space for coming out as bisexual, resources and a sense of community, and space for other alternative sexualities. Contributors said for instance:

> BiCon is still white, but the openness in terms of diversity and diversities I found in BiCon is really rare... I usually attend the workshops

in diversity because they are so, every time there is something that I gain from that in terms of understanding other differences, not taking for granted things that for me are ordinary, but for other people it is not the case.

(Pia, who is of Southern European origin)

Pia then went on to note that lighter-skinned BME people (like herself) seemed to be more welcome at BiCon than darker skinned ones, indicating that racism is present.

The UK, being predominantly white in ethnic/racial and cultural terms, is a good place from which to examine whiteness and bisexuality (see the introduction of this chapter). It was noticeable, when asked about their identity, that those research contributors who were white and British did not discuss their own ethnicity or race, whilst those who were of colour and or/non-British of origin did. Further research would be needed to ascertain reasons for this; it could in some cases be due to a lack of awareness concerning racial privilege. A lack of awareness amongst white people about racialised privilege was indicated in other parts of the research findings. For example, BME people become framed, by white people, as the educators or experts, removing the responsibility for learning about race from them, as indicated in the following quote:

I remember going to the first Bis of Colour [at BiCon], a white woman stopped me in the corridor and said 'how the hell am I going to learn about Bis of Colour if you don't tell me' I said 'I've got enough on my plate', there are resources these days, there is the internet. (Jacqui)

Are organised predominantly white bisexual groups racist? The organisations and groups discussed by contributors varied widely in terms of the levels of awareness experienced around racial and ethnic diversity, with experiences ranging from direct racism (in a women's bisexual group some years ago) to a BiFest which had a clear code of conduct and which was described very positively by black British research contributor Jacqui. However, at the time of the fieldwork, there was evidence that difficulties with racism and ethnocentrism were very real within the community associated with BiCon. These manifest as a tolerance of overtly racist behaviour, as well as assumptions of secularism, an alcohol-oriented culture which excludes some people of faith, and a lack of awareness of white hegemony. For example, Jacqui described the way in which a white individual tried to stop specific groups forming at BiCon (black and trans) because they would feel excluded; as Jacqui said 'The fact they don't like feeling excluded for 75 minutes, if that's not institutional racism I don't know what is... I still have emails from people saying they will not be coming to BiCon because of that event [trans and BME people]'. Overtly racist behaviour is also discussed in the following quote:

> A couple of us ran a session at a BiCon three years ago called Bis of Colour, specifically for Bis who were also black or minority ethnic, we made the definition because we didn't want to exclude people who needed it. But that session was quite [pause] astonishing, because we had into double figures... every single person in that room had had a racist experience at BiCon. And that includes people asking you if you are in the right place. I have had that on more than one occasion, where people would ask me if I knew where I was, or if I was in the right place, which mirrors experiences I have had on the gay scene... there were things like bringing up instances of racism and people not believing it, people denying it, there are things like discussions of race that are characterised as drama rather than serious issues. (Camel)

Other experiences of racism that BME people have had at BiCon or other bisexual organisations include:

- Getting blank stares when attempting to take part in conversations
- Being treated as exotic, including in one instance being told 'you look like an African queen'
- White people assuming that a BME person's family of origin are biphobic and that they are closeted with their family
- White people assuming that bisexual spaces will be non-oppressive
- Being included in a tokenistic way without any changes to the white power structures (being 'ornamental ethnics', for example, on posters)

It is important to see the racial structuring of the bisexual communities in terms of the predominant whiteness of those communities, which renders the issues and identities of BME bisexuals marginal. The hegemonic whiteness of the organised bisexual community is partially constituted by the alternative cultures that are prominent within it. These include the goth community, the fan community, the pagan community, the kink scene (BDSM), and the poly community, all of which are very white. For example, Jacqui noted that 'the only scene that's whiter than the poly scene is the kink scene, a tin of white paint spilled over... the poly scene the only big difference I can see from the bi scene is there are a heck of a lot more pagans in the poly scene'. Class intersections provide another dynamic, with contributor Jacqui remarking that bisexual people's activities that are marked as 'middle class' also alienating (some) BME people; 'unless you've read certain books or watched certain... or had a background in research, or certain comics, you can get completely left out of the conversation. That is probably one of the *whitest* parts of it'. An understanding of whiteness and subcultures helps to explain the persistent nature of racism in the bisexual communities. Subcultures tend to exist within particular social strata (Gelder and Thornton, 1997, see Chapter 4); for the bisexual community in the UK, this is a white middle-class strata. The subculture element of the community makes it hard to incorporate diversity because it involves changing the basis for identification.

The intersectional marginalisation of BME people by the white cultures and subcultures associated with the organised bisexual community can be seen as unacceptable for a community that aims to support all bisexuals. However, the situation is complicated by the fact that some of the alternative subcultures, and the people within them, are themselves socially marginalised. Some of them (such as the pagan faith communities) are of key importance to some white bisexual people's identities, in the same way as socially accepted faiths (such as Christianity) are to some BME (and white) bisexual people. Therefore, several processes of intracategorical intersectionality are apparent, and these sometimes conflict with each other, especially when other marginalising factors, such as mental distress, are also part of the picture.

Cultures associated with whiteness, and overtly racist actions, mesh together to form a structure of racism which has material effects on the lives of bisexual people of colour in the UK. Racism can lead to self-exclusion from the organised bisexual community, so that BME people who wish to access that community then have to deal with the effects of both biphobia *and* racism in a way that can fuel mental distress and isolation, affecting their capacities to contribute to wider society and to access economic and social opportunities. The issues are described by Camel as similar to the racism on the lesbian and gay 'scene', but the combined (intersectional) effects of dealing with heterosexism, marginalisation within the lesbian and gay communities and then a lack of acceptance of minority ethnic status by the bisexual community can be experienced as 'really damaging and painful' (Camel).

The organised bisexual community is making efforts to deal with patterns of racism and ignorance, for example, by running race diversity awareness training at a bisexual activist event, and providing support for a BME asylum seeker (see UK Bisexual Community Outraged by Deportation, 2014). Important developments concerning bisexuality and ethnicity are also taking place outside of the organised (predominantly white) bisexual community. For example, a 'Bis of Colour' group has recently been established separately from BiCon by BME bisexual activists (http://bisofcolour.tumblr.com/), organising events, networking, and providing positive images. More broadly, there are a range of other organised groups in the UK for LGBTQI people of colour and faith which include bisexual people, for example the Safra Project serves Muslim lesbian, bisexual, and trans women (Safra, 2013).

This section of the chapter has addressed the UK bisexual communities from an intersectional perspective. It mentioned some of the ways in which bisexual people in the UK view intersectionality theory, and briefly introduced some dynamics regarding ability, age, gender, and socio-economic class. The chapter then provided a more in-depth analysis of the UK bisexual communities from a perspective centred on the experiences of BME bisexuals.

To summarise, this chapter has introduced intersectionality theory and provided an overview of three strands of intersectionality theory as developed by McCall (2005): anticategorical, intercategorical, and intracategorical. It has applied intersectionality theory to one Southern country, India. In doing so it has provided some postcolonial contextualisation generally, followed by a historical overview of the development of gender and sexual categories in India, and then an analysis of Indian bisexualities and related sexualities using a primarily intercategorical approach. The chapter then addressed UK bisexualities, focusing on an analysis of whiteness, ethnicity, and racism within the organised bisexual communities, drawing on all of McCalls's approaches to intersectionality theory.

Summary

- Intersectionality theory was initially developed by black feminists to address the marginalisation of black women in the USA, drawing on materialist analysis.
- It has been developed along a range of trajectories; this chapter uses the anticategorical (deconstructing categories), intercategorical (looking at how different social forces interact), and intracategorical

(examining how forces forge specific subjectivities) approach, following Leslie McCall (2005).
- Intersectionality theory can be further expanded on by introducing a postcolonial element, addressing the way that bisexuality and other sexual identity categories have been constructed as part of the colonising process and the ways in which this plays out in previously colonised countries.
- India forms a case study; intersectionality theory is useful in explaining why, and how, gender, nationality, socio-economic class and caste, faith, and spatiality intersect to forge different types of bisexual and other non-heterosexual subjectivities.
- The UK forms a second case study, demonstrating the utility of intercategorical and intracategorical intersectionality theories in tracing different social forces that shape UK bisexual people's lives, and focusing on the operation of whiteness and racism in the organised bisexual communities.
- Anticategorical intersectionality theory is shown to have particular relevance for people who are not, due to intersectional pressures, willing or able to assume bisexuality as a master identity.

The next chapter explores bisexual people's experiences of sexuality, relationships, kinship, and community. It also discusses the interfaces and differences between the bisexual and some other communities.

4
Sex, Relationships, Kinship, and Community

How do bisexual people live their lives? How do they 'do' sex and relationships, parenting, and care for others? What networks and communities are important to bisexual people? This chapter focuses on the lived experiences of bisexual people and other non-LGH people in relation to these matters. It also provides some analyses of the social spaces that bisexual people may engage in, including not only the organised bisexual communities but also those relating to BDSM. Whilst the combination of these different aspects of lifestyle and community within one chapter might seem startling, it does enable the interrogation of some of the underlying values and processes that take place across these different spheres. The chapter also includes a discussion of the relationship between bisexual people and the lesbian and gay communities. This last section stands in contrast to the others, in that the cultural norms and values of the bisexual communities, and the lesbian and gay 'scene', diverge in some important ways.

The chapter 'speaks to' a number of bodies of literature within sociology and feminist scholarship, including literature about care and the family, and non-heterosexual care and kinship networks (see Hines, 2007). It adds to the growing literature about new forms of family, including, for example, Elisabetta Ruspini's (2013) text which addresses a variety of family forms and parenting models. The chapter is relevant to discussions about welfare, particularly in countries where there is a governmental expectation that welfare (care) requirements will be met within the private realm (see Prideaux, 2005). A particular set of 'sexual stories' are relayed in this chapter, following the tradition established by Plummer (1995), but adding a new, bisexual dimension. The chapter addresses various intimacies; sexual, emotional, and kinship-related, but it does not conceptualise them in terms of intimate citizenship (Plummer, 2001); rather, the emphasis is on providing a picture of bisexual and other non-LGH people's lived experiences.

The work of Pierre Bourdieu (1977) is drawn on for this chapter, because Bourdeusian concepts can be used to provide insights into the formation and operation of communities that are other to those revealed by the theories that I have already used in the book. Bourdieu occupies 'a political and theoretical space constructed out of the divergent currents of Marx, Weber, and Durkheim, structuralism and interactionism, pessimistic determinism and a celebratory belief in the improvisatory creative potential of human practice' (Jenkins, 1992, p.10). Bourdieu had a 'pragmatic relationship' with various authors (see Jenkins, 1992, p.11), and it is in a pragmatic fashion that I shall be applying some of the concepts drawn from his work. Some sexuality theorists have drawn on Bourdieu, for example Yvette Taylor in her (2009) analysis of UK lesbian and gay parenting; however, there is a dearth of discussion concerning Bourdieu and bisexuality, which this chapter addresses. The chapter does not seek to provide a critical analysis of Bourdieu's work per se (see, for example, Adkins and Skeggs, 2004).

The chapter requires some caveats, as follows. To start with, it does not engage with the large amount of international literature about MSM and MSMW which addresses sexual practices (see, for example, Yun et al., 2012), nor does it add to this literature. I purposefully focus, in this chapter, on the UK, in order to provide some depth of analysis. Bisexual community organising appears to have begun in the USA, and the development of both US and UK bisexual communities historically is well-documented elsewhere (see Hutchins, 1996; Rust, 2000; Monro, 2005; Richardson and Monro, 2012).

The chapter is mostly focused on the organised bisexual communities and other organised erotic communities, and more research is required about the familial, intimate, and community experiences of bisexual and other non-LGH people who are not involved in these. Also, the UK bisexuality research showed that some bisexual people have experienced sexual abuse as children, and other studies show that intimate partner abuse can take place amongst bisexuals (Head and Milton, 2014). Sexual violence and abuse will not be addressed in this chapter. It is also worth noting that some of the contributors to the UK bisexuality research discussed other communities that they are involved with, for example, professional networks, but that these are not addressed here. Lastly, there are other trajectories of analysis that could be pursued elsewhere. For example, the norms and practices that have developed within the bisexual communities concerning care and support, and social and erotic capital, could be seen as a contribution to civil society (using concepts drawn from Robert Putnam (1993)). 'Cultural capital' is defined here as a type of social resource that is associated with tastes, consumption patterns, and attributes that are authorised within a particular culture (see Webb *et al.*, 2002). Social, and erotic, forms of capital complement more 'tangible' forms of capital such as economic resources.

I begin the chapter with two sections that are inclusive of a range of bisexual people, including those involved in bisexual communities, and those who are not. These sections concern, firstly, sex and relationships, and secondly, kinship and care. The chapter then looks at the organised bisexual communities and at some related communities, before providing, by way of contrast, some thoughts about the lesbian and gay communities and the ways they diverge from the bisexual communities.

Relationships, intimacy, and sex

It is impossible to do justice to the richness and variety of bisexual people's relationships and sexualities in a short chapter section. This part of the chapter therefore traces some relevant patterns and dynamics in a UK context. It begins by outlining different types of bisexual relationship form and sexual expression, and then looks at these in relation to gendered and sexual normativities, before briefly discussing some of the challenges facing bisexuals.

Bisexual people and other non-LGH people have a very wide range of different types of relationship identities. Those involved in the UK research project discussed asexuality (where someone does not experience sexual attraction), celibacy (where they do not have sex – this can be chosen or involuntary), single but engaged in casual sexual liaisons, monogamously partnered, poly partnered, poly-identified but single, partnered and in a non-monogamous setup, and in one case paying for sexual services. There are other forms of sexual/relationship setup that are described in the literature, including internet sex (see for example, Hartman-Link, 2014) and covert same-sex sexualities between women who identify as heterosexual (Walker, 2014). In terms of actual sexual practices amongst the UK bisexuality project contributors, these also ranged very widely, from masturbation, to traditional forms of sex within monogamous relationships, to threesomes, casual sex in spaces such as saunas, BDSM play (which may or may not be sexual), and group sex. It would not be possible to quantify the extent to which different forms of sex take place, but it is important to warn against framing bisexuals as promiscuous and/or involved in multiple relationships. For example, research contributor Pablo discussed being single as a positive choice, and said that:

> I like the idea that you don't necessarily have to demand everything from one partner, and you can have a relationship to serve a smaller series of purposes... and that actually chimes quite well with me, so maybe that's something that will happen in the future.

Bisexual people's relationships and sexualities are gendered in varied ways. A minority of the bisexuality research contributors were actively critical of heteronormative models, for example Lena said that 'We do not have to destroy coupledom, because that's human instinct, but it would not have to be two people, it could be three, four, five, six people'. Others bypassed heteronormative models and the scripts provided by other fairly established scenes, as the following quote shows:

> because we didn't have anything to do with the poly community or really have much experience of it, we were able to make it up as we went along, so we didn't get sucked into it 'well if you are going to do this shape relationship this is how it has to be done, if it is a V this is how it has to be done' ['V' is a particular poly relationship model]... As far as I am concerned I am incredibly lucky – I have two major partners who both love and respect me and mores to the point love and respect each other. (Lee)

Here, Lee described the way in which he and his partners established their own relationship scripts (see Chapter 2) in a different way to those established within the poly community, showing that even within a relationship model, variations exist.

Normativities

One theme to emerge from both the interviews and participant observation is the prevalence of male-female primary relationships within the organised bisexual community. In other words, bisexual people in male-female couples might or might not engage in sex and/or relationships outside of their main relationship, but the main relationship is usually between a woman and a man. For example, research contributor Grant reported:

> I think people that have ongoing life-relationships with same-sex partners are visible in the bi community, on the edges of it... it is not as obviously visible, there's a lot more flirting but I think a lot of the relationships that you see as ongoing tend to be more male-female... there is a very strong idea of support [for same-sex relationships] but what you actually see is [opposite sex relationships] there is a lot of discussion about changing that, and celebration of people doing what they want to do, a hedonism or freedom, but not talking about the difficulties of doing it. (Grant)

Despite the prevalence of a dominant heteronormative model of bisexuality, there is also evidence of gender diverse and queer sexualities and relationships. For example, Dave, who is a trans man, talked about the bisexual community potentially providing a 'pool of people who would potentially be attracted to a trans person without threat' because bisexual people potentially welcome partners with a range of genital configurations and are therefore less likely to reject trans partners. There are also signs that some bisexual sexualities combine and possibly disrupt normative relationship models in complex ways, as shown in the following interview section:

> Kay: a previous boyfriend was very happy to get involved with other men and me. That didn't just involve me and the other guy touching, it involved him and the other guy touching.
> Interviewer: Was this at a party?
> Kay: Oh, plenty of parties [laughs]
> Interviewer: Would it be possible for you to say a little bit more about the setup for these parties?
> Kay: Alright, it was a group of friends, I was with my boyfriend, lots and lots of couples that would go out and we'd go clubbing, you know obviously have quite a few drinks, dance the night away then come back and all meet at somebody's house where it was suitable for us to stay up all night, big, and people got a bit fruity and just went off into different corners or wherever, or we'd all end up in the same room and we'd be touching and kissing [pause] it wasn't swinging as such, it was just people enjoying being around other people that they loved.

Here, whilst the public-facing relationship model might be heterosexual, the intimate story is more nuanced. This shows that it is difficult to analyse relationships in dichotomous transgressive/heteronormative ways; sexualities can be either, or both, depending on context.

Challenges facing bisexuals

Bisexual people face challenges in their relationships, including not only overt biphobic discrimination (see Chapters 1 and 2) but also invisibilities and marginalisations. For example, Angela Breno and M. Paz Galupo delineate the ways in which:

> Bisexual identity remains largely invisible within the context of relationships as sexual orientation is often presumed based on whether the coupling is same- or other-sex (Ochs, 1996). This may lead to a feeling of disconnect between communities and increasing isolation, especially when bisexual individuals change partners.
>
> (2008, p.221)

The challenges of existing outside of mainstream relationship norms can take a major toll on bisexual people's lives. For example, Yaz talked about how her relationship with her girlfriend broke down because the girlfriend wanted to have sex with other people but Yaz was 'too in love with her to be able to do that', whilst Merina talked about how she found the way in which a poly partner informed all their other partners of their relationship developments very intrusive, because she is a 'very private person'. Because these relationship formats take place outside of the usual sexual scripts (see Chapter 2), emotional work is required to develop alternative sexual scripts. There was considerable evidence of bisexual people finding ways to develop sexual and relationship scripts that worked for them, for example Kate discussed the process she went through with her husband:

> I didn't talk to anyone, and it was very stressful, because all I could think about was 'If I'm a lesbian, then I can't be married to [husband] so what am I going to do?' So he came back from his trip, and we did the usual thing, and then I said 'look I've got to talk to you about something'... he was really, really, really sweet, kind of like 'I don't really understand what is going on but we'll figure it out'.

It is apparent in the above discussions that personal choice and affective bonds such as love and desire are central to the sexuality and relationship formations found amongst the bisexual interviewees. The findings overall reflect Antony Gidden's (1992) notion of a 'pure' relationship; contributors discussed the basis for sexual engagements and relationships being about sex, expressing love, emotional connections, shared interests, and happiness for everyone involved. When asked about the basis for sexual relationships, the contributors unanimously rejected structural reasons for relationships (such as economic security). However, the two contributors who were in parenting relationships did describe structural constraints on their bisexual expression (see below) and some others discussed 'building a life together' as involving caring responsibilities. These themes are discussed in the next section of the chapter.

Kinship and care

Whilst care and intimacy have been addressed in the literatures about gay men, lesbians, and transgender people (see Hines, 2007), there has been no such analysis of bisexual practices of care, beyond some anecdotal material (for example, Arden, 1996) and texts that include bisexual people in their title but have no bi-specific content (for example, Cahill and Tobias, 2007; Chapman *et al.*, 2011). 'Care' can be defined as 'day-to-day activities which are central to the sustaining of family lives and personal relationships – helping, tending, looking out for, thinking about, talking, sharing, and offering a shoulder to cry on' (Williams, 2004, p.17, cited in Hines, 2007, p.35). This section of the chapter shall demonstrate some of the ways in which bisexual people and their allies care for each other as friends, family, lovers, and partners.

The bisexual communities and care

The organised bisexual communities in the UK actively support mutual care, in recognition of the minority stress, discrimination, and related mental health problems that bisexual people face (see Barker *et al.*, 2012). Care is manifest in a whole range of ways, including, for example, the volunteer counselling provided at BiCon, cuddle and massage workshops, and the culture of cake-eating. Self-care is an explicit aspect of the agenda, as exemplified by Anon's (2012) article in Bi Community News about self-care at BiCon.

The emphasis on safer sex in organised bisexual spaces, as demonstrated by the widespread provision of safer sex supplies and workshops on safer sex at events such as BiCon, is also an aspect of caring within the bisexual communities. Research internationally shows some links between behavioural male bisexuality and unsafe sex practices; this is challenged by the steps that the bisexual communities have taken to minimise risk. There is also evidence from the USA that bisexual men take more care about condom use with female partners, as compared to heterosexual men (Jeffries and Dodge, 2007).

Contributors to UK bisexuality research indicated that safer sex practice, and other practices to ensure emotional safety around sex and intimacies (including mechanisms to ensure consent during BDSM play; see Bauer, 2014), are key parts of the cultures associated with events such as BiCon. Such practices may be shared with other communities such as the gay men's sex scenes and the BDSM communities (see, for example, Landers *et al.*, 2011). The research findings indicated that there is a culture of safer sex competence within the bisexual communities, which together with capacities concerning communication and eroticism form a type of intimate capital.

Traditionally, the sociology of the family has privileged heterosexual nuclear families over other familial forms (see, for example, Roseneil and Budgeon, 2004 cited in Hines, 2007). However, scholarship is emerging (for example, Ruspini, 2013) that challenges this. Bisexual family forms may also offer challenges to heterosexist notions of the family. This section of the chapter looks at bisexual people's relationships with their birth families, and at the families that they have built. It includes some discussion of care within the family.

Families of origin, parenting, and care

The contributors to the UK research had very varied relationships with their families of origin, ranging from distant links with families based in other continents, to regular, mutually supportive contact. Some participants were 'out' to their families; of these, several discussed the subject as difficult, and some contributors remained closeted about their sexual identity. Ethnic origins had some impact on this, for example Yaz said that 'they have met my girlfriends on occasion, but I would never be able to tell them directly because they wouldn't understand' (see Chapter 3).

Some bisexuals, like some LGT people, create alternative families with lovers, ex-lovers, and friends (see, for example, Hines, 2007). There is a history of bisexual people having children, often by traditional means (within male-female partnerships), and BiCons have sometimes provided crèches. Overall, there has been a baby boom in recent years amongst UK-based bisexuals and some contributors discussed the way in which 'It's [BiCon] becoming a more family-oriented community as more event organisers have children and want to continue being involved in the community' (Nancy). There are workshops at BiCon that focus on bisexual people as parents, and poly parenting, as well as some child-friendly events such as craft workshops. However, as contributor Grant noted, 'Some people do not want to have kids at BiCon because they want to keep it highly sexualised. There is a tension which will come up more – whether childcare should be provided, what events you can take kids to'.

Parenting clearly structures bisexual people's identities and activities, although this depends on their relationship setups. As noted above, two of the research contributors had children. Both of them were in monogamous, male-female relationships and their interviews showed that they privileged their parenting over the sexual expression with other people and/or engagement with sexually cosmopolitan social scenes that they had enjoyed before having children. Neither of them was out as bisexual to their children (who were all under ten years old). Contributor Dave discussed this as follows:

> one thing is I always expected to be open with my kids about my gender identity and my sexual orientation... with them being adopted... I have found it very difficult to talk about those things with them... in fact I have never talked about dating anyone other than their mother with them... I feel they are a bit too young to understand the nuances of who I am as a person... and the other thing is, I have never tried to have kids and date, but I imagine that would be difficult. (Dave)

Being closeted with children may be a challenge for bisexual people, adding another layer of minority stress in a similar way to the stress that may be experienced by closeted lesbian, gay, and trans parents. However, those bisexual parents who maintain the appearance of heterosexuality will access heterosexual privilege in a way that 'out' partnered lesbians and gay men cannot.

The closets that some bisexual parents maintain also include some of the other identities discussed later in the chapter, which are more heavily sanctioned socially (BDSM and swinger, for example). Some of these are explicitly sexual and require 'adult-only' boundaries for child protection reasons rather than convenience. Cultures of care amongst the organised bisexual communities (in this case, awareness of the need to protect children from inappropriate sexual influences) were evident in the research findings.

Moving on now to look at caring more generally, it was clear from the interviews with UK bisexual people that caring relationships varied considerably depending on the relationship status of the research participant. Interviewees were asked who they would turn to if they got ill. Some of the single people indicated that they were isolated, and said that they either looked after themselves and/or exchanged mutual support with friends. Those interviewees who were in committed couples felt that these were the site of caring responsibilities, even where other sexual partners were in the picture. The interviewees who were in poly relationships reported that the live-in partner(s) formed the core caring unit, although there could be caring links with other partners, too. For example:

> My partners are listed as my emergency contacts at work! If my geographically-closer partner got ill I would take care of them, if necessary rearranging things so that I could live with them. We would try to take financial care of each other too, probably with help from family of origin and chosen/domestic family. They would take care of me if I got ill in a similar way. With the partner who lives further away it's more likely that their domestic partner would be a primary carer but I would do what I could to take care of them too, as I think they would with me. (Nancy)

This chapter sub-section on care in the bisexual communities, parenting, and care within families of choice has reflected the diversities that are found in the bisexual communities. The research demonstrated the high levels of agency that bisexual people are exercising in creating cultures of care that are non-traditional, in areas as diverse as sexual practice, parenting, and care in the community. There were however areas where care was less present; notably amongst single bisexual people, who face bisexual minority stress but do not benefit from the welfare provided within bisexual families and partnerships. Some interesting tensions were also apparent, for example, between sexual rights agendas and parenting agendas, as played out in arenas such as BiCon. The next section of the chapter looks at the organised bisexual communities in more depth.

The bisexual communities: fields, habitus, and subcultures

The statement that 'As bisexuals we have to create a safe supportive atmosphere in our lives' (Hutchins and Kaahamanu, 1991, p.132) provides a good opening for a discussion of bisexuality and community in the UK. This section of the chapter investigates the norms, values, and processes associated with the bisexual communities, using a number of concepts drawn from the work of Bourdieu (for example, 1977), specifically 'fields', 'doxa', and 'habitus'. In the last part of the section, some ideas from subculture studies are also applied, complementing the previous discussions.

The organised bisexual communities can be understood as a set of 'fields', following Bourdieu:

> a field, in Bourdieu's sense, is a social arena within which struggles or manoeuvers take place over specific resources or stakes and access to them... A field, therefore, is a structured system of social positions – occupied either by individuals or institutions – the nature of which defines the situation for their occupants.
>
> (Jenkins, 1992, p.85–86)

The bisexual communities can be seen as a 'field'. They have been created by bisexual people and their allies to provide 'space' to be bisexual; to connect with others, to explore identity issues, to find refuge from the heterosexism and mononormativity of mainstream society, and to organise politically (see Firestein, 1996). There is a substantial network of bisexual groups and events in the UK (Bisexuality in the UK, 2014) and groups are structured in various ways. For example, Jen Yockney reflects on the formation of Biphoria, a Manchester-based bi group formed in 1994 and the oldest bi group in the UK:

> every month's meeting had a defined topic with workshops planned out for months ahead. That seemed to be the case for most other bi groups at the time... we had day-long events to mark Bi Visibility Day in 2001 and 2002... another BiCon in 2004 was our last big blow-out, since when there have been small to mid-size events each year.
>
> (Yockney, 2012)

The importance of bisexual space is demonstrated in some of the research findings, for example Pia said that 'The first time I went to [BiCon] was the one in Wales, oh it was so brilliant. I wasn't expecting to see so many people and also because it was in the countryside it felt like it was only *us* there'. Bisexual community spaces can also be interpreted as fields because they involve a particular set of practices which are separate to mainstream society and also to the gay and lesbian fields, although there are overlaps and engagements (see below), for example bisexual group meetings are held at the Manchester Lesbian and Gay Centre. The bisexual communities also involve struggles over particular stakes. For example, Chapter 3 illustrated some of the tensions concerning processes of belonging and exclusion that take place in the bisexual communities.

Bourdieu has presented other ideas which are relevant to understanding the UK bisexual communities. These concepts mirror the interactionist theories outlined in Chapter 2, but with particular relevance to groups and communities. Bourdieu argued that a field manifests via a 'doxa': a core set of values and discourses which are taken for granted (see Webb *et al.*, 2002). He also adapted the term 'habitus' (a Latin word meaning 'habitual or typical condition') to mean:

> an acquired system of generative schemes objectively adjusted to the particular conditions in which it is constituted, the habitus engenders all the thoughts, all the perceptions, and all the conditions consistent with those conditions, and no others.
>
> (Bourdieu, 1977, p.95)

In other words, the habitus in which each individual finds themselves is a historically grounded set of cultural and social practices (including norms and values), which the individual takes for granted and then, by default, reproduces, in interaction with other people and the wider environment. The habitus disposes people to act in a certain way; people adjust their actions to the external world on the basis of the social programming that they already have, and can then also influence the external world, effecting change.

There is a particular type of habitus associated with BiCon and other events associated with the bisexual communities, such as BiFest. It concerns shared identity issues, activism, lifestyle politics, a broadly left-wing political orientation, non-commercialism, the inclusion of gender and bodily diversity, and voluntary organising. Some core values underpin the bisexual communities; these include support for sexually diverse identities and expressions between consenting adults; support for the ethical frameworks and care (see above); particular organisational processes and rules that frame the events; anti-commercialism and anti-hierarchy; and high levels of tactile and emotional expression. Some of these values and related practices can be highly confluent with individual bisexual people's identities, as illustrated by Jacqui's description of her first BiCon:

> it was brilliant, the open affection from people, being hugged more in the last 24 hours than I had in my entire life... It felt that I could be myself, I went to a drag event... it felt almost like getting into a warm bath, I could just relax.

The habitus associated with the organised bisexual communities (notably BiCon, and BiFests (which are day-long bisexual community gatherings)) is also delineated by a particular set of cultural markers and behaviours which are apparent in the following section of an interview with Grant:

> Interviewer: When you talk about the 'cool' crowd in the bi community can you say a bit more about that?
> Grant: They were highly comfortable with who they are, or entirely comfortable with the bi aspects of that [identity], whether or not they actually were, they said that they were happy with that and it's wonderful, and these feelings of oppression or argument against [bi] were something to be annoyed about, rather than something that was scary... a higher preponderance of highly coloured hair, piercings, that sort of thing... lots more dressed up, high goth, wearing a lot more piercings... badges... androgynous sort of style, bright coloured hair, something alternative.

These markers and behaviours also point to a subculture interpretation of the communities that make up BiCon and the BiFest. A broad definition of 'subculture' is of groups of people who have something in common, distinguishing them from members of other social groups; typical descriptors could be 'disenfranchised', 'disaffected', 'creative', 'informal', 'organic', 'deviant', and 'oppositional to the mainstream' (Gelder and Thornton, 1997). Some of the other behaviours characteristic of BiCon could also be interpreted as subcultural, for example the use of name tags which individuals decorate with coloured symbols to indicate characteristics such as relationship status, sexual availability, and interests, and the informal rule that people ask each other's consent before hugging.

Sometimes people in subcultures re-negotiate their socially subordinate position within wider society by creating internal hierarchies or alternative forms of status, differentiating themselves from those outside of the subculture and creating a group identity (Gelder and Thornton, 1997). The 'in-crowd' at BiCon appears to have reconfigured mainstream norms, valorising subculture markers such as alternative appearance and sexual confidence. This may inadvertently exclude those who either do not identify with these, or who lack the necessary social and cultural capital to embody them. Some of the research contributors who had been to BiCon expressed feelings of alienation concerning the BiCon-related communities, due to being socially marginalised in a field where alternative forms of habitus render them 'uncool', or in some cases due to a lack of shared habitus. For example, Dave (who is married, middle class, male, middle-aged, and white) found BiCon and BiFest to be unfriendly and so he stopped attending, and Reggie (who is a single, middle class, older white male) experienced BiCon as cliquey and overly sexualised. Another example of the ways in which subculture norms and processes can marginalise people is provided by Andy, who was speaking about a local bisexual group:

> I remember one time a guy came down, he was a young farmer, I remember thinking 'he doesn't really fit in with our group', because we mostly tended to be on the left politically, we had a shared intent about how we looked at sexuality and the social issues around it, and the reasons for the existence of the group, so when he came along he sort of couldn't find a way in really.

Some of the research contributors also discussed the ways in which once they had experienced the relief and pleasure of being in bisexual-friendly space, they realised that there were other pressures to conform, for example, to poly and BDSM norms (see below), although it is important to note that BiCon supports all consensual adult sexual identities including asexuality and monogamy. It is also necessary to emphasise the diversity of experiences that people have at BiCon. For example, at a workshop titled 'Fitting and Misfitting in the Bisexual Community' (BiCon 2012) a young man from a rural area who was at BiCon for the first time described how he felt comfortable and welcomed (consent was given for this material to be included in the research).

The fact that there is space at BiCon for concerns about 'fitting in' to be raised demonstrates the reflexive nature of the community, but, nonetheless, analysis concerning habitus and the ways in which subcultures create internal hierarchies remains pertinent. These form 'doxa', meaning that is can be hard for people who are embedded within the field to perceive them, in a similar way to the difficulties that white bisexual people have in perceiving racism (see Chapter 3). The next section of the chapter addresses a set of communities which have fields that overlap with the bisexual communities, and largely confluent sets of habitus.

Erotic communities related to the bisexual communities

There are several erotic communities in the UK that overlap with the organised bisexual communities, but that have their own distinct habitus; these are the BDSM (also known as 'kink'), fetish, poly, and swinger communities. A few specifically bisexual sex clubs exist, for example BiBaby in London. There are other networks that may include bisexual activities, including MSM (for example cruising and cottaging), adult sex work (Boris et al., 2010), behavioural bisexuality on the 'party' (clubbing, rave) scene, and dogging (group/voyeuristic sex in secluded public places), all of which are generally consensual and between adults, and therefore largely confluent with the habitus of the organised bisexual communities. Activities such as paedophilia, which can be behaviourally bisexual, but are criminal and non-consensual, are strongly non-confluent with the habitus of the organised bisexual communities.

Before looking at the UK erotic communities, it is important to state that the development of sexual and erotic cultures takes place within specific national contexts. For example, there are bisexual-relevant networks in the USA which are less apparent in the UK. In particular, the Human Potential Movement in the USA has fuelled the development of notions of sexuality as spiritual, healing, and transcendent, in some cases taking inspiration from ancient Eastern cultural archetypes, for example the idea of the 'sacred whore' as discussed by Lorraine Hutchins (2011). Another related development in the USA is the 'expanded' model of sexuality, which is based on energy exchange rather than specific physiology, as experienced by Annie Sprinkle (1991) who discussed sexual engagements within nature (for example with waterfalls and winds) as well as with several humans. Serena Anderlini-D'Onofrio (2009) frames bisexuality (and poly) as follows: 'sharing emotional, physical, and affectional resources empower players to generate abundance out of scarcity, hope out of fear, gayness out of sadness, peace out of war' (2009, p.xxiv–xxv), and she argues that 'These amorous arts produce affection, pleasure, and emotional sustainability. They are *shy of any normativity* because by definition they are artistic, creative, and imaginative' (2009, p.xxiv, my italics). Of course, whilst these erotic exchanges may indeed generate emotional resources for their participants, the idea that they are intrinsically non-normative is highly problematic. Other, quite different, forms of sexual networks are also located primarily in the USA, including the 'Down Low' lifestyle (MSM, mostly amongst men of colour) (Sandfort and Dodge, 2008; Heath and Goggin, 2009) which was discussed briefly in Chapter 1.

The US situation indicates some of the ways in which sexual communities are culturally situated. The UK provides a different picture. This section of the chapter will address bisexuality and the BDSM communities, using data from the research on the UK BDSM scenes as well as the UK bisexuality research. Before beginning, two other erotic communities need to be mentioned; the poly and swinger communities. The poly community is largely inclusive of bisexuals. According to some of the UK bisexuality research contributors, it has influenced the bisexual communities considerably; key shared areas of habitus concern the importance of openness, negotiation and communication, and a tendency to develop community-specific terms and labels.

The swinger community was reported by some of the research contributors to be very inclusive of female bisexuality, but much less inclusive of male bisexuality. A minority of the bisexual contributors have some knowledge of the swinger 'scenes'. For example, Grant suggested that the more 'progressive' parts of the swingers scene, those that are connected with other erotic communities, 'are pretty friendly towards bisexuality, they feel that there is more in common with bisexuals than there is with say the gay community'. Andy, who has been to swingers clubs, reported that male bisexuality is unusual but that female bisexuality is welcomed because it forms erotic entertainment for the men:

> if the women accept it and obviously the men accept it because they [the men] can enjoy the object of their gaze, enjoy it without it compromising their own sexual identity, and it feels like they're saying, 'oh that's great, there's going to be more stuff happening, more fun', whereas men [male-male sex] it's special circumstances required for that, a special night.

These findings indicate that whilst there appears to be an unequal gender-based structuring of sexuality within the swinger scenes, this may vary across the different swinger sub-scenes and related communities. This stands in contrast to the goth scene which also influences, and overlaps into, the bisexual communities; the goth scene was reported by research contributors to be largely accepting of bisexuality because of a general emphasis on outsider status and gender ambiguity.

BDSM and bisexuality

The research with BDSM practitioners (people who 'do' BDSM) and club organisers showed that the UK has developed erotic communities based around BDSM and fetish interests. BDSM practitioners engage in activities (known as 'play') including role-play, corporal punishment, and bondage. The fetish scene is worth mentioning because it overlaps with the BDSM scene; it involves dressing up in particular eroticised ways (for example in latex outfits). The bondage and domination aspect of BDSM involves people taking roles as 'tops' or 'doms' (dominants), 'bottoms' or 'subs' (submissives) or 'switches' ('top' or 'bottom' at different times).

The BDSM 'scenes' can be interpreted as Bourdeusian fields (see above) and they have their own habitus, and doxa. For BDSM club events, there are very clear guidelines about conduct and methods for enforcing these. For example, 'Dungeon Managers' (a form of bouncer) manage the spaces, and those that I interviewed reported actively regulating club attendees who transgress the guidelines (including expelling them from the club).

There are various differences across the BDSM and fetish scenes, depending on the type of audience and play. However, key underpinning norms are those of consent and mutual trust; these norms are shared with the organised bisexual communities, as noted by the bisexuality project contributor Grant who said that 'there should be a very clear "this is what people want or are willing to do with their bodies" shared across the bi and BDSM communities'. Another set of shared norms concerns tolerance of a wide range of sexual diversity. Overall, there was broad consensus amongst contributors to the BDSM research that, as the organisers of two different clubs said:

> There is...far less bigotry within the BDSM and also the fetish communities...it's hypocritical of the community as a whole to be critical of a minority when we don't want to be seen as an outside, just a bit different. (Duncan)

Another area of partially shared habitus between the BDSM 'scenes' and the bisexual communities concerns gender variance. However, whilst the bisexual communities are inclusive of all genders, the BDSM 'scenes' vary in their levels of inclusivity. Contributors to the BDSM research reported that transvestites (TVs) are ubiquitous across the different parts of the 'scene' because cross-dressing is an accepted form of fetish. However, there were a few reports of prejudice against transvestites, as evidenced, for example, in the idea of 'death by trannie' (the stigmatising idea that having too many TVs in a club is problematic). Beyond this, attitudes to trans and gender variant people differed depending on the segment of the scene in question. Trans men, and butch women, were seen as less welcome on the 'straight' BDSM scene, and some contributors reported more conservative gender norms generally on the straight fetish scene, including fetish fairs which may have restricted gender roles (for example male doms and female doms). These gender-normative types of habitus contrast with those of the queer-oriented clubs such as Club Lash in Manchester, which is inclusive of gender variance (and was described as pangender and pansexual by one of the organisers) and some other organisations, such as SM Dykes in Manchester, which although women-centred, welcomes trans men. One area of notable gender difference that cuts across both straight and mixed queer BDSM scenes concerns the issue of predatory straight men. Straight men were described by research contributors as overrepresented in clubs, and several club organisers talked about findings ways to manage what they called 'wandering wankers'. This derogatory term is used for men who watch BDSM play for their own sexual stimulation, without this being welcomed by players. 'Wandering wankers' can be seen to transgress core values concerning consent, and they would not be tolerated in the organised bisexual communities (outside of sex clubs, which are not under discussion here). The phenomenon of 'wandering wankers' may be related to the unequal access that individuals have to various 'scenes' (with, for example, older, individuals or those seen as 'less attractive' being less welcome), but it is specifically gendered; an issue with female 'wandering wankers' has not been reported. The unequal gendered structuring of the BDSM 'scenes' would form an interesting topic for further research, however this chapter now moves on to address BDSM and bisexuality.

Bisexuality and the BDSM 'scenes'

How do the BDSM 'scenes' deal with bisexuality? The research findings indicated that sexuality is modelled differently on the BDSM scenes as compared to mainstream society, with sexualities being based around roles (sub/dom/switch), and preferred BDSM activities, as well as gender and LGBH identities. This alternative form of sexual habitus is fairly confluent with that found in the bisexual communities, particularly when BDSM practitioners privilege activity preference and/or role over gender, and where trust between players is seen as more important than gender. There are also complexities of gendered sexualities that are found on the BDSM scenes that shine light on different forms of bisexuality. For example, contributor Daisy, who is a female switch, said that she goes to BDSM clubs as a femme when she is subbing and butch if she is topping, whilst male contributor Duncan said:

> A lot of people look at switches in a slightly different light to pure doms or subs. For example, my other half [female] is very submissive to me but also dominant towards women, but not towards men. This is confusing for many people as she is not a true switch. A bi [bisexual] switch would play with men and women.

Another twist in the BDSM bisexuality story concerns the way in which a few individuals used the term 'bisexual' to mean 'into a range of sexual activities', for example Cherry said that 'in general its better in the BDSM scene because people are more bisexual – they understand that different activities can turn people on', and in one case, a player was reported to use the term 'bisexual' to mean 'non-monogamous'. These alternative definitions of 'bisexual' indicates divergence from the habitus of the organised bisexual communities, where 'bisexual' quite clearly does not mean sexuality active, sexually varied, or non-monogamous, and where discourses regarding the validity of asexuality, monogamy and non-BDSM sex are common if somewhat marginal.

BiCon and BDSM

This chapter section now looks at the BDSM 'scene' that is part of BiCon, and at areas of divergence and shared ground with the BDSM 'sciences'. Participant observation shows that BiCon is other, in terms of environment, from the spaces found on the commercial BDSM scenes; for a start, there are no dimmed lights and large pieces of bondage equipment. Some BiCon attendees organise, or take part in, workshops that are run about BDSM, which involve, for example, learning how to tie knots and use whips safely, as well as or instead of going to private parties. The 'beginner' levels of these workshops are open to non-BDSM players. The habitus is also different to that found in BDSM clubs, for example:

> there are a lot more people talking, a lot more people teaching and learning, which I really like, people do have their own private parties

at BiCon, kitchen parties, you feel a lot safer, there isn't blaring music which you get at clubs, very different. I really like the whole thing; they will have a workshop [at BiCon] just on spanking, or just on ropes. There are people wanting to pass on information... also with BiCon you've got a helluva lot more time... people talking about subjects on kink and they will start talking on the Friday afternoon and they will stop on Sunday when they go. (Jacqui)

Overall, there are clear divergences between BiCon BDSM environments and those associated with the BDSM 'scenes', in terms of space, activities, and field. However, going back to the points made earlier about the habitus of the organised bisexual communities, there are also high levels of shared habitus between the BDSM scenes and the bisexual communities. These concern core values such as consent, communication, and positivity about eroticism and sexual diversity, as well as shared lexicons and preferred 'looks', including fetish outfits. These shared territories mean that bisexual people who are 'into' BDSM and/or fetish may tend to feel more of a sense of belonging at events such as BiCon than those who are not. The BDSM-positive habitus of BiCon also diverges from more conventional heterosexual, and lesbian and gay, cultures. The issue of divergences between the bisexual communities, and the mainstream lesbian and gay communities, forms the focus of the next and final chapter section.

The lesbian and gay communities: divergent from the bisexual communities?

The roots of the UK gay, lesbian, and bisexual communities are all found in struggles for sexual rights that took place in the last century (and previously) as well as in the erotic communities that evolved in the underground social spaces that emerged as a reaction to persecution. However, the evolution of these communities has subsequently taken divergent trajectories, for a number of reasons (see Feinberg, 1996; Richardson and Seidman, 2002; Richardson and Monro, 2012). Biphobia, as discussed in Chapters 1 and 2, has been an issue within the lesbian and gay communities. This manifests in very real ways, as the following quotes show:

I go clubbing quite a lot, and even at clubs where there are quite a few bi people there, up until a few years ago, clubs that market themselves as LGBT friendly and then see a man and a woman together in a queue get angry and say, 'you're straight'; there is not enough awareness. (Pierrette)

> Why, for example, do we have safer sex packs [at a community centre that purports to be for lesbians, gays and bisexuals], one for the gay men, one for lesbians, and when you open the women one, there is no condom or anything [raises hands in disbelief]... It doesn't cater for all women. It is only for women who don't have sex with men or who don't use [pause]... sex toys, and share them. (Pia)

This section of the chapter will not focus on these elements of the bisexual-lesbian-gay community relationships per se, rather it will show that by considering the divergences of habitus of these communities, the biphobia that has been an unfortunate aspect of the lesbian and gay communities becomes easier to comprehend. Space limitations preclude a detailed examination of the gay and lesbian communities as fields in themselves, but it is important to note that these groupings are very diverse and that there are also big differences between lesbians and gay men. The ideas presented here are indicative and further research is needed to address different sections of the lesbian and gay communities in relation to bisexuality.

Before looking at divergences, it is important to flag up the overlaps between the lesbian and gay communities, and the bisexual ones. Many organisations that are primarily focused on gay men and lesbians are actively supportive of bisexual people; moreover, the overlap in bisexual, and lesbian and gay identities means that habitus can be experienced as confluent. For example, one bisexual research contributor described the way in which her local LGB community centre had paired her with a woman she thought was lesbian, in order to help her develop the confidence she needed to access the lesbian and gay scene, and that she was finding this helpful. There seemed overall to be some indications of a cultural shift towards bisexual inclusion by networks that are predominantly LG, as discussed in the following interview snippet:

> Kay: I think it was more fear than anything, if you weren't part of that community then they didn't want to let you in because they didn't want trouble, I can understand that. Pride events these days are just *so much happier*, so much, all encompassing, they seem to welcome people from all walks of life, and I do think Pride events help... the bisexual message anyway, because you can mix together and you can talk and people understand you more.
> Interviewer: What has helped things to change?
> Kay: I don't know... legislation changes and improvements for the gay and lesbian community has helped them chill out in a sense

and start thinking about the bigger picture, not just about gay and lesbian people, also about transgender people and bisexual people as well, they even acknowledge that [bisexuality] exists (sic).

There are elements of this shift that are very much about activism, struggle, and wider frameworks (legislative, policy and institutional) and these shall be addressed in Chapter 7. This part of the chapter will now flag up a number of divergences in the habitus associated with the lesbian and gay (LG) communities, as compared to the bisexual ones. The types of divergence that are considered are as follows: commercialism, discrete sexual identities, and mononormativity.

Commercialism

Various authors, such as Mark Casey (2007) and Taylor (2007), analyse the ways in which the mainstream lesbian and gay 'scenes' are commercialised, requiring certain types of capital in order to successfully access them (for example being young, physically able, and middle class in terms of clothing and presentation). The fields associated with the commercial lesbian and gay 'scenes' act to exclude lesbians and gay men who do not have these credentials. They also exclude bisexuals; not just those bisexual people who fail to have the required economic capital, but also those who dislike or do not adhere to the commercial and cultural style of the mainstream gay and lesbian scenes. For example, Andy reported:

> I would go to gay venues because that's the space where you can feel comfortable but began to realise I could not stand the music and it was actually spoiling the night... it maybe helps you define what you are not, and bisexuality, maybe it's a benefit that it's [bisexuality] not that tightly tied to a set of cultural markers like being gay can seem to be.

It will be obvious to anyone who knows the LG 'scenes' in the UK that the types of bisexual community habitus described earlier in the chapter (such as multiple piercings, 'goth' looks, and alternative clothes and hairstyles) are unlikely to 'fit' with the 'looks' associated with many of the lesbian and gay scenes. The organised bisexual communities also show enthusiasm about a large range of gender and bodily diversities, in contrast to the commercial lesbian and gay 'scenes' (see Casey, 2007). In addition, the various subcultural-type practices and lexicons that are particular to the bisexual field and some adjacent fields such as the

BDSM scenes could be incomprehensible to some people within mainstream LG fields. The bisexual community emphasis on consent, trust, and communication may also be less present in lesbian and gay spaces, as indicated in the following quote about an experience of BiCon:

> Just being with 200 other people, and talking about bisexuality, bisexual politics [pause] I don't know, I found a level of [pause] discussions, and quite deep, something that I didn't experience in the lesbian group... to me it was another level of politics. (Merina)

A further issue is that the bisexual communities are, in contrast to the LG scenes, non-commercialised and volunteer-run, and are virtually non-existent in economic terms as compared to the large 'pink pound' economy. The anti-commercial nature of the bisexual communities renders them of little interest to organised commercial interests (see Chapter 5), and the grassroots affiliations have also made them easy to exclude by professionalised national lesbian and gay-dominated organisations (see Chapter 7). Overall, therefore, the counter-culture, non-commercialised characteristics of the organised bisexual communities stand in contrast to those of the commercialised, professionalised LG communities.

Discrete sexual identities and mononormativity

Another area of stark divergence between the bisexual and the LG communities concerns models of gender and sexuality. The bisexual communities support a wide range of sexual identities and expressions as opposed to the mononormative sexualities that predominate within the mainstream lesbian scenes (mononormativity is far less common amongst gay men). For the more queer-oriented bisexuals, the emphasis on particular forms of identity that relate only to same-sex desire can be stifling. For example, Lena said that 'I dipped toes into the lesbian scene in [city] and found it very exclusive and very, I didn't want my identity to be contained by my sexuality, I found that really reductive and really depressing'.

The mononormative element of the lesbian and gay communities can fuel prejudice concerning bisexuality (for example the ideas that bisexuals are undecided or promiscuous, see Barker *et al.*, 2012). Mononormativity can negatively affect the lived experiences of bisexual people, as demonstrated in the following quote from Anne:

> I have been in this relationship with a woman for 21 years, and most of the other relationships I have had have been with women, and

when I had a relationship with a man (short lived), which was a bit of a surprise I have to say because it had been some time, the [lesbian] community of which we are a part were really quite angry, rude... they were saying my partner 'should change the locks and kick me out; that behaviour is completely unacceptable' which is pretty extreme... [the relationship was an open one and her partner knew she was bisexual].

The issue of divergence between the bisexual and the LG communities concerning mononormativity/multiple relationship forms goes beyond values and norms in that there is a structural element to it. Whilst the UK bisexual community has supported same-sex marriage, the granting of marriage rights to same-sex couples acts to socially and economically privilege couples over single people and those in plural relationships in an unfair way by giving them access to economic and social capital that others do not have. Critiques of marriage are well rehearsed generally (for example, Williams, 2008) but they are especially relevant to bisexual people because of the wide variety of relationship styles that bisexual people have (see above). Same-sex marriage also exemplifies the domesticisation of lesbian and gay politics. This domesticisation, in which lesbians and gays are framed in respect of identities rather than sexual preferences and expressions, may underpin some of the tensions between the bisexual and the LG communities.

Domesticisation, and sanitisation, has not taken place within the bisexual communities, which retain a robust emphasis on actual sex, as opposed to identities. Such wilful celebration of sexuality, especially alternative sexual expressions, may render the bisexual communities repugnant to a mainstream lesbian and gay field intent on representing itself as 'respectable' (see Richardson and Monro, 2012 and Chapter 6).

To summarise, then, there are some key areas of divergence between the bisexual, and the lesbian and gay, communities. These revolve around several axes; these include the LG communities as commercialised and the bisexual communities as grassroots and non-commercialised; the LG communities as reliant on, and reinforcing of, discrete gender-binary and sexually binary identities as opposed to the bisexual communities, which celebrate sex/gender diversities; and the LG community as primarily mononormative, in contrast to the mixed relationship styles supported by the bisexual communities.

This chapter has provided an empirically grounded contribution to the sociology of the family and community, and to an analysis of informal care-giving, as well as to sexuality studies. It places analysis of sexualities, relationship forms, the bisexual and the BDSM communities,

108 *Bisexuality*

and the lesbian and gay communities together within a Bourdeusian analytical framework, drawing also on notions of subculture. In discussing the ways in which the bisexual and other communities can be seen as fields, and the types of habitus and doxa that are present within them, the chapter enables an examination of the divergences and commonalities across these communities. In addition, the chapter provides some analysis of the gendered and heteronormative patterning of the bisexual and sexual fringe communities, as well as the ways that these are resisted or complexified.

Summary

- Bisexual people have a wide range of relationship forms and types of sexual identity and expression. These vary across country, with some types occurring in the USA that are less common in the UK.
- Parenting and informal care giving (both to significant others and more generally) are found amongst UK bisexuals, forming resources that can be seen as a kind of social capital.
- The organised bisexual communities operate as 'fields' within which specific dynamics are evident. Specific markers of bisexual communities include support for gender variance and for people with a wide range of appearances, and 'alternative' dress codes including 'fetish' looks.
- The habitus found within the bisexual communities can mean that people who do not fit the norms of the communities can be inadvertently marginalised.
- The habitus associated with the organised bisexual communities, which can also be interpreted as a form of subculture, is at odds both with the heterosexual mainstream and the organised lesbian and gay communities.
- The bisexual communities share considerable habitus with some of the sexual fringe communities; the chapter addresses in particular the BDSM 'scenes'.

The following chapter addresses a different but overlapping set of issues: organisations and consumerism in relation to bisexuality.

5
Bisexuality, Organisations, and Capitalism

This chapter addresses bisexuality, organisations, and capitalism. It focuses, firstly, on bisexual people as actors within workplace organisations, and secondly, on the ways in which certain bisexualities are commodified in order to generate profit. Commodification is defined here as the transformation of social processes and identities into 'things' that can be used to make money. The chapter explores the ways in which the commodification of bisexuality takes place in different ways in various sectors, including the sex industries and the media.

The chapter aims to help remedy the bias in the existing bisexuality-related literature, which is weighted towards issues of identity and of sexualities within private and community spheres. It also addresses the relative deficit of scholarship concerning sexuality in organisations (see Hearn and Parkin, 2001; Wilson, 2003). The chapter speaks to the literature concerning the equality of LGB people in organisations (see Colgan *et al.*, 2007, 2009; Monro, 2007; Richardson and Monro, 2012). It focuses on providing an overview of bisexual people's experiences of employment, and an analysis of their views regarding the sectors where bisexuality is commodified. The chapter is focused on two countries where bisexual people have some human rights (the UK and USA, although the legal situation for bisexuals varies across different US states), and other forms of analysis are required for countries where this is not the case.

This chapter argues that bisexuality is rendered marginal within the statutory, voluntary, and private sectors of employment. In contrast, some types of bisexuality are an important part of the practices present in organisations which commodify sexualities, particularly the sex industries (see, for example, Capiola *et al.*, 2014). The chapter is underpinned by the observation that variations across these sectors are related to the operation of capitalism, together with heterosexism and mononormativity. Within workplace contexts, processes of heterosexualised domesticisation and desexualisation may render bisexual people unable to express their identities in the ways that heterosexual people can (for example being able to talk about partners at work). This leads to bisexual marginalisation and erasure, and it may be linked to organisational anxieties about non-heterosexualities generally (see Richardson and Monro, 2013). The erasures of bisexuality within the public sphere of mainstream employment may fuel the relegation of (certain) visible bisexual behaviours to sex industry or dating website spaces, which means that people may have to pay if they wish to access them. This relegation of bisexuality away from quotidian spaces and into the commercialised sex industries works to fuel neoliberal accumulation; if all bisexual sexualities were socially acceptable, there might be less of a commercial market for images and activities that are framed as 'bisexual'.

The chapter addresses bisexual hypersexualisation, which is a theme cutting across both mainstream workplace organisations and the sex industries. 'Hypersexualised bisexuality' refers to the discursive framing of bisexual people (and others involved in bisexual behaviours) in such a way as to prioritise their sexuality over other aspects of their identity, and also to frame bisexuals as being people who are very sexual in particular ways (for example promiscuous and sexually adventurous). The hypersexualised construction of bisexuality means that bisexuals are likely to be especially marginalised in mainstream organisations, given the way in which they are constructed as public spaces and 'sexuality is [seen as] the antithesis of what organisation is about. Organisation is about control, instrumental rationality and the suppression of instinct as emotion' (Wilson, 2003, p.193). The hypersexualisation of bisexual people is an issue that emerges from the research about bisexuality in the UK as well as elsewhere; it underpins some of the stigma that bisexual people face within workplace organisations and elsewhere. In contrast to lesbian and gay identities, which have been subject to a degree of domesticisation (see Chapters 1, 4, and 6), bisexuality continues to be associated, within dominant discursive frameworks, primarily with sex and sexuality.

The chapter adopts a materialist feminist framework (see Evans, 1993; Richardson *et al.*, 2006; Hines, 2010), building on the themes outlined in Chapter 2, and speaking to Monro's (2010a) assertions about the need for a materialist turn in sexuality and gender studies. In particular there is a concern in this chapter with lived and socially situated experience, and with structural inequalities relating to the distribution of resources. The chapter also speaks to interactionist theory in its discussion of workplace bisexualities, where an understanding of the ways in which micro-relations can forge the organisational inclusion or exclusion of bisexual people is important. It is necessary to point out that the research findings indicated that bisexual and other non-heterosexual people acted with considerable agency in negotiating their way around (and sometimes challenging) heterosexist regimes of power, and that institutions are evidently changing in some ways in relation to bisexualities. Therefore, determinist materialist interpretations of bisexuality, in which bisexual people are framed purely as pawns in a neoliberal system of capital accumulation, would be untenable. It should be noted that other forms of conceptualisation, for example, along post-structuralist lines, would be useful, as would analysis of bisexual queer and anarchist counter-publics as organisations (see Jeppesen, 2010), but that these are not explored here.

The chapter begins with a discussion of bisexual people and employment, using material from the UK study and from the USA. The chapter then addresses bisexuality in other workplace contexts, focusing on the media, and the sex industry, from the perspectives of bisexual people, before beginning to develop some conclusions concerning organisations, capitalism and bisexualities. The data used in this chapter is partial. For example, bisexual people working in the sex industries were not interviewed (with the exception of a fetish club organiser) and further research is required to represent their views. There is also underrepresentation of working class bisexual people. Another of the omissions the UK research concerned bisexual people who were not engaged in paid work or study; given the high levels of impairment amongst UK bisexual people involved in the bisexual communities, especially mental health issues (see Yockney, 2013), this is an important gap which requires further research. In addition, there are many other sectors in which analysis of bisexuality could be developed (for example the profession of counselling and psychotherapy in relation to bisexuality (see Matteson, 1996), sexual health and education (Brown, 2009), and the diversity industry (see Richardson and Monro, 2012)) but space precludes the inclusion of these here.

Bisexual people's experiences of the workplace in the UK

Whilst much of the scholarship regarding sexual identities and the workplace addresses LGB people as a grouping (for example, Colgan *et al.*, 2007, 2009), there is some literature that deals with the specificities of bisexual people's experiences and with organisational cultures and strategies concerning bisexuality. The research indicates that bisexual people experience high levels of discrimination in the UK workplace (Chamberlain, 2009; Keeble *et al.*, 2011). Brett Chamberlain's (2009) UK study found widespread evidence of biphobia in the workplace:

> Overall, participants said that prejudice and stereotypes of bisexuality extended into the workplace and colleagues often portrayed them as untrustworthy, indecisive or troublemakers at work... the stereotypes that surround bisexuality result in bisexual employees being labelled by colleagues as being uncertain, indecisive, and even unstable.
> (Chamberlain, 2009, p.6–7)

Examples of discrimination against bisexuals in the workplace include bisexual people being constantly questioned about their sexuality whilst at work, and colleagues expressing disapproval about bisexuality. An example of biphobia (see Chapter 1) in the workplace is cited in Meg John Barker *et al.* (using material from The Bisexual Index) as follows:

> Ever since I told my boss I was going to a bi event she seems to treat me like a flake. She makes little comments all the time about how I can't stick to things, how I'm not a team player. One time she told me not to apply for promotion, because they wanted 'someone loyal, who could commit'.
> (2012, p.24)

On an organisational level, the findings from the *Organisational Change, Resistance and Democracy* project conducted between 2007 and 2010 (Richardson and Monro, 2012, 2013; Monro and Richardson, 2014) showed that bisexuality was both marginalised and stigmatised within public sector organisations (specifically local authorities) in England, Wales, and Northern Ireland. Whilst bisexuality is a part of the 'LGBT' acronym in the UK, in practice it was frequently omitted from conversation about equality and diversity within these organisations, with any discussion about sexuality equalities issues only addressing lesbians and gay men. The project included groups of statutory sector actors engaging in action research, and in one action research session, bisexuality was described as 'completely off the radar' (this was in a locality where addressing lesbian and gay issues was seen as very difficult). Prejudice against bisexuals was reported by some participants in the research project, for example a local authority officer said, 'How can you be bi, and fancy both? It's seen as indecisive and kind of having your cake and eating it'.

There are ways of dealing with workplace biphobias. In the UK, there are developments taking place in some areas of employment strategy and infrastructure, for example, Carola Towle (2011) details the ways in which UNISON, a British public service trade union, has become proactive regarding bisexual equalities since 2005. Chamberlain's (2009) and Barker *et al.*'s (2012) reports discuss the importance of workplace strategies in tackling the patterns of discrimination and marginalisation that can render bisexual employees unable to work in a fully effective way, and they suggest training, awareness raising, policy statements, bisexual role models, and inclusive employee networks.

Overall, a varied picture concerning bisexuality in the workplace emerged from the UK bisexuality research, mirroring existing research that demonstrates biphobia, as well as strategy and research documents outlining ways to address biphobia. In some workplaces, bisexual people felt supported, whilst others experienced marginalisation and discrimination. However, the sample was small and that almost all of the contributors who discussed their workplace identified as middle class. The next section of the chapter delineates bisexual people's experiences regarding their workplace, starting with positive experiences, then experiences of workplace activisms, followed by invisible bisexualities and the impact of employment precariousness, and finishing with direct biphobia.

Positive experiences and 'good practice'

Some of the UK bisexuality research contributors discussed routinely positive experiences of being bisexual in the workplace. For example, Pia, who worked in social care, was out as bisexual and did not feel that there were any difficulties with this. The ease associated with being out was, for her, related to the length of her time at this workplace (three years) and the fact that some of her colleagues have lesbian and gay friends. Similarly, Nancy stated that 'I work full time in charity administration. I am out at work and have been out at all my workplaces. The reception has always been fairly neutral'. Anne, who was an alternative health practitioner, reported that most of her experiences of being bisexual in the workplace were good: 'I think because I'm comfortable with my sexual identity and don't feel a need to hide it, I think that helps other people to feel comfortable with it'. The ability to be out at work is important for bisexual people. As a large US-based survey of bisexual people at work shows, 'dissatisfaction in the workplace, as well as in life in general, can be correlated with the degree to which a person keeps his or her bisexuality a secret' (Green, 2011, p.300). Similarly, in a German survey of bisexual employees, Thomas Köllen (2013) demonstrated that a climate of greater openness about bisexuality in the workplace supports bisexual employees.

Turning around difficulties/workplace activisms

In contrast to the positive or neutral experiences outlined above, Kay, who works for a public sector organisation (civil service), found coming out as bisexual at work difficult but was prompted to do so because of her role within UNISON (see Towle, 2011). She had been bullied at work (not particularly in relation to her sexual identity), and she responded to this by becoming active within the union and taking the lead in terms of the 'bisexuality' part of the 'LGBT' diversity role within the union in order to help others who were having difficulty at work. This had, for Kay, been empowering on a personal level and she discussed her satisfaction at challenging colleagues' stereotypical attitudes about sexuality. Colleagues held these attitudes partly because her partner was a man and she identified as bisexual rather than heterosexual. Another narrative that demonstrates high levels of agency concerning bisexuality comes from Lee, who worked for private sector organisations and also provided professional consultancy about diversities:

> Lee: The classic one is going into a new space, workplace, the assumption is that I am a heterosexual male, a cis male, biological male, so those assumptions are made, and because I am in a poly relationship, I have a wife and a boyfriend. So if I talk about one, it is assumed that, if its [name] my wife, it's assumed that I'm heterosexual. If I talk about [name] my boyfriend, it's assumed I am homosexual. And therefore I try and get both into the conversation so they understand all of it and don't assume one or the other.
> Interviewer: What sort of reactions have you had?
> Lee: Generally shock at first, it was not what they were expecting, especially the trans stuff [laughs]. Once they have come back down to earth, interest, and generally wanting to understand where I am coming from.

What is apparent in both Kay and Lee's narratives is not just individual agency but also the mutability of workplace attitudes towards sexualities; both related ways in which they challenged the assumptions of colleagues. Kay also discussed structural changes within the workplace, including higher levels of bisexual representation within Unison at a national level, and the use of *The Bisexuality Report* (Barker *et al.*, 2012) to enable her to leverage an institutional focus on bisexuality and diversity.

Invisibility and assumptions of heterosexuality

The above narratives concern a public bisexuality, one of 'outness' and increasing normalisation. They contrast with the experiences of several other research contributors, for whom bisexuality was largely invisible; perhaps they were out to a few people in the workplace but would not generally discuss their sexual identity. For some contributors, sexual identity was seen as a private matter, whilst others thought that their sexual identity was irrelevant to the workplace. Some contributors did not identify as any sexual identity in particular (although they might be behaviourally bisexual) so they felt that there was nothing to come out about. For other bisexual people, being out at work was seen as socially inconvenient, as is evident in the following quote from Kate, who was married to a man and who stayed overnight during the winter with her girlfriend close to the public sector organisation where she worked:

> I talked to [girlfriend] a couple of weeks ago, said 'people are talking about road conditions' and she said 'oh just tell them you are staying with a friend' that seems much [more] straightforward – I was going to go down the whole route of telling them, [but] it's more practical, does not feel being dishonest but 'without full disclosure'.

This quote demonstrates the way in which Kate exercised agency in managing potential biphobia in the workplace. It also shows how for those bisexual people who are in male-female relationships, it is possible to hide behind a primary relationship that is presented as heterosexual, and avoid stigmatisation. This dynamic may lead to a vicious cycle, where people hide their sexual identity in the workplace, which then contributes to the social erasure of bisexuality.

Employment precariousness

A number of the UK bisexual contributors stressed the strategic nature of their workplace sexual identity, for example stating that they would be out if this was needed but not otherwise. For some people, the precarious nature of their employment, and the dangers of stigmatisation that they identified within their workplace, meant that they were actively closeted all the time at work. For instance Dave, who worked on a temporary contract for a public sector organisation and was a trans man who had a young family, stated that he came across as heterosexual at work (because he is married) and that he was worried that being 'out' as bisexual would complicate people's understanding of his identity. For Dave, the risk of coming out as bisexual when he had another stigmatised identity (as trans) was too big to take. Dave, Yaz, and Merina were (or had been) part of marginal workforces and this impacted on their ability to be 'out'. Yaz did sessional work for a public sector employer and was worried that colleagues would gossip about her if she came out, so she stayed closeted. Merina, who was in temporary employment with a local council (statutory sector body representing local communities and providing services), was the only bisexual person at the workplace LGBT network of this large organisation, and she felt marginalised by the LGBT network and withdrew from it. In her subsequent employment in a small private firm, Merina did not come out due to worries about potential victimisation by a manager she experienced as generally untrustworthy. In all of these cases, bisexual people assessed their employment status as relatively weak and adjusted their levels of 'outness' accordingly. They were all BME (one white American, one Southern European, and one British Asian) and intersectional discriminations may also have played a role both in their insecure employment situations, and their responses to employment insecurity. Like the contributors to the above section, they exercised agency, and their stories demonstrate the ways in which bisexuality can be hidden within workplace organisations.

Biphobia

The UK bisexuality research showed that overt prejudice is present in some workplaces. For example, Andy, who worked for a private company wholesaling hardware, discussed the way in which he presented himself as masculine and straight at work in order to survive, including alterations to his voice (taking on a more pronounced regional accent) and body language. He said that:

> It is a very straight male environment, verbally racist, misogynist, homophobic, like people talking about the weather...talking about faggots...you are outnumbered so there is no point standing up and giving people a lecture, and I am not going to come out because it would make life intolerable. I am basically a middle class ex-student and to them a student is also code for homosexual [laughs] also the

way the word 'gay' is used these days, it can just mean a bit posh, a bit effete, different to yourselves.

Here, homosexuality appears to have been framed as class identity that the working class men in Andy's environment rejected; this also impacted negatively on Andy as a bisexual colleague. In other environments, the workplace itself may not be overtly homophobic and biphobic, but being 'out' at work can mean an onslaught of stigmatising attention. This was particularly apparent for Meg John, who worked for a public sector organisation. Meg John spoke about the way in which:

> I came out as bi and poly in my work because I was studying those things, as part of author reflexivity... it got in the newspapers and stuff, and by then it was too late to go back in the closet, not that I would have wanted to.

In Meg John's situation, wider biphobic and mononormative processes impacted on her workplace experiences in a very direct way. It is useful to remember that workplace organisations operate within a web of dynamics, so that whilst they may be able to provide positive environments for bisexual employees, they will not be immune to stigmatisation via the media. There is also a class element to the ways that biphobia can be managed within the workplace. Meg John, who had a middle class occupation, recounted very positive workplace experiences with a different employer, but this was not the case for Andy, whose working class occupation rendered him unable to challenge prejudice in the workplace. However, working class environments are not necessarily homophobic and biphobic, as demonstrated in Pia's positive account of working in social care (above).

This sub-section of the chapter has explored a range of experiences, as presented by the UK bisexuality research contributors. The next sub-section of the chapter provides insight into the workplace experiences of bisexual people in the USA.

Bisexual people's experiences of the workplace in the USA

The USA can be used as a comparison with the UK when considering bisexuals in employment. Some of the US bisexuality literature discusses bisexual people in the workplace, albeit in a tangential fashion. Weinberg *et al.* (1994) describe the majority of their 100 research contributors as being mostly heterosexual in orientation, who had little incentive to come out regarding what Weinberg *et al.* describe as 'secondary associations' (same-sex sexualities) given the levels of stigmatisation these could provoke. This finding mirrors some of the UK bisexuality research findings in that a number of the contributors were conveniently closeted and passed as heterosexual at work. Weinberg *et al.* (1994) also found that bisexual people were less likely to 'come out' at work than gay men and lesbians. Unintended outing was described by some contributors to their study and more research would be needed to ascertain the impact of this when it occurs.

A large international survey (Green *et al.*, 2011; 822 respondents (68 per cent from the USA)) which used a snowball sample produced some interesting results, many of which reflect the UK research findings (Chamberlain, 2009; Barker *et al.*, 2012; Richardson and Monro, 2012). They described the way in which, in the USA and in some other countries, there are company-sponsored affinity-based LGBT groups (Employee Resource Groups). However, these groups commonly fail to provide resources or programming concerning bisexuality; because the need for this is unproven it is not seen as justifiable. Heidi Bruin Green *et al.*'s study (2011) showed that 50 per cent of the bisexual respondents felt misunderstood by gay and straight co-workers. Forty-five per cent of the sample reported that there are unique issues for bisexuals, for example being seen as unreliable and un-promotable by management, and being distrusted by lesbian and gay colleagues. There was also a tendency for bisexual people to be treated as allies of a workplace LGBT group rather than full members, and being excluded from full participation in workplace LGBT networks. Green *et al.* (2011) emphasise the importance of being 'out' in terms of bisexual people's wellbeing and mental health. Those who were not out were likely to be more isolated and to suffer from dissatisfaction with their work life and depression. Green *et al.* (2011) make several recommendations, including the need for company equalities policies to include bisexual people specifically and that this is supported as much as LG and T initiatives and the need for more bisexual people to be out at work. They also indicate that bisexual 'outness' is necessary for those bisexual people involved in diversities or advocacy work; this is mirrored in some of the UK interviews discussed above, specifically Kay and Lee.

Robyn Och's (2009) collection of life stories also contains some information regarding US bisexual people and work. These narratives illustrate the close ties between bisexual and LG employment rights. For example, contributor Melinda commented that two of the largest employers in her locality have domestic partner benefits for same-sex couples, as well as material demonstrating the contributions that bisexual people make to the LGBT communities more broadly through their employment. For Melinda, support for same-sex partnerships goes together with support for bisexual people, in a workplace context. Another example of this trend is provided by Jan, who is a physician. She founded a small LGBT group at her workplace and said that she made her office for queer teenagers by placing information about LGBT groups in accessible places. Och's collection also flags up the importance of intersectional employment dynamics that affect bisexual people, for instance, Richard M. Juang (who is Chinese-American) described the way in which he grew up in a climate where 'the model-minority myth... portrayed Asian immigrants as hard-working and docile' (2009, p.95) and that this impacted on the development of his sexual identity.

Whilst analysis of more material about workplace bisexualities in the USA is needed, these pieces of research and narrative reflect, overall, some of the findings from the UK bisexuality research. They highlight the pervasive nature of workplace prejudice against bisexual people, and the processes by which bisexual people remain hidden in the workplace. The US research also reveals the extent of the tie between lesbian and gay, and bisexual rights in organisations. Whilst lesbian and gay stigmatisation of bisexuals remains an issue, there are also areas of common purpose, most obviously in campaigns for same-sex partnership rights in the workplace.

This part of this chapter explored the issue of bisexual people as employees within public sector, and to a lesser extent, private and third sector organisations; organisations which all contribute to the capitalist neo-liberal project. It showed that both UK and US research to date indicates that there are strong patterns of marginalisation, erasure, and discrimination with regards to bisexuality, and that this impacts negatively on bisexual employees and perhaps the organisations within which they work. By drawing on more recent research findings from the UK bisexuality project, the chapter section also indicated that bisexual people in the UK have varied experiences of the workplace. Some of these experiences were negative, but a few demonstrated a work environment as being bisexual-positive (or tolerant). Other accounts illustrate the ways in which bisexual individuals manage stigma strategically, and in some cases effectively challenge it, set in a context of broader pro-diversity workplace policies and structures and professionalised or public sector employment sectors. The next part of the chapter addresses different aspects of employment and bisexuality; those employment sectors where bisexuality is commodified.

The commodification of (certain) bisexualities

The commodification of some forms of bisexuality is an important topic for investigation, partly because it demonstrates one of the ways in which sexualities come to be constructed within a neo-liberal capitalist environment, but also because the commodification of bisexuality can be seen as lying at the root of some negative stereotyping that plagues bisexual people and others today. This stereotyping is bound up with what Breanne Fahs (2009) terms 'performative bisexuality'. Performative bisexuality is bisexuality that is expressed in interaction with viewers whose gaze constructs the bisexual subjects in a particular way; typically it involves women being sexual with each other for the pleasure of men, or to attract men.

This section of the chapter presents insights from the UK bisexual people about commodified performative bisexuality, the gendered underpinnings of this, and its negative impacts. I also discuss the ambivalence that can exist concerning the commodification of bisexuality. The chapter section provides some analysis of two sites in which hypersexualised bisexualities are visible; the media, and sexual services.

Before proceeding, it is important to point out that another form of capitalist accumulation – that which is supported by 'good citizens' who work, pay taxes, consume goods, take out interest-bearing loans, and contribute to the labour market via procreation (see Chapter 6) – can also be 'read' from a critical perspective. For some bisexual people, the assimilationist trend in lesbian and gay (and perhaps bisexual) politics, where people attempt to 'fit into' mainstream society, can be interpreted as buying into the consumerist neoliberal system. An assimilationist trend stands in contrast to radical bisexual critiques of hegemonic norms, including not only heteronormative relationship models but also capitalist imperatives concerning employment and reproduction. It is questionable whether supporting neoliberalism via 'good citizenship' is fundamentally different to supporting it via voluntary involvement in, for example, the sex trade. However, whilst 'good citizenship' involves a domesticisation and desexualisation of bisexual and other non-heterosexual identities, the commodification of bisexuality discussed in this part of the chapter refers to performative and hypersexualised bisexualities.

The chapter does not make a clear distinction between the commodification of performative bisexualities in everyday settings (for example the two girls who kiss at a club in order to 'get boyfriends') and those in more elite settings (the music and film industries) or illicit ones (the pornography and sex work industries). This is because the hypersexualisation of a certain type of bisexuality appears to cut across all of these sectors, as was shown in the interviews with UK bisexual people. However, the chapter addresses, in particular, two sites (the media and the sex industries) because these were highlighted in the research as being important sites for the construction of hypersexualised performative bisexualities.

Hypersexualisation

The UK research findings suggested that some bisexuals revel in consensual, celebratory sexualities, which could be seen as hypersexual. The difficulties with hypersexualisation are that it can mean that all bisexual people become seen as hypersexualised, which diminishes other aspects of their identities, and erases those bisexuals who are asexual or average in their sexual proclivities. As research contributor Kate remarked, 'Framing something as titillating... causes a problem because it seems like it gets framed solely as that, and nothing goes beyond that'. The majority of the research participants were critical of the commodification of bisexuality, with responses to the question 'what do you think about the commodification of bisexuality?' ranging from 'not great' to 'it makes me sick'.

There are indications that the hypersexualised construction of bisexuality is not limited to Western societies. For example, Jo, talking of the situation in China, described female-female sexual behaviour in films as not being taken seriously; 'it's just double pleasure for a male audience to see two girls together'. It is this production of pleasure for a male audience which is central to hypersexualised and commodified bisexualities.

In a Western context, there are specific cultural attributes associated with bisexuality, as the following quote demonstrates:

> The way its [bisexuality] been commodified, that was always going to happen... there's a whole sort of discourse around bisexuality, its exotic, maybe it goes back to the old holiday stars, Dietrich and Garber and Talullah Bankhead, they were all living these bohemian bisexual lives. It's seen as an essential part of living a bohemian lifestyle. That bohemian angle, it masks the actuality of being a bisexual person even in this day and age. (Lena)

Here, the discursive framing of bisexuality as 'exotic' sits alongside, and contributes to, the 'othering' of bisexuality that also takes place when bisexuality is hypersexualised. The notion of 'exotic' bisexual lifestyles is apparent in the ways that bisexuality is commodified – framed as something sexy, exotic, titillating, and wild. Such images of bisexuality conflict with the lived experiences of many bisexual people, and they fuel prejudice amongst more conservative elements of society.

Bigotry towards bisexuals is partially underpinned by a set of broader prejudices concerning non-procreative sexualities, and non-monogamous relationships and sexual activities. As Chapter 4 showed, bisexual people have many types of sexual identity and relationship form, including asexual, celibate, and monogamous. However it is the stereotype of bisexual people as hypersexual, and as promiscuous, which continues to haunt the bisexual community as a whole, contributing to the biphobia which can then be institutionalised through organisational and cultural practices.

Gender and patriarchy

The hypersexualisation of bisexuality is constructed in a heavily gendered way. As indicated above, the type of bisexuality that is commodified is usually one in which two or more females are engaged in erotic contact for the benefit of the male viewer. Sometimes this is termed 'lesbian sex'. However, it is not 'lesbian' in the usual sense of the word (I define 'lesbian' as female-female desire and sexuality without any male involvement). The appropriation of the term 'lesbian' by the media and sex industries can be seen as a manifestation of the heteropatriarchal commercialisation of sexuality. A rather different interpretation of lesbianism, in relation to bisexuality, is discussed in one of the UK bisexuality interviews as follows:

> Yaz: ... I think bisexuality can be encouraged within mainstream *male* thinking because it's considered sexual, it's considered *amorous*, it's considered quite sort of *exotic*. In terms of a male porno fantasy. So if a woman tells a straight man that she's a lesbian, there will be a different reaction to if she tells a straight man that she's bisexual
> Interviewer: Just to check what you mean, with a lesbian that would be unavailable to that man, where as a bisexual woman might be available and/or be sexually titillating?
> Yaz: Exactly. That is exactly what I mean
> Interviewer: So am I right in thinking that that kind of bisexuality is not challenging to men's sense of their sexuality?
> Yaz: Yes, that's right, and it doesn't affect their male superiority in any way.

Here, lesbianism is seen as threatening to the patriarchal dominance of men (because they are excluded), whilst commodified bisexuality can be interpreted as non-threatening to men; a titillating diversion that does not challenge male dominance. This line of thinking was supported by some of the other contributors. Their interviews suggested that, whilst pop culture tends to reject lesbians because of stereotypes concerning feminism and 'man-hating' (in other words, perceived potential threats to dominant heterosexist relations of power), bisexual women are perceived as novel and sexually interesting, rendering bisexuality depoliticised. Commodified notions and models of both 'lesbian' and 'bisexual' are appropriated and used to make money. However, the dynamics are rather different, because 'bisexual' does include men as objects of desire or as sexual actors. It seems overall that 'lesbianism' and 'bisexuality' can both be assimilated within heteropatriarchy via processes of sexualised commodification, but that this is easier with bisexuality.

What about the commodification of male bisexualities? The UK bisexuality research revealed a startling absence of male bisexual subjects in the discussion of commodified bisexualities. There was little mention of men and commodified bisexuality in the research findings, although contributor Lena suggested that male bisexuals are part of the 'bisexual bohemian lifestyle', but are generally less visible, because male-male sex is more available than female-female sex, and men are not objectified in the same way that women are. The issue of the non-commercialisation of male bisexuality is one that requires further attention. Bisexual commodification is clearly heavily gendered. Whilst women are objectified for male consumers, female consumers have less spending power and perhaps less interest in objectified 'male on male' sexualities. Consumers of 'gay' porn prefer men-only action, even if the men who produce the porn are actually bisexual. It may be that the potential radicalism of bisexuality (the possibility that it can disrupt heteropatriarchal, mononormative social norms and structures and to open up new possibilities for sex and relationships) is managed in different ways for males and females. For males, bisexuality is erased within commercialised spaces as a viable possibility, whilst for females, it is commodified and contained.

There was no discussion amongst the UK bisexuality research contributors of the commodification of trans bisexualities. However, there is some research internationally on the commodification of gender-diverse people's sexualities. For example, a study of trans sex workers in Thailand (Sanders, 2010) indicates that Western females are involved in the consumption of the sexual services provided by lady boys in Thailand, albeit in different ways to males. This underscores the importance of context (for example the power imbalances between Western tourists and Thai sex workers) as well as the complexities associated with the gendering of the sexual service sector. Therefore, whilst the commodification of bisexualities in the UK does seem to be very gendered (hypersexualised bisexual females, absent bisexual males), this may be altered when transgender is considered, in different sectors of the commercialised sexual markets, and internationally.

Negative stereotyping and its impact

The UK research strongly indicated that the commodification of bisexuality as it currently stands contributes to biphobia (see Chapter 1), with the majority of contributors being critical of commodification because of this. For example, contributor Nancy stated that 'it perpetuates harmful stereotypes of bi people as being (for example) universally sexually available and inconsistent'. The hypersexualised commodification of female-female bisexuality was seen to fuel antipathy amongst lesbians towards bisexual women; lesbians may see bisexual women wishing to have relationships with other women as untrustworthy. More broadly, because bisexuality is framed in a titillating way, some individuals may (according to contributor Kay) define themselves as bisexual just to get media (or other) attention, which then further trivialises the identity. There are also body-discrimination dynamics taking place in bisexual commodification, as the following two quotes show:

> conventionally attractive female bisexuality, mostly, that's it basically, that is the one acceptable meme of bisexuality that will always be used and that is a sure fire ratings booster if you like, because everybody has the language of it in their head and it doesn't upset people like if would if you had two men. (Anne)

> people make money off that kind of bisexuality – making money off a pornified version. I don't think that kind of body form is reflective of what most bisexual people have so it doesn't help... and I've heard people making horrible comments about actual groups of bi people because they are comparing them against this ideal pornified type of bisexuality, saying 'oh you're all fat, you're all ugly'. (Meg John)

In these two quotes, we see the way in which a sexually commodified depiction of bisexuality acts not just to consolidate stereotypical notions of female attractiveness, but also to socially stigmatise bisexual people who either do not wish to, or cannot, fit with stereotypical notions of attractiveness. This dynamic can be interpreted from an intersectional perspective (see Chapter 3), in that participant observation of the UK bisexuality 'scenes' showed that many bisexual people are, for example, older, disabled, or large, and therefore fall outside of mainstream attractiveness ideals. From a materialist feminist perspective, the social marginalisation and denigration of people on the basis of their looks can be seen as a powerful tool by which non-normative groups are stigmatised. It can be argued that producers of the media shape notions of attractiveness in such a way as to maximise capital accumulation, not just via the sale of media products but also by fostering a beauty industry where people (mostly women) feel pressurised to spend money on cosmetic products and services.

Another of the themes to emerge from the findings was the way in which performative, hypersexualised, ideas of bisexuality can create pressures on bisexual women and others to engage in same-sex sexualities in order to seem 'sexy' (often for males), and to do this in particular ways (see Fahs, 2009). This is, for research contributors such as Lena, part of a broader erotic imperative imposed on women (where they are supposed to be sexually active and enjoying this) which problematically clashes with some women's priorities, such as economic survival, work, health and well-being, or childrearing. The bisexual erotic imperative goes beyond actual sexualities to include the supposed 'trendiness' that goes along with the 'bohemian' trappings of bisexuality discussed above. The UK bisexuality research participants were asked about the notion of bisexual trendiness, which they saw as located amongst the celebrity class of bisexuals (contributors mentioned, for example, David Bowie and Suede). More ordinary bisexual people are, according to contributor Meg John, untrendy and in fact (as was discussed in Chapter 4) the organised bisexual community is anti-fashion in its norms and values, and it celebrates at least some non-normative sexualities. The disjunction between commodified, celebrity, and fashionable bisexualities, and more ordinary, DIY bisexual identities, may be one reason for the social marginalisation of the bisexual community generally and for its historical lack of political purchase (see Chapter 7).

Ambivalences about commodification

The commodification of bisexuality is contested rather than as a uniformly negative process. Bisexual commodification can sometimes be forged in a way that asserts non-normative sexualities. These can be queer sexualities, or may challenge notions of a 'pure' relationship (where a 'pure' relationship is seen as one based on love and affection rather than a concern with money, security and property (Giddens, 1992)). This is evident in, for example, bisexual anthologies such as *Best Bisexual Erotica* (published by US-based Bill Brent and colleagues (see Henkin, 2012)).

The UK bisexuality research revealed some ambivalences about bisexual commodification. Whilst the majority of contributors were critical of the commodification of bisexuality (see above), there were some exceptions. For example, Jo said that she did not mind the commodification of sexuality in the context of sex work. In some cases, divergent attitudes played out in individual's intimate lives, for example Anne and Reggie both described ambivalent feelings towards commercial pornography, finding it sexually exciting but worrying about the possible exploitation of the actors. There was also some ambivalence about the commercialisation of bisexuality, as Rosie commented:

> sex will always sell, and men like to look at girls snogging, so it's a commodity, and it's like, 'yawn', if anyone thinks that that's radical or that it's positioning lesbianism or bisexuality or queerness on screen then they kind of need to wake up really. On the other hand if that image makes a small 8 year old child think 'ooh that looks nice, maybe that's me' one day, maybe that's worth it. I can remember being a lonely, isolated queer kid, when I was little... when I saw things that were slightly out of the ordinary on television I took notice.

Here, commodified sexualities provide a site for awareness raising concerning sexual identities (albeit in a limited way), at the same time as consolidating certain heteropatriarchal norms, demonstrating complex and contextualised processes.

The media

Addressing the media and bisexuality in any depth is beyond the scope of this chapter, but it is worth noting that Fahs (2009) emphasises the commercialisation of performative bisexuality in the (anglophone) media, and the way in which bisexuality is often portrayed as 'just a phase'. Talking of female bisexualities, she states that there has been 'a dramatic increase in the number of television shows that rely on performative bisexuality as a form of entertainment' (2009, p.435), whilst films such as *Girls Gone Wild* exploit women's behavioural bisexuality for commercial gain.

Within the UK, Barker *et al.* (2012) argue that bisexual invisibility in the UK media (UK and international material) is standard, with few portrayals of bisexual people, and a tendency for fictional characters who demonstrate attraction for people of more than one gender to be portrayed as transitioning between gay/lesbian and straight, or vice versa. The representation of bisexual people in the media is gendered (see above); women tend to be portrayed as promiscuous or titillating whilst bisexual men are more likely to be invisible. This may affect the organised bisexual community negatively. For example, contributor Meg John remarked, 'Just recently Bi UK [a research and activist organisation supporting the rights of bisexuals] got asked to provide a 'hot bi babe' to be photographed...it doesn't help matters that is associated with a certain type of, women particularly, the stereotype, bi curious, just titillating men'.

The portrayal of bisexual people in the media may be changing to a degree; Bisexual Media Watch provides analysis of contemporary media and bisexual representation which shows that some programmes shown in the UK provide positive portrayals of bisexual characters, for example the USA show *Revenge*, which had a male bisexual character (Jules, 2012). In the UK, mainstream media coverage occasionally includes bisexual and pansexual people. For example, Hattie Collins (2013) discusses out bisexual/pansexual rappers such as Syd Tha Kid and Azealia Banks, and bisexual celebrities singer-songwriter Jessie J and TV personality Craig Revel Horwood were both included on the Guardian newspaper's World Pride Power List 2013 (McGrath, 2013). However, the tendency for female bisexual hypersexualisation and male bisexual erasure is a theme that, as argued above, tends to cut across the sector. Overall, the use of 'bisexual' imagery in films and advertising is described by contributors such as Anne as 'a little frisson of trying to portray an image of broadmindedness, or adventurousness, or edgy, or decadence, a thing that is just designed for a particular target, consumer, and it's not *honest*, it's not really about that'. Specific micro-encounters described by some of the bisexual research contributors demonstrated the negative impact of the hypersexualisation and commodification of female same-sex sexualities, as the following quote demonstrates:

> We were in a jazz club, we had a kiss, and a man came up to us and said 'oh my god, you guys look amazing, I'm a photographer from a magazine and I'd really like to photograph you'. And I was so angry.

And [girlfriend] really liked it, she was really flattered by it, and we had a big fight about it. (Yaz)

This quote shows how a relationship was disrupted by someone seeking to capitalise on it. However, it also demonstrates the way which amorous bisexuality can quickly become performative bisexuality and that this can be interpreted differently even amongst people in an intimate relationship.

Sexual services (sex work and pornography)

The field of sexual services is a substantial one, with multifaceted accounts now emerging which emphasise context, location, and agency as opposed to either pro or anti-sex work stances (see for, example, Boris *et al.*, 2010; Hardy *et al.*, 2010). This section of the chapter will not seek to engage substantially with this body of literature but will rather highlight some key themes to emerge from the UK bisexual project research findings in relation to sex work and pornography. It is worth noting that, whilst there is research about behavioural bisexuals (who may identify as heterosexual or lesbian/gay, for example; see, for instance, McCaghy and Skipper Jr., 2000), there is little research about bisexual people as sex workers. One exception is provided by Browne *et al.* (2010) who, in surveys of LGBT people in the UK seaside town of Brighton, found that 10.6 per cent of bisexual respondents had taken pay for sex (as compared to 3.7 per cent of lesbians, 13 per cent of gay men, and 17.9 per cent of those identifying as queer). The study did not provide a bisexual-specific analysis, but for the sample overall one key issue was the impact of structural pressures such as homelessness, youth, poverty, and housing shortages on LGBT people's choices to take part in sex work. These factors were mediated by other aspects, such as the way that some people who sold sex enjoyed it, and the fact that the boundary between paid-for and other forms of sex can be blurred. Whilst little data was forthcoming from the UK bisexuality project about sex work, what data there was supported a nuanced analysis. For example, Jo reported that two sex workers she knows provided paid-for sexual services to females despite identifying as straight and that they said they did not mind doing so, and Grant said 'I know some sex workers who are bi and most of their work as female sex workers is with men... [there is] quite a lot of female-female connection in female sex work, especially the more highly paid [parts of the sector]'. More research would be required to understand the specifics of, firstly, the lived experiences of sex workers who identify as bisexual, and secondly, bisexualities performed by sex workers who do not identify as bisexual (for example group sex with a male-female couple as the client).

The research yielded some insights about pornography which quite clearly support the materialist analysis of bisexual hypersexuality which is developed above. Firstly, the pornified (sexually commodified) version of bisexuality was explicitly discussed, for example, in the following interview segment:

> Lena: This commodified bisexuality has been in porn for heterosexual men for a long long time but it's got to the point where it's actually compulsory.
> Interviewer: It's a mainstay of mainstream porn?
> Lena: Yes...the men are threatened for the sight of other men, so [they want] to have men out of the picture, on a base level.
> Interviewer: So they don't want to have just one woman there being on show, they want some sort of interaction?
> Lena: But they don't want to see a hairy man, yes [both laugh].
> Interviewer: What is it about male sexuality, do you think, that commodifies?
> Lena: I don't know, maybe just if you are a straight man who likes women, what more, as many women in the same room as possible is really nice? Obviously that's on the level of the person consuming the porn, but on the level of the industry...its worrying...if the straight male consumer actually came across a bisexual women he would probably run for the hills [laughs].

The dynamics evident in this interview section mirror those described above; hypersexualised bisexualities exist within a commercial context, and they do not challenge heterosexism.

Although there is clearly a normative pattern taking place within the pornography industry, there are also indications of a more subversive reworking of porn. For example, Zoe Williams provides journalistic coverage of ethical porn which does not exploit participants, and she remarks that 'the more the sex industry tries to hammer us into one sexual identity, the more we rebel with riotous weirdness' (Williams, 2014, p.45). The ethical producers of porn include directors such as Madison Young, whose 'imaginatively plotted, BDSM-flavoured porn...I want to call bisexual, but don't feel that quite conveys the unpindownability of its sexual leaning' (Williams, 2014, p.41). This type of porn does not necessarily fail to challenge heteronormativity and may indeed provide space for its disruption.

Most of the UK bisexuality researcher contributors did not use any type of pornography. Some engaged in DIY sexualities, for example Anne said that 'I have a very active pornographic mind thank you very much, which may be being influenced by culture and society', whilst others expressed antipathy to commercialised pornography. For instance Dave said that whilst he was not against pornography per se, 'it's a big turn off actually when girls are kissing each other for the benefit of the guy, I don't like it'. Some of the contributors discussed the context for the production of the pornography as being important, notably Rosie who said:

> it's about who is making it for who, what's the audience, what's the production like, who is it being created by... I have seen some really good lesbian porn *made by lesbians for lesbians* and its very very different to heterosexual porn or even so-called 'lesbian porn' made by male directors using *crack heads* which is the abuse of humans.

Overall, the UK bisexuality research findings indicate that bisexual people are critical of commercial pornography, although there were exceptions. Some contributors spoke of the widespread use of female-female and so-called 'bisexual' sexualities within the pornography industries (see above). One contributor discussed the way in which the porn industries colonise the social media with porn, for example the 'bisexual' tag on Tumblr is reported to be full of links to porn in comparison to other tags. This may indicate that there is a large market for 'bisexual' porn, perhaps reaching many times more people than there are identity-based bisexuals. The appropriation of the term 'bisexual' by the porn industry and its frequent portrayal as meaning promiscuous and sexually adventurous may be fuelling a trend in which the term 'bisexuality' becomes synonymous with certain sexual activities, rather than with the multifaceted social identities of bisexual people. This can be analysed from a critical perspective, which traces the operation of neo-liberal capitalist processes in shaping notions of sexuality, and in particular hypersexualised bisexualities that may make money, but that also render bisexual people subject to social stigmatisation.

This chapter has examined bisexuality in relation to the production of wealth within neo-liberal capitalist countries, focusing on the UK and the USA. It has addressed two key sites in which bisexualities are relevant: mainstream workplaces and industries where bisexuality is commodified. The chapter has examined how bisexual people are marginalised in some workplace organisations, with bisexuality tending to be erased, and some bisexual people facing overt discrimination and prejudice. Material from the UK bisexuality project demonstrated, however, that some bisexual people experience supportive workplaces, and also that bisexuals exercise considerable agency in dodging, and in some cases challenging, workplace biphobias. In the USA, studies also showed patterns of discrimination and concurrent tendencies for bisexual people to stay closeted to avoid discrimination. In both countries, bisexual employment rights agendas were related to policies and strategies regarding lesbian and gay employment rights, whilst at the same time, bisexuals sometimes face greater marginalisation than lesbians and gay men. The lives of both UK and US bisexuals appeared to be crosscut by intersectional forces, such as those relating to socio-economic class.

The chapter then went on to address the commodification and hypersexualisation of bisexuality, focusing on the media and the sex industries (specifically, sex work and pornography). It explored the discursive framing of bisexuality as exotic, sexy, and titillating, and the ways in which this is used to sell commodities such as porn. This hypersexualisation of bisexuality impacts on bisexual people in negative ways; by framing bisexuality in an overly sexualised way, the other aspects of bisexual people's identities are overlooked, and bisexuality can be stigmatised by those who are anti-sex and mononormative. Processes of sexism also operate in the sectors associated with hypersexualised bisexuality. The research found, however, that there are ambivalences about the media, and porn, within the narratives of the bisexual research contributors. Paradoxically, the subversion and resistance of dominant norms may take place in such fora, and bisexual people can engage with them in agentic ways. The commodification of bisexuality appears overall to contribute to the stigmatisation of bisexual people, but sectors such as the media and sex work remain contested territories.

Summary

- Bisexual people within mainstream employment sometimes face marginalisation and stigmatisation.
- Bisexuality tends to be more hidden than lesbian and gay identities within workplaces, due to a combination of bisexual closeting and organisational silencing and discrimination.
- In the UK, bisexual people have a range of positive and negative experiences of the workplace.

- UK and US bisexuals exercise agency in a number of ways in their workplaces – including strategic closeting and challenging biphobia.
- Within the media and the sexual services, female bisexuality is framed in hypersexualised ways for the benefit of (mostly) male audiences; it is commodified and used to sell products and services.
- Male bisexuality is largely erased within the media and the sexual services.
- The hypersexualisation of bisexuality is linked with the stigmatisation of bisexuality within the wider population because bisexuals come to be seen as promiscuous and 'other'.
- However, the process is not uniform, and the media and sex industries may also be sites where bisexuality is supported and bisexuals operate with agency.

The next chapter of the book applies citizenship theories to bisexuality, and in doing so contributes to some debates within citizenship studies.

6
Bisexuality and Citizenship

This chapter explores some of the conceptual tools that citizenship studies provide, and the debates such studies raise, in relation to bisexuality. In so doing it aims to provide insight into the issues facing bisexuals, and also to inform the development of citizenship studies, particularly in relation to sexuality and intimacy. Citizenship rights are important for bisexual people given the ways in which bisexuals are marginalised and stigmatised, as discussed in the earlier chapters of the book. Some of the issues concerning citizenship that are relevant to bisexuals and other non-heterosexual people include sexual expression, relationship form, reproduction, freedom from harassment and abuse, social inclusion, and identity recognition.

What does 'citizenship' mean? The idea of 'citizenship' has traditionally been associated with the rights and responsibilities of people living within a particular country, in other words, personal protections and privileges on the one hand, and obligations on the other (see Monro and Richardson, 2014). The classical model of citizenship is associated with the work of T.H. Marshall (1950), a British sociologist who defined citizenship in terms of three sets of rights: civil or legal rights, political rights, and social rights. Civil or legal rights are institutionalised through the law and include the right to own property, freedom of speech, liberty of the person, and the right to justice. Political rights are institutionalised in parliamentary political systems, civil services, and regional and local governments and they include the right to vote and participate in the exercise of political power. Social rights include the right to a certain level of economic welfare and security, as well as rights that are institutionalised in the welfare state in countries where a welfare state exists (Monro and Richardson, 2014). The classical model is complemented by others, such as civic republicanism. In this tradition, citizenship is seen as communal (as opposed to individualistic models found in the liberal Marshallian tradition); citizens are people whose lives are interlinked through shared traditions and understandings that form the basis for the pursuit of the 'common good' (Delanty, 2000). Although debates about communitarianism will not be much developed in this chapter, it is noticeable that the organised UK bisexual communities are marked by norms of care and interdependence, as are some of the other communities with which they overlap (see Chapter 4). In addition, the bisexual communities have shared goals, such as increased bisexual visibility and solidarity, which suggests that it could be useful to pursue a communitarian analysis in more depth.

Since the 1990s, debates over the inadequacies of the traditional models of citizenship have led to the development of new ideas about citizenship. It is in the context of such developments that notions of gendered and sexual citizenships have emerged, much of it fuelled by the work of feminist, and lesbian, gay, or queer, scholars. These scholars have challenged some of the assumptions that were embedded in the traditional models of citizenship, such as the idea that citizenship concerns only the public sphere. Their work forms a basis for the discussion of bisexual citizenship that is provided in this chapter.

It is important to note that modern notions of citizenship emerged in neo-liberal democratic states and the transposition of central citizenship notions such as 'rights and responsibilities' to nation states which are non-democratic is problematic. Some of these countries are anti-LGBT (see Itaborahy and Zhu, 2014), and one key issue is that in countries, or localised communities, where homosexuality is illegal or heavily sanctioned, people's methods of managing their sexualities will be different from those where some level of citizenship rights are in place. Therefore, rather than seeking recognition for their sexual identities via citizenship claims, as is increasingly the case in countries such as the UK, bisexuals may keep their sexual identities hidden in order to avoid persecution. Bisexual and others non-heterosexual people living in countries where fundamental human rights are lacking will have less agency than those living elsewhere. This issue has been recognised by some scholars, notably Ken Plummer. Plummer highlights the way that intimate sexual and intimate citizenship discourses emphasise the 'right to choose' – in terms of partners, sexual activities, and whether to marry or not (Plummer, 2006, p.25). This is highly problematic for people whose agency is impeded by a punitive state regime, or by factors such as poverty. Therefore, it can be argued that critical approaches to bisexual citizenship need to situate analysis within a framework that considers international and national dynamics and inequalities.

This chapter uses empirical material from the UK, which is characterised by its colonial history, neo-liberal economic system, and current relatively progressive legislative framework (with respect to sexuality and gender). In this context, the importance of individual agency, recognition, and rights claims are central to discussions about citizenship. However, as shown in Chapters 3 and 4, bisexual and other non-heterosexual people who are not white, British nationals, or middle class, may not be able to relate to the values found in the UK bisexual communities, which emphasise freedom of expression and visibility. This means that even within a UK context, some key aspects of liberal approaches to citizenship, such as the focus on individual agency, are limited.

The chapter takes a UK focus in order to gain some depth of analysis, whilst recognising that the sample used for the research was limited and that more work is required, both in the UK and elsewhere. The chapter begins with a brief review of existing literature on bisexual citizenships, and then outlines some conceptual tools provided by feminist and sexual citizenships. It provides understandings of the ways in which bisexual people are marginalised by mainstream models of citizenship, developing bisexual critiques of heterosexist and gender-binary citizenships. In doing so it addresses a key debate about the assimilationist nature of citizenship, in contrast to the arguably radical potentials of bisexuality. The chapter then moves on to look at another set of debates, concerning whether a bisexual-specific model of citizenship (particularist model) is useful, or whether models of citizenship that include everyone (universalist) are better. The chapter does not address the important areas of civil, legislative, and political citizenships, which are considered to an extent in the following chapter.

Bisexual citizenships

There is little literature about specifically bisexual citizenships. Exceptions include David Evan's (1993) seminal text on sexual citizenships, which documents the prejudiced construction of bisexuality by psychologists, sexologists, psychiatrists, and social scientists. Evans discussed the evolution of the bisexual movement in the West and the bisexual activist claims of the 1980s and 1990s. He also analysed the processes by which lesbian and gay communities have marginalised bisexuals, and highlighted key issues such as the fluidity of bisexuality and the difficulties with which this interfaces with identity-based citizenship claims. Surya Monro also began to map out the terrain, arguing that bisexual citizenship can be seen to be unique because bisexual identities are different from lesbian, gay, and heterosexual identities in a number of ways. Bisexuality typically includes the experience of fluid and multiple desires. Some bisexual people are attracted to people on the basis of characteristics other than sex; others desire men, women, and others simultaneously, while others shift in cycles between desire for women and men. Bisexuality is subjectively different from monosexuality (Monro, 2005, p.155–156).

The existing literature suggests that bisexual citizenship claims concern the recognition of bisexuality as a valid identity, and acceptance that desire can be fluid. This entails support for lesbian and gay rights but also an understanding that sexuality can be changeable, and that people with more fluid or complex identities and multiple (rather than monogamous) relationship forms also require citizenship rights (Monro, 2005; Richardson and Monro, 2012). It is possible to build on existing work concerning bisexual citizenship by using ideas drawn from feminist scholarship on citizenship, and the chapter now turns to these.

Feminist approaches to citizenship

Feminist approaches to citizenship have provided a crucial challenge to the traditional approaches (see, for example, Monro and Richardson, 2014). Feminist citizenship studies is pertinent to bisexuality in two key ways: firstly, gendered inequalities affect bisexual people, and secondly, some of the key theoretical developments of relevance to bisexual citizenships stem from feminist approaches. This section of the chapter explains some aspects of feminist citizenship theory and outlines ways in which this might apply to bisexual citizenships. It includes a short discussion of trans theory; trans theory and citizenship studies are relevant to bisexual citizenships because of gender diversity amongst bisexuals, but also as gender pluralist theories, and deconstructionist approaches to gender, are useful in relation to understanding bisexuality.

There are a wide range of feminist approaches to citizenship, many of them grounded in empirical studies of particular geo-political and social contexts. They address issues as diverse as trafficked sex workers (Andrijasevic, 2010), motherhood and migration (Erel, 2011), and EU policies (Lombardo and Meier, 2011). The key conceptual contribution that feminist approaches make is that they challenge the masculinist bias inherent in traditional forms of citizenship theory (Pateman, 1988; Lister, 1997, 2003). In other words, traditional citizenship theorists developed their ideas with men in mind, overlooking the ways in which this excludes women, and the possibilities that their theories might work to consolidate the greater power and economic resources that men – as a group – have in comparison with women. For those readers who are unfamiliar with citizenship debates, traditional citizenship theorists assumed that the locus of citizenship is the public sphere (including paid employment, cultural activities, civil society, and political engagement) and that this public sphere is mostly inhabited by men. The masculine bias of traditional citizenship studies has been challenged by theorists such as Ruth Lister:

> feminist theory and research have significantly transformed the theorization of citizenship. And, in challenging the false universalism of the 'malestream', it has contributed to a more differentiated analysis.
> (2011, p.27)

What is meant here by the idea of 'false universalism' is that a citizenship focus which foregrounds the interests of men, in the public sphere, but presents itself as universal (applicable to everyone) is flawed. This type of universalism overlooks the interests of women, their contribution to the public sphere, and also citizenship issues pertaining to the private sphere (which could include domestic life, caring roles, and intimacies). The next section of the chapter provides more insight into public/private citizenship issues with respect to bisexuality.

Public and private

As indicated above, traditional models of citizenship rely on a separation between the public and private spheres, and this has been challenged by feminist theorists. The extension of mainstream notions of citizenship to include women includes a reformulation of the public and private divide, with a need for greater focus on the involvement of women in public life (see Monro, 2005) as well as a re-privileging of unpaid caring, as opposed to paid work (Lister, 1997). Notions of public and private are changing, for example Diane Richardson (see 2000a,b) discussed a shift in the locus of citizenship, as practices that had previously been thought of as 'private' are increasingly becoming thought about as a basis for citizenship, whilst Ken Plummer notes that 'personal and the public cannot be so readily split up' (2003, p.69). However, it appears that a consideration of the public/private divide is relevant for bisexuals.

For UK-based bisexuals, issues relating to the public/private divide concern the right to be out as bisexual within the public realm, claims for the recognition of bisexuality as a valid identity, and a number of intimate citizenship issues (see below). The research findings indicated that bisexuality is substantially pushed into the private realm in the UK, although commodified bisexualities are an exception (see Chapter 5). The bisexual communities have mostly formed separately from mainstream public spaces and discourses, and although bisexuality is included in the 'LGBT' acronym used in equalities work, in practice there is limited engagement with specifically bisexual interests (see Richardson and Monro, 2012). Social prejudice and heteropatriarchal norms keep bisexuality in the private realm within wider society, as the following quote may show:

> Lena: I think people find [bisexual] activism really difficult in its traditional, conventional form.
> Interviewer: You mean ordinary people?
> Lena: Yeah.
> Interviewer: Can you say why?
> Lena: I don't know [sighs] there is that cliché 'we don't mind what you do so long as you don't shove it in my face' attitude... if I'm being more understanding I guess for some people it *is* frightening, it's frightening to see what they think of as their safe kind of unchanging world changing.

It is not just bisexual-identified activists who get pushed into the private realm. Behavioural bisexuals who have covert same-sex encounters provide a particularly sharp example of bisexuality as privatised. However, the people who engage in them exist within citizenship frameworks, which underpin rights, such as the right to be free from violent hate crime when cruising for sexual partners in public spaces. At the same time, they may be deeply affected by the dominant models of citizenship, which tend to assume that society is founded on heterosexual, monogamous relationships. The privatisation of behavioural bisexualities renders them ineffective in terms of potential change within the political, public realm (see Chapter 7).

Another issue concerns the disjunction between the public/private dynamics concerning bisexuality within mainstream society in the UK, and those found within the bisexual communities. BiCon is a particularly good example, as the conference often includes sessions on topics that usually pertain to the private realm within mainstream society (such as cuddling, emotional intimacy, sex toys, and BDSM) alongside sessions on topics such as activism and the media which could be seen as belonging to the public realm. It may be that this blurring of public and private is one reason why the bisexual communities have so far failed to assimilate (or be assimilated) into the more public-facing lesbian and gay voluntary and community-sector organisations and state machinery. In their troubling of the public-private divide that is part of heterosexist, mononormative mainstream society, they remain outside of mainstream 'ways of doing things'.

This part of the chapter has addressed a key concern for feminist citizenship scholars in relation to bisexuality: the public/private divide. The next chapter section analyses transgender citizenships and bisexuality.

Transgender citizenships

The majority of feminist citizenship scholarship concerns the interests of cisgender females. There are exceptions, including Monro's (2003, 2005) and Monro and Warren's (2004) work, which analyses transgender in relation to different forms of citizenship. Trans citizenships are relevant to bisexuals because a substantial number of bisexual people are also gender-diverse. Also, trans theory, as shown in Chapter 2, includes models that deconstruct the binary gender system, and gender pluralist models. Such models are important for bisexual people. The 'moving beyond genders' approach to gender diversity could be used, together with citizenship-related notions of communitarianism, to forge a new basis for bisexual citizenship. This could rely on values such as mutual care, agency, consent, and self-determination, rather than models of citizenship which reinscribe gender binaries via legislative and welfare systems that divide people into 'male' and 'female', and homosexual/heterosexual. This might not foreground bisexuality per se, but it could form a broad basis for citizenship that supports non-heterosexual, as well as heterosexual, people.

The gender pluralism approach also applies to bisexual citizenship. It could be used to open up a much broader range of gendered and sexed subject positions and desires, many of which are not currently named (at least within mainstream society), for example desires between people who identify as androgynous. These may then become institutionalised into sets of rights and responsibilities regarding aspects of social life, such as partnership rights, reproduction, caring, and access to welfare, so that people with these identities and desires gain citizenship rights. A gender-plural model of citizenship could revolutionise the two-gender system on which citizenship in the UK is currently based, giving bisexual people and others more space to identify in different ways.

Despite appeals to a more nuanced, gender-diverse model of citizenship as a means of supporting bisexual citizenships, as well as those of other people, it is necessary to point out that the institutionalisation of fluidity and multiplicity poses a difficulty. This is partly because of bureaucratic processes (for instance forms that monitor, and consolidate, gender identity and marital status). These processes and mechanisms act to regulate subjects and create static, solid social identities. These identities form one of the underpinnings of social institutions including the law, welfare, and healthcare. The institutionalisation of gender and sexual fluidity and diversity could also be seen as difficult because gendered regulatory processes are central to other goals associated with citizenship, such as the control of immigration and preservation of the nation-state. This is of course very problematic from critical postcolonial perspectives; the institutional forging of discrete sexed, sexualised, and gendered identities being inextricably tied to global relations of inequality (see Chapter 3). However, this chapter will not address these concerns now; rather, it will turn to a discussion of sexual and intimate citizenships.

Sexual and intimate citizenships

Theories of sexual and intimate citizenship developed in the West by linking discourses about citizenship with those of sexualities (Wilson, 2009). They subsequently gained international purchase, being taken up and developed in, for example, Vasu Reddy's (2009) discussion of sexual citizenship in South Africa. There is a substantial literature on sexual and intimate citizenship across a range of disciples (see, for example, Berlant, 1997; Weeks, 1998; Bell and Binnie, 2000; Richardson, 2000a, 2000b; Phelan, 2001; Plummer, 2001; Cooper, 2006; Oleksy et al., 2011; Richardson and Monro, 2012, 2014).

What are sexual and intimate citizenships? Sexual citizenship concerns bodily autonomy and sexual responsibilities, such as the non-exploitation and non-oppression of others (Brown, 1997, p.5 cited in Hearn *et al.*, 2011). It directs attention to the cultural, political, and legal aspects of sexual activities and expression (Hearn *et al.*, 2011, p.7). The related notion of 'intimate citizenship' can be broadly defined as a cluster of concerns over the right to choose what we do with our bodies, our feelings, our identities, our relationships, our genders, our eroticisms, and our representations (Plummer, 1995, p.17). Like sexual citizenship, intimate citizenship can be understood in terms of both political and social status, constituted through everyday practices.

Ideas of sexual citizenship have been developed in various ways (see Monro and Richardson, 2014). Those that deal directly with sex and sexuality include Jeff Hearn's (1992) approach to socio-spatial aspects of sexuality, which looks at where sexual partners are found and where sex acts take place, and David Bell and Jon Binnie's (2000) argument for greater consideration of sexual practices. There are also consumer models of sexual citizenship, drawing on David Evan's ideas about 'partial, private and primarily leisure and lifestyle membership' (Evans, 1993, p.64). For Evans, the sexual citizen is someone whose sexual rights are expressed primarily through 'participation in commercial "private" territories' (Evans, 1993, p.64).

For bisexual people, and others who have sexual desires for people of more than one gender, these ideas of sexual and intimate citizenship are highly relevant. Plummer's notion of intimate citizenship may be particularly useful for behavioural bisexuals who reject identity categories, as it deals with sets of practices and desires, rather than particular relationship formations or sexual identities. There was a great deal of support amongst the contributors to the UK bisexuality research for choice and consent-based sexual and intimate self-expression, across many types of sexual proclivity (including celibacy and asexuality) and relationship formation (see Chapter 4). The micro-level, individualised citizenships emphasised in intimate citizenship discourses are highlighted in the UK bisexuality research contributors' narratives, with much less discussion about the institutional formation of sexualities, and social and political rights beyond the right to self-identify as bisexual. Bisexual participation in 'private' territories, following Evans, is also very noticeable and clearly forms a resource for the construction of sexual identities for some bisexual people (see Chapter 2). These territories are far less commercialised than both the gay scene and heterosexual 'sexual' spaces such as nightclubs, pointing more to alternative 'scenes' as spaces where counter-mainstream sexual rights can be forged and articulated. However, Evan's (1993) idea of commercial, private zones where sexualities can be enacted is problematic for contemporary bisexuals, given the heteronormative, sexist ways in which commercial bisexualities are structured (see Chapter 5). It also leads to questions about who is included in sexual citizenship, given the unequal ways in which access to consumption is structured (Bell and Binnie,

2000; Richardson and Monro, 2012). One of the themes to emerge from a discussion of sexual and intimate citizenship is that of challenges to heteronormativity, and this forms the topic of the next chapter section.

Challenges to heteronormativity

Sexual citizenship theorists have challenged the heteronormativity of traditional models of citizenship, mirroring the challenges to the masculinist bias of traditional notions of citizenship that have been provided by feminists. As Richardson and Monro (2012) have noted, it has been argued by a number of writers that hegemonic forms of heterosexuality underpin the construction of the 'normal citizen' (see Richardson, 1998; Bell and Binnie, 2000; Cossman, 2007). It is important to recognize that this is a dynamic process: such constructions of citizenship both reflect *and* reproduce the privileging of heterosexuality (see Richardson, 2000a,b).

Critiques of the heterosexist construction of citizenship are relevant to bisexual people, but sexual citizenship authors have not always considered the specific characteristics of bisexuality, including fluidity, complexity, and multiplicity, when making such critiques. It is not just heteronormativity that bisexuality can challenge; it is also the normative notion that people have static sexual identities, with desires that are directed towards persons of only one sex. This static, unidirectional construction of sexual identity underpins both heterosexual and lesbian/gay identity constructions, and it also underpins traditional notions of citizenship. Moreover, a substantial proportion of bisexual persons are openly non-monogamous, prompting critiques of the mononormativity that is so central to lesbian and gay, and heterosexual, claims to citizenship (see the discussion about homonormativity, below). In addition, bisexual people have specific citizenship issues, partially due to the nature of discrimination against them. For example, research contributor Kay explained that some people may be fluid long term about their sexual identity. She said:

> you've got pressure from family or friends, whatever, 'be straight, get married, do this, do that' pressure from the other side which may be your gay friends saying 'you've got to pick and choose, be one or the other, you've got to settle down, pick out who you want'. There is discrimination from sides... you can't be someone in-between, you can't be multisexual, or metrosexual... there is so much peer pressure

and society pressure to decide either way, why do people need to know what your sexuality is? They seem to be so hung up on it.

The mononormative and rigidly structured underpinnings of heterosexual, and lesbian and gay, citizenships can be understood by considering the trend towards reformist politics that has taken place in countries such as the UK. Lesbians and gays, and sometimes transgender people and bisexuals, have sought to reform social institutions such as the law and welfare in order to make them incorporate some of their citizenship rights and interests. UK-based reformist moves have taken place at the same time as the globalisation of lesbian, gay, bisexual, and transgender organising and advocacy (see Adam, Duyvendak, and Krawel, 1999), with the establishment of transnational networks as well as international organisations (Kollman and Waites, 2009).

Reformist politics can be seen as 'assimilationist', because some LGBT people are trying to become part of the mainstream, using established institutions such as the law to achieve this goal. As Richardson and Monro (2012) suggest, this development is in contrast to queer or directly radical challenges to these social institutions. A good example would be the successful campaign for same-sex marriage in the UK, which is a very different type of activism than that associated with attempts to get rid of the institution of marriage altogether. Critiques of assimilationism stem from feminist, as well as sexual citizenship, authors. For example, Sasha Roseneil discusses the 'spectre of incorporation' (2013, p.4) that haunts feminist engagements with citizenship. The issue is that radical political moves may end up being incorporated into existing institutions, defusing their critical and radical edges without fundamentally changing these institutions. Some theorists question whether the 'turn to citizenship' in LGBT politics is a narrowing of political space that fails to adequately address wider transformations that feminist and queer writers seek (Lustiger-Thaler *et al.*, 2011).

Has assimilation taken place in the UK? Lesbian and gay activism has, so far, failed to address sexual fluidity and to include the full spectrum of identities and relationship forms that bisexual people have, such as poly and asexuality. In this sense, the lesbian and gay activist agenda in the UK does appear to have been assimilated into one which valorises same-sex partnerships and gains greater citizenship rights for some lesbians and gay men, but in doing so marginalises others, including many bisexuals. This is discussed by research contributor Camel, who also highlights the ways in which the stigmatisation of bisexuals by assimilationist lesbian and gay activists becomes bound up with prejudice against certain parts of the bisexual population, in a way that stigmatises the whole bisexual community:

> there are a set of people who want to draw lines between themselves and the rest of us so they can fit into the norm, and it's very convenient for [organisation] and other sets of people who feel represented by [organisation] to draw one of those lines at 'lesbian and gay' and to say that 'bisexual' means poly, S and M and it means all sort of other things, which it doesn't.

The redrawing of citizenship boundaries to include some types of lesbian and gay identities has implications for all bisexuals. Those who are engaged in publicly monogamous relationships will be at least partially included within the citizenship remit. However, others (those in openly poly or non-monogamous relationships, single or asexual bisexuals, and those with fluid or multiple gender/sexual identities and/or relationships) are excluded. Again, the situation may be dynamic, as powerful institutions and organisations change in response to pressure from bisexuals and others who support bisexual rights. However, it is likely that 'good' bisexual citizens (those who are monogamous, or who are private about non-monogamy) may be assimilated, potentially fragmenting the basis for a radical bisexual identity politics.

In the UK, bisexual assimilationist or reformist political moves have been largely absent or invisible, at least until recently with the publication of *The Bisexuality Report* (2012) and subsequent political engagements (see Chapter 7). The UK bisexuality movement, with its grassroots style and non-hierarchical, privatised structures, could be seen as a case study of a non-reformist, non-assimilationist movement, although there are tensions within the community regarding whether to take reformist, or radical, approaches to activism. The historically 'outside' status of the UK bisexual communities may partly explain the lack of prominence that bisexual politics has within the 'LGBT' acronym and the lack of visibility of bisexuality within more mainstream LGBT equality structures and policies. At the same time, outsider status can be seen as a strength because the movement has not been (fully) co-opted into homonormative forms of citizenship.

The concept of 'homonormativity' provides another way of thinking about bisexual citizenship issues. Lisa Duggan (2002), coined the term 'new homonormativity' which 'does not contest dominant heteronormative assumptions and institutions but upholds and sustains them, while promising the possibility of a demobilised gay constituency and a privatised, depoliticised gay culture anchored in domesticity and consumption' (Duggan, 2002, p.50). Homonormativity denotes certain types of citizen (those in stable monogamous relationships, who contribute to the economy and who provide care for each other, thus avoiding being a burden on the welfare state) who are seen as 'good' citizens while others are not (see also Richardson and Monro, 2012). Some aspects of bisexual culture, in particular the privatised nature of it, may reinforce homonormativity. As noted in the chapter on Sex, Relationships, Kinship, and Community, many bisexuals are in primary male-female relationships; they may pass as heterosexual in public, and they provide welfare and reproductive functions in similar ways to heterosexual couples. There seems to be a pattern of private diversities and public normalcy amongst some bisexuals, which can also be seen amongst other erotic communities. For example, UK bisexuality research contributor Grant discussed 'an insularity, not necessarily wanting to change the outside world so long as your personal life is going well' amongst sections of the bisexual and swinger communities. Another, connected, aspect of the privatisation of bisexuality is that some bisexual people (those in heterosexual relationships or who pass as heterosexual) benefit from the citizenship rights afforded to heterosexuals. However, there are also signs that both homonormativity and heteronormativity are resisted within some parts of the bisexual communities, and overlapping communities such as the poly communities, and that different agendas regarding citizenship agendas exist. Some of these different agendas are discussed in a section of the interview with Meg John:

> Meg John: There is definitely a tension, at poly events we have had like a sort of queer group, and the swingers groups coming, and there has been a real tension around sort of the...swingers can be quite heteronormative, and the bicuriosity, as opposed to bisexuality going on. That's not [the case] for everybody, but there can be a...not troubling gender norms, being quite couple-based or whatever.
> Interviewer: How does that actually play out?
> Meg John: I think at polyday [event for poly people] there was a real tension...especially around marriage rights, whether they should be fought for, I don't see that many swingers coming to BiCon.

Clearly, the bisexual and poly communities form a contested territory with regards to homonormativity and other forms of normativity. The next section of the chapter looks in a bit more depth at the challenges that bisexuality poses to homonormativity, and heterosexism, within the context of citizenships. It focuses on queer and anarchist bisexualities in relation to citizenship.

Queer and anarchist bisexualities and citizenship

As we saw in Chapter 2, the term 'queer' has various meanings. Where 'queer' is used to mean 'a politics of difference' that seeks to be more inclusive of sexual and gender diversity, and all sexual and gender minorities, it is closely aligned to the types of identities associated with bisexuality. It might in this case be possible to talk of a 'queer citizenship', alongside other forms of intimate citizenship. This would speak to some of the visions provided by the UK bisexuality research contributors. For example, Meg John said, 'I would like to see sexuality in a utopian way, an opening up of what we see sex as, and certainly beyond gender.' The 'queer as a politics of sexual difference' approach would also support broad-based coalitions for sexual rights, as reflected in some of the UK bisexuality research findings. For example, Nancy noted, 'I think there's some overlap [with bisexual activism] in the more radical queer parts of the lesbian and gay activist movements,' and Grant discussed shared activisms with other communities:

> there are parts that I have come across [of the swingers community], that are the more progressive, or outgoing, or politically connected with a wider umbrella of sexuality groups, and those are pretty friendly towards bisexuality, they feel that there is more in common with bisexuals than there is with say gay community... the feeling 'they are like us, they fit under the sexuality umbrella' more than exclusively gay people do. So I think there is absolutely a kinship... physically, this idea of hedonism and enjoyment.

These phenomena all fall within the remit of intimate citizenship, as well as a 'queer as a politics of sexual difference' type of citizenship, although whether they challenge heteronormativity and mononormativity is open to debate.

There are other definitions of 'queer' that are harder to fit within the remit of citizenship. Where 'queer' concerns an anti-identity politics that displaced the categories of lesbian, gay, and heterosexual (see Richardson, 1996), it becomes more difficult to develop ideas of queer citizenship. This issue is demonstrated in the following quote provided by Rosie:

there are gay people, male and female, out there who see [sighs] being gay is just like being straight really except who you sleep with, and being queer has never been that for me, for me being queer is a lot more than who I choose to go to bed with, to quote the inspirational Peter Tatchell 'I am not looking for equality I'm looking for liberation', not equal to heterosexuals if equality means marriage, children – lovely if people want that, not for me to say they shouldn't, but I don't see gay marriage as some wonderful step forward, it basically just means 'you're towing the line'.

Queer seems, here, to be positioned against not only discrete sexual identities but also against the institutions and structures that are central to mainstream citizenships, such as marriage. Institutions such as marriage, and civil partnership, consolidate frameworks for privatised welfare and reproduction, which sit within assimilationist citizenship frameworks associated with notions of rights and responsibility. This type of queer works, then, against the assimilationist pull of citizenship, and it has much in common with anarchism (see Heckert and Cleminson, 2011). Some of the bisexual research contributors showed insight into the contradictions and tensions between anarchist and queer politics on the one hand and assimilationist politics on the other. For example, contributor Lawrence self-identified as an anarchist, which he defined as 'neither master nor gods'. I asked him the following question: 'Do you think bi activists and allies should be trying to change the mainstream?' and he replied:

Yes. As an anarchist I should say 'no' but I say 'yes', basically, it should be changing, the law and associated law at the local level... [as] individuals we have the capacity to socially organise ourselves without the need for leadership or government or governing forces.

Lawrence explained that, for him, changing law was a short-term goal, and that his ultimate goal was the dissolution of marriage and for people to construct their own marriage contracts. Meg John took a similarly strategic approach, arguing that bisexual politics are somewhat different from queer politics. This does not necessarily mean that bisexual politics are assimilationist, but that they engage with citizenship claims and issues:

I think for example with same-sex marriage the bi activists were arguing it's important to call it same-sex marriage rather than gay marriage... to make it a level playing field for bis. Obviously there are people with a range of politics, mine would be more towards the queer end, I am not convinced of the value of marriage, but I think the overall flavour within a bi activist meeting would be 'we'll support something like gay marriage but let's make sure the bis are included', or 'This is why bisexuals need to be taken into account' rather than 'let's move to a queer utopia where none of the labels are important', we are maybe more seeing it as a stepping stone to that ideal future, but it's so far away we need a stepping stone

What is apparent in these discourses is a strategic politics, which may enable hegemonies to be challenged, depending on how activist interventions play out in particular contexts. In terms of citizenship debates, they reveal that the dichotomy between radical and assimilationist politics is ultimately a false one; both forces may be taking place within bisexual activisms and activists may take different approaches at different times. However, it is also apparent that there are ongoing tensions between radical, queer, and anarchist bisexual activisms, and reformist, citizenship-oriented ones. The next section of the chapter addresses a different dichotomy: universalism versus particularism.

Bisexuality and the universalism/particularism debate

The universalism/particularism debate forms another means by which bisexual citizenship can be examined. In essence, universalist approaches to citizenship include everyone and may seek to treat everyone the same in terms of rights and responsibilities. Particularist approaches, on the other hand, address the rights and responsibilities of different groups, paying attention to their specific characteristics and issues.

The universalism/particularism debate is centrally important to bisexual politics because of the lack of visibility of bisexuality and the way in which bisexuality tends to be subsumed into the larger categories of 'LGBT' or indeed 'queer', which can be seen as a universalist tendency. To focus specifically on bisexuality is a particularist turn; bisexuals are a specific category of person, as opposed to a larger category of LGBT people, which require a more universalist approach. It is worth noting that focusing on LGBT people could also be seen as particularist, because the LGBT population are a specific group, albeit a larger one than bisexuals. A completely universalist approach would consider the sexual citizenship rights of everyone, including LGBT and heterosexual people.

The particularist turn in citizenship studies can take a number of trajectories, focusing on site-specific (for example, national-level) analysis, or analysis concerning identity-based communities such as bisexuals, migrants, or fathers. Particularist approaches are found in the work of, for example, Elsbieta Oleksy *et al.* (2011) who also take a position that, whilst recognising broad trends concerning the gendering of citizenship, focuses on different levels of analysis. They contend that 'Though it is often constructed in a universal way, it is not possible to interpret and indeed understand citizenship without situating it within a specific political, legal, cultural, social, or historical context' (Hearn *et al.*, 2011, p.3).

In this book, I have taken a primarily particularist approach, addressing the individual concerns (see Lister, 2011) of specific set of populations (bisexual and non-LGH) within specific contexts (mostly the UK, Colombia, India, and the USA). This particularist approach is supported in a number of ways by the data provided by the research contributors. In both Colombia and the UK, the research indicated a need for bisexual-specific, or particularist, activist interventions (see Chapter 7). UK contributors said for example:

> There's a tendency for all LGBT sexuality to get subsumed under gay men's sexuality. Highlighting bisexuality can remind people that all the letters in LGBT are unique and have their own difficulties. (Elizabeth)

> another thing that is important to me is to bring more bisexual films to the cinema...the LG [lesbian and gay] film festival do not bring bisexual films...also bisexual books in the libraries, reading is important to me but I find it difficult to find them, so I spend my money online. (Pia)

The research contributors' discussion of a need for bisexual-specific citizenship rights went beyond visibility and representation in the media, and included issues concerning bisexual people's health and well-being, employment rights, relationship options, parenting options, and many other aspects of their lives. Also, there is a need to tackle the specific discriminations that take place against bisexuals, which arguably demands a particularist approach to bisexual citizenship (see Barker *et al.*, 2012). The research contributors described biphobia (see Chapters 1 and 2) and they also discussed bisexual-specific mental and sexual health issues, marriage and civil partnerships, tax allowances, asylum applications, and children. Support for particularism is demonstrated in the following quotes:

> If I have a partner of either biological sex, I might need a triple bed instead of a double bed... if I was dying in a hospice, who would be my next of kin? Both partners might equally be, but legally they can't be... most of us might not think about that because we are not in that situation. (Meg John)

> there needs to be a clear understanding in research... surveys and suchlike, that bisexuals may have different issues to lesbians and gays, that they can't just be missed out, or added in, that needs to be given a separate understanding... I know that mental health issues are stronger in the bi community than the gay community, so if surveys are carried out in which the data from bisexuals is added into the lesbian and gay, then the picture is lost, or it might just change the data. (Kate)

It can therefore be argued that a particularist approach to bisexual citizenship is needed in the UK. This may extend to other countries where there is a human rights framework that supports (or at least tolerates) same-sex relationships. In countries where people engaging in same-sex sexualities are persecuted, there may be a need to seek more universalist fundamental rights for those engaging in same-sex (usually known internationally as 'homosexual') acts first, whether those individuals are sexually involved with someone/people of just one other gender, or more than one gender. What is central here is the *act* not the *identity*; identities such as 'gay' and 'bisexual' with their particularist connotations, may not be useful. This may be especially the case where the 'LGBT' categories and identities are seen as not indigenous and/or where indigenous sexuality/gender formations are different (at least in some social contexts), for example India (see Chapter 3).

Moving on now to look at universalism, it is important to mention the strong arguments for a universalist approach to gender and sexual citizenship generally, for example the political utility of claiming equal allocation of gendered citizenship rights regardless of gender (see Lister, 2011). The framing of LGBT politics that is increasingly dominant in numerous national settings is set within human rights discourse (Kollman and Waites, 2009) and is grounded in the liberal democratic tradition with its universalist rhetoric (Phillips, 2006), as opposed to the kind of particularist stances described above. Drawing on human rights discourses could imply the adoption of a universalistic rather than a differentiated model of sexual citizenship.

The argument for a universalist approach to bisexual citizenship was not very evident amongst the UK bisexuality research interviewees. However, there were two themes within the interviews that did support a universalist approach. The first is support for a broader-based notion of citizenship that includes ideas of self-expression, tolerance, consent, and an ethics of care. This broad-based model of bisexual citizenship includes non-transgressive sexual identities, as well as those identities that are transgressive of social norms concerning sexuality. It is exemplified in the following quote from Reggie:

> I am not sure I would want to be recognised as a bisexual, and maybe this is a cop-out, I do think it's about a more generalised thing re people being tolerant of each other's sexuality and not judgemental, this sounds very pink and fluffy... it would be nice in an ideal world if we could talk and communicate as adults and not be judgemental... and understanding, bearing in mind that person may not understand themselves anyway.

There is another, different reason for supporting some level of universalism, which draws on Kelly Kollman and Matthew Waite's (2009) scholarship concerning broader human rights frameworks. Debates about bisexual identities and citizenship rights – and the overt expression of such rights within quasi-public spaces such as BiCon – are only possible because of the fundamental rights that bisexual people and others enjoy in the UK, including the legal right to engage in same-sex sexualities, to be free of sexuality-related violence and hate crime, and to express opinions and beliefs. These rights are universal, although as indicated above in Chapter 3, not everyone will be able to exercise them.

Overall, therefore, it seems that a combination of universal and differentiated approaches to bisexual citizenship is required. Universal approaches are important for two reasons: [i] where identity-based approaches to citizenship are rejected, either because of a desire for rights based on general principles such as consent, and/or because the categories of 'LGBT' are seen as not useful; [ii] because universal human rights principles and directives underpin bisexual people's rights, as well as other people's rights. However, particularist approaches are also crucial in supporting a marginalised, partially hidden population which has specific needs and issues. The argument for a combination of universalist and particularist approaches to citizenship follows scholars such as Jeff Hearn *et al.* (2011) who contend that the concept of citizenship is broad enough to include both the universal (which they see as being the level at which equality claims are made, which for bisexuals could mean some claims to universal rights such as freedom of expression) and the particular (the level at which claims for the recognition of differences are made, which for bisexuals could mean recognition of bisexual-specific discriminations and issues). As Lister (2011) suggests, a 'differentiated universalism' 'which attempts to capture the idea that the achievement of the universal is contingent upon attention to difference and the particular, as a way of working with the creative tension between the two' (2011, p.30) may be the most useful approach. This is recognised by some of the UK bisexuality research contributors. For example, Lee suggested that:

> although there are some overlapping things between GLB and T, there are some specific to bi and therefore it is just important they have a voice, and feel represented, and feel safe, and have legal recognition as well.

Coming back to discussions about intersectionality, there is a further argument for a differentiated universalism. This comes into play in the accounts of some of the minority ethnic contributors in the UK. For example, Merina discussed the way in which she was marginalised as a bisexual volunteer within an immigration support group, but she was unable to get any support from either the (white-dominated) local bisexual support group, or the (lesbian-dominated) immigration support group. What is apparent here is that bisexual people face different types of intersectional discrimination. In order for these marginalisations to be addressed, particularist approaches to citizenship are required along a number of lines, for example citizenship claims based on ethnicity and race, as well as on sexuality. Arguments for a combination of universalist and particularist approaches to bisexuality and citizenship could be extended to include particularist bisexual disability citizenships, bisexual trans citizenships, and bisexual elder citizenships, for example. A combined approach could also include a plethora of sexuality/gender identities and related citizenship characteristics and claims, perhaps tied into a broader umbrella of gender pluralism or queer. This appears to be supported by some of the interview material, as follows:

> recognition of all identities is important – but going back to the overarching queer label idea, it's very difficult to expect every single

person to understand every single label that exists... I think there are so many different acronyms and all the different queer lifestyles that even for someone within those communities it can be quite difficult when somebody comes up with a new term. (Pierrette)

Overall, it is clear that a particularist approach to bisexual citizenship is especially important in countries such as the UK, which already have fundamental human rights frameworks addressing same-sex sexualities. Particularist citizenship enables biphobia to be tackled, and the specific interests of bisexual people to be addressed. In countries where rights are lacking, a more universalist approach which supports the fundamental rights of all people, including bisexuals, to engage in intimate relationships, is crucial. Overall, both universalist and particularist approaches are important for bisexuals, pertaining as they do to different levels of rights claims, set within specific contexts.

This chapter has explored different strands of citizenship theory, applying them to bisexuality. It is based on the UK situation, enabling some depth of analysis to be developed, located within a specific national context, whilst maintaining some awareness of international dynamics regarding citizenship. The chapter uses conceptual tools from feminist, sexual citizenship and intimate citizenship theorists. It addresses transgender, queer, and anarchism in relation to citizenship debates. The chapter shows the ways in which bisexuality is marginalised within existing bodies of citizenship literature, and it begins to develop a bisexual critique of existing approaches to citizenship studies and to explore bisexual-centric issues within a citizenship framework. The chapter looks, in particular, at a number of related themes: the public/private divide; assimilation/radicalism debates; and universalism/particularism debates.

Summary

- There is some scholarship concerning bisexual citizenship to date, but this is limited.
- Citizenship is relevant to bisexuals because it addresses rights and responsibilities, within a range of different spheres (such as civil and legal, social, political, and intimate). The rights associated with citizenship in countries such as the UK make it possible for bisexual (and other non-heterosexual) people to have consensual adult private sex, and talk about bisexual sexualities and desires, whilst having some protection against persecution and hate crime.

- Traditional approaches to citizenship, whilst useful, have consolidated stereotypical models of gender and sexuality; they contain assumptions that it is mostly men who inhabit the public sphere, that the private sphere is not part of the citizenship remit, and that relationships are heterosexual. Bisexuality troubles such assumptions.
- Feminist and sexual/intimate citizenship theorists have provided an important set of tools for questioning traditional approaches to citizenship.
- From a bisexual citizenship perspective, other critiques can be added to those of feminist and lesbian and gay-focused sexual citizenship theorists, such as critiques of mononormative models of sexual citizenship and those which reify rigid, mono-directional sexual identities (such as heterosexual and gay).
- Trans theory, especially approaches that reject gender binaries and those that envisage spectrum models of gender, are useful in developing ideas of bisexual citizenship.
- Some of the UK bisexuality research contributors have queer or anarchist perspectives, and some take strategic political approaches; these dynamics can be used to inform discussions about citizenship.
- Both universal and particularist approaches to bisexual citizenship are useful, but in different ways. Universal approaches can be used to support claims for fundamental human rights, whereas particularist approaches are needed to tackle bisexual erasure, invisibility, and biphobia.

In the final chapter I use another set of approaches, drawn from political science, in looking at bisexual activism and democracy in Colombia and the UK.

7
Bisexuality, Activism, Democracy, and the State

How is it possible to make the world into a better place for bisexuals, and other people who do not identify as heterosexual, lesbian, or gay? How do activists engage with social institutions and structures in order to gain equality, visibility, and the right to self-expression? What social movements have developed to support bisexual people's rights? This chapter addresses these questions, framing them broadly within political science.

It is difficult to talk about a bisexual political science due to the absence of bisexual-specific literature. Mainstream and feminist political scientists have largely overlooked LGBT issues (see, for example, Sulkunen *et al.*, 2009). There is a fairly substantial body of political science literature about LGBT issues in the USA and Canada (for example, Bristow and Wilson, 1993; Blasius, 2001; Werum and Winders, 2001; Currah *et al.*, 2006; Smith, 2008), whilst a range of contributions stem from Latin America (Fajardo, 2006; Sanabria, 2006; Viveros, 2006; Corrales and Pecheney, 2010) and elsewhere (see Chapter 1). Whilst important, the scholarship to date has tended to address either LGBT people taken together as a group, or lesbians and gay men. In both cases, bisexuals, with their specific identities and concerns, can be erased. For example, Miriam Smith's (2008) book on lesbian and gay rights and political institutions includes sections on same-sex marriage, but there is no acknowledgement that same-sex marriage may take place between bisexual people or one bisexual person and one gay man or lesbian.

Some signs can be seen of an emergent bisexual political science. There are a few specifically bi-focused contributions. In Colombia, for example, the first specific study was Oscar Garcia's (2006) *Bisexualidad: De la Tercería a la Ruptura de Dicotomías* (Bisexuality: From third positions to ruptured dichotomies) which was followed by the work of other authors (Salazar and Galvis, 2008, 2009; Salazar, 2009, 2009a). Other relevant Colombian authors include José Fernando Serrano (2003, 2010). An emergent bisexual political science can also be identified when bisexuality-specific work is included in broader contributions. In some political science texts, distinctions are made between the different groups included within LGB or LGBT acronyms, which supports the development of a bisexual political science. For example:

> Gays and lesbians (and, in recent times, many would add bisexuals and transgendered persons) have transitioned from outsiders to insiders in the political process, from the liberationists of the sixties and seventies to the lobbyists of the nineties.
> (Riggle and Tadlock, 1999, p.2)

In others texts, practice is varied. For example, in Manon Tremblay *et al.*'s (2011) collection, the majority of the contributions barely acknowledge bisexuality or ignore it completely. However, Kelly Kollman and Matthew Waites' UK-based chapter includes bisexuals as part of an LGB acronym (see also Waites, 2009, 2009a). The authors note the issue of erasure of bisexuality and alternative sexualities within political science, and they briefly discuss bisexual challenges to identities politics based on discrete heterosexual and gay/lesbian identities. For Kollman and Waites, the BiCon bisexual conference (see earlier chapters) is interpreted as part of a set of developments that may escape from identity politics based on the homo-hetero dichotomy, towards a more pluralistic approach to sexual diversity. They suggest that:

> There is now an opportunity for the 'lesbian and gay movement' – perhaps to be articulated by new groupings in relation to an implicitly 'queer' agenda for sexual diversity – to be owned and led by anyone who wishes to challenge the privileging of heterosexuality.
> (2011, p.192)

There is also inclusion of some discussion of bisexual politics within interdisciplinary LGBT studies. For instance, Monro (2005) and Monro and Richardson (2012) address the emergence of bisexual movements alongside (and as part of) the lesbian, gay, and transgender movements, and the reasons for bisexual erasure and marginalisation by non-bisexual activists.

To summarise then, mainstream and feminist political science has tended of overlook LGBT issues. However, a body of literature has developed internationally which analyses issues such as the development of lesbian and gay movements as new social movements. Bisexuality is often rendered invisible in this literature but there are some signs of an emergent political science of bisexuality.

This chapter, then, aims to make a contribution to the field of bisexual political science. It takes a broadly comparative approach, tracing the development of bisexual activism in two democratic states; firstly Colombia, and secondly the UK. Each state is taken as the unit of analysis from which comparisons can be made. However, it should be noted that there are substantial differences across Colombia and the UK (see, for example, Serrano, 2010; Monro and Richardson, 2014). In addition, the context in which bisexual activism takes place is increasingly shaped by the activities of global infrastructure organisations such as the World Trade Organisation (WTO), as well as (to a lesser degree) transnational interest groups attempting to implement social standards, such as the International Lesbian and Gay Association (ILGA) (see Elliott, 2005). Globalisation favours the wealthier nation-states and powerful economic interests, at the expense of the poor (Sandbrook *et al.*, 2007). Therefore, whilst an explicitly materialist analysis will not be provided in this chapter, it should be assumed that bisexual activism will be striated by material factors, such as the resources available to individual activists, and the availability of funding to support activist engagement with the state. Other structuring factors also shape bisexual people's lives and activist trajectories; specifically in the context of this chapter, these include the armed conflict in Colombia (see Zea *et al.*, 2013).

The chapter takes a primarily empirical (rather than theoretical) approach, focusing on the development of activism and social movements, and the participative democratic processes by which activists interface with state institutions. The term 'participative democracy' concerns the ways in which members of a population can engage with, and potentially influence, institutions associated with the state via processes such as lobbying and consultation. The idea of the 'state' is used here to mean the nexus of institutions, processes, and actors that together make up the structures that govern, support, and regulate human affairs in particular geographical areas. As Julian Lee points out, states are not monolithic and 'the impact on sexuality of any given State often varies greatly according to which arm of the State is being considered' (2011, p.3). There are a large number of ways in which political analysis of bisexuality could be further developed, several of which are outside of the scope of this text. Future bisexual political analysis could address, for example, the following topics: electoral democracy (the representation of the population by elected politicians); the branches of the state associated with the executive (the part of government with responsibility for implementing state powers); legislature (for example, Congress or Parliament, where legislation is debated) and the judiciary (the courts and related institutions, where legislation is tested and enforced).

As noted above, this chapter will address activism, participative democracy, and the state in two contrasting localities: Colombia and the UK. The next section of the chapter will focus on Colombia, providing a snapshot of the context for bisexual activism, an outline of the ways it has developed, and some analysis of key themes. The section draws on both the fieldwork and analysis provided by the Colombian researcher, Camilo Tamayo Gómez.

Colombia

Colombia was colonised by the Spanish in the 16th century and has a legacy of colonial relations which places the Afro-Colombian and native peoples in a socially marginal position. Scholars such as R. Ardila (1998) and C. Prieto (2011) argue that bisexuality is widespread in Colombia, particularly in regions such as the Caribbean lowlands and the principal urban cities. This is because some Afro-Descendent population that live along the Caribbean Coast of Colombia and in the cities recognize bisexuality as part of their sexual identity roots, which are linked to ancestral sexuality practices.

There are powerful structures and forces supporting LGBT people's rights in Colombia. The 1991 Colombian Constitution has promoted a range of legal measures to protect LGBT people in sectors such as education (Republic of Colombia, 1991; Serrano, 2009). According to Serrano (2009), the Constitutional Court (judicial strand) has been most important in supporting LGBT rights overall in Colombia. In addition, the Roman Catholic Church has a key role in dealing with generic human rights abuses. Since 1991, the Catholic Church has also actively supported many LGBT organisations and individuals (see Serrano, 2009).

At the same time as the trends towards support for the human rights of LGBT people, including bisexuals, there are many challenges. Violence levels are high in Colombia generally, reflecting the socio-political conflict and related humanitarian difficulties (Serrano, 2010). Serrano asserts that:

> LGBT people have been the victims of homicides, and extrajudicial killings that have not been properly investigated. Arbitrary

detentions, cruel degradations, and inhuman treatments committed by police members against LGBT persons have been denounced.
(2010, p.90)

Serrano (2010) describes how human rights activists have documented murder squads targeting LGBT people, especially *travestis* (trans people). Displacement due to socio-political conflict is also a major issue for LGBT people in Colombia; it can place bisexual people at risk of sexual violence as well as HIV/AIDS (Zea *et al.*, 2013).

It is against this backdrop of democracy, human rights frameworks, conflict, and marked difficulties that the bisexual movement has begun to emerge in Colombia. The next sections of this chapter document the ways in which bisexual activism has developed, from its roots within a generic LGBT movement towards a more bisexual-specific set of interventions.

Early stages of bisexual activism in Colombia

The development of organisations based around sexual orientation or gender identity in Colombia can be traced back to the 1970s, in the context of feminism, emergent social movements, processes of democratisation, and academics' discussions around sex and politics influenced by European authors (Ardila, 1998; Fajardo, 2006). By the 1980s, diverse lesbian, gay, and mixed organisations existed in many Colombian cities (Fajardo, 2006). The end of the 1980s and the beginning of the 1990s heralded the development of new LGBT organisations of lesbian, gay, and mixed groups organised around issues such as support and identity affirmation, religion, cultural activities, academic discussions, and rights advocacy (Fajardo, 2006).

Colombian bisexual activism 2000+

The development of a more specifically bisexual politics in Colombia initially took place as part of the LGBT Colombian movement that started around 2000. This was a time when different LGBT organisations and activists articulated their support for actions to link LGBT rights with peace building activities in order to claim recognition and respect for different sexual orientations in the middle of the Colombian armed conflict. With the support of the Non-governmental organisation (NGO) *Planeta Paz*, different organisations, collectives, activists, and supporters of sexual rights started to use the acronym 'LGBT' as a strategy to connect 'the grievances of organizations with the international lobby around gender identity and sexual orientation rights and to create a collective identity to articulate particular initiatives' (Serrano, 2010, p.96).

The initiative *The body, first territory of peace* (Planeta Paz, 2002) was the first collective action of LGBT groups in the Colombian locale to claim respect for the human rights of the LGBT community and stop the violence against them. It was in this context that bisexuality began to gain visibility, as an aspect of LGBT activism.

Some scholars (see Garcia, 2006) argue that at the beginning of 2000 it is not possible to suggest that there was a bisexual movement in Colombia, but that there were different groups and sexual rights activists trying to support this sexual orientation in the public sphere. Lesbian groups such as *Triangulo Negro* (Black Triangle) in 1996, or *Mujeres al Borde* (Women on the Border) in 2000, developed some collective processes in order to make bisexual people's needs and demands visible inside the LGT community. Some scholars (for instance Sanabria, 2006) contend that the inclusion of the B in the acronym LGBT at the beginning of 2000 was really important. They argue that it was because of this inclusion within the 'LGBT' umbrella that the bisexual community started to be publically visible in Colombia. It is suggested that the integration of the bisexual community at the beginning of the LGBT movement in Colombia opened the door to this group being involved in a powerful social movement, and bisexuality not being treated in a ghettoising way (Viveros, 2006).

It is important to make two assertions about the period of activism that took place around 2000. Firstly, it is possible to argue that some bisexual organisations, academics and bisexual activists have contested the use of the acronym 'LGBT' in the Colombian context (see Salazar, 2009; Serrano, 2010). This is because of its supposed unity and its blurring of inner differences inside this social movement. Secondly, the bisexual community may be employed as a 'commodity' for the lesbian, gay, and transgender movement to use in order to be engaged with international discourses, economic resources and projects about gender, identity and sexual rights around the world, at the same time as being internally discriminated against, within LGBT organisations. The stigmatisation of bisexuality by lesbians and gay men was described by several Colombian contributors to the research (see Chapter 1). These dynamics mean that whilst Colombian bisexual activism has its roots in the LGT movement, there are at the same time some tensions and divergences between bisexual, and lesbian and gay, activists.

Developments from 2006 onwards

Before the creation of bisexual-specific groups, some bisexuals organised in a group inside the LGBT movement called *Bisexuales Unidos* (Bisexuals

United), but without political representation or 'voice' inside the LGBT rights activism.

The phrase 'Bisexuality as a political identity' (Salazar and Galvis, 2008, 2009; Salazar, 2009) began to gain visibility in 2006. At this time, the category of 'bisexuality' was used by some bisexual communities outside the LGBT movement in Colombia in 2006 in order to distance themselves from the LGBT movement as a whole. This was done so as to claim recognition, dignity, respect, and protection for this specific sexual orientation, and to claim visibility in the public sphere of the country. Some of the issues that Colombian bisexual people face are reflected in the narratives of the research contributors, for instance:

> For me, if you want to have a bisexual identity, you have to overcome three closets...gays and lesbians say all the time that you have to 'come out of the closet' and be proud of your sexual identity, but for bisexuals, we have to do a step more... the first closet is with yourself, recognize you as a bisexual; the second closet is with the Gay, Lesbian and Transgender community, because sometimes they can't accept you as a bisexual and it's really difficult to try to construct your bisexual identity when non-heterosexual people, 'your friends' judge you all the time; and finally, with the society in general. (Liliam)

During the 2006 period to the present, a number of specifically bisexual groups and organisations were formed in Colombia, for example the organisation *Sentido Bisexual* (Bisexual Sense) in Bogotá. Bisexual Sense focused on political actions to fight against the discrimination experienced by bisexual people in Colombia, and against the public/private representation of bisexual people as not being a 'right' sexual orientation. As Liliam Salazar states:

> talking about a bisexual movement some years ago is a fallacy. We have been included in the acronym LGBT but the work in favour of the bisexual community did not exist, and talk of a bisexual community was not allowed. In 2007, with the creation of *Bisexual Sense*, the first group of Bisexual people in the country, we could start to talk about of a kind of 'institutionalization' of the bisexual community.
> (Salazar, 2009, p.1)

Bisexual Sense has worked with different city councils in the country in order to create specific public policies in favour of this community (see below). During this period, there were also the first bisexual-specific public demonstrations. For example, academic Liliam Salazar, who contributed also to the research, said in her interview that: 'The year of 2007 is the first year that for first time the bisexual community as a group developed a public demonstration in order to be visible inside the Bogotá LGBT pride parade'. Since 2007, these two groups (*Sentido Bisexual* and *Dimensión Bi*) and other bisexual communities across the country (*Colectivo Bi al Ataque, Sentimos Diverso*) started to use the bisexual pride flag as a symbol of unity and attempting with these actions to acknowledge diversity within the LGBT movement as a whole.

In 2008, another bisexual organisation was born, called *Dimensión Bi* (Bi Dimension), which focused on developing academic reflections about bisexuality, given a lack of research. In order to consolidate the beginning of this 'Independent Movement of Bisexual People in Colombia' (Salazar, 2009; Salazar and Galvis, 2009), in 2008 *Sentido Bisexual* and *Dimensión Bi*, with the economic support of the National University of Colombia and The Institute for Participation and Community Action (IDPAC) of the Bogotá City Council, organised the First District Conference about Bisexuality in Bogotá. The conference was held in order to discuss bisexual issues, to encourage studies about bisexuality in Colombia, and to develop a state-of-the-art bisexual movement in Colombia.

Alongside the collaborations between academics and activists that were taking place, some groups of bisexuals started to transmit a weekly radio show in 2008 which was called *Doble Vía* (Two ways) on one of the most important LGBT radio stations of Colombia: Radio Diversia (Diverse Radio – http://www.radiodiversia.com). This show provided quality information about bisexual issues, and fought against wrong stereotypes inside the LGT community such as 'bisexuality is not an identity', 'bisexuality is just a transitory period of time', and 'bisexuals want everything because they do not want to have to pick'. The show provided a sense of social cohesion inside the Colombian bisexual community (Salazar and Galvis, 2009). The targets of this radio programme were the Colombian gay, lesbian, and transgender communities, and the presenters used different strategies such as open radio workshops, plural radio debates, and LGBT magazines in order to create a 'space of tolerance' between the LGT community and the bisexual community.

The developments concerning bisexual activism in Colombia have taken place in the context of considerable state support in some localities for interventions to support the fundamental rights of LGBT people. The interviews with Colombian bisexual people showed that between 2004 and 2012 the Bogotá City Council invested around four million dollars to support activities related to LGBT rights in the city; this was seen as a result of LGBT activism and political lobbying in recent years. The creation of an LGBT Community Centre in one of the most popular LGBT neighbourhoods in Bogotá (Chapinero neighbourhood), the organisation of the LGBT Citizenship Parade every year to celebrate sexual diversity in the city, and the developing of programmes and activities to protect and promote LGBT rights in public schools of the Capital City of Colombia provide examples of political action where the bisexual community were involved. In 2011, The Planning Department of Bogotá's City Council developed the campaign 'In Bogotá you can be... (Gay, Lesbian, Bisexual or Transgender)' in order to promote LGBT rights and respect for different sexual orientations in the city. This included a state-sponsored bisexual awareness campaign using posters. Overall, therefore, in at least some parts of the country, a considerable amount and range of activism concerning bisexuality has taken place.

Analysis – Colombia

The researcher for the Colombian bisexuality project, Camilo Tamayo Gómez, suggests that, overall, there is an interconnection between the emergence of the category of 'bisexuality' in Colombia and the beginnings of a bisexual movement in the country in recent years. Both of these support the recognition of a 'bisexual identity' in the public sphere. He identified several themes to emerge from the interviews and literature.

Firstly, the incipient bisexual movement in Colombia has gained recognition in the three largest Colombian cities (Bogotá, Medellin, and Cali) and some intermediate cities such as Barranquilla or Santa Marta, but it is principally an urban middle and upper-class movement (see Chapter 3). The relationship between this movement and the high levels of bisexuality reported throughout the country is unclear. There is also uncertainty amongst some research contributors about whether a specifically bisexual movement existed at the time of the fieldwork (in 2012):

> I think you cannot say that in Colombia there exists a 'bisexual movement' at the moment... you definitely can find bisexual leaders in some Colombian cities and maybe in the future it could be possible to start a movement... for example, it is a fact that when different organizations want to do some research about bisexual people, or create some statistics about our community, finding bisexual people to interview is really really difficult. (Liliam)

This shows that whilst there are some bisexual-specific activist trends, and organisations, the movement may not itself be permanently established.

The second theme is that bisexual groups have focused on direct political actions in some cities such as Bogotá and Medellin in order to be recognised and included in social policies. Their work with some LGBT Community Centres to develop plans of public policies; their political articulation with some city councils to coordinate public efforts to protect and promote bisexual rights; and the use of the slogan 'Bisexuality as a political identity' in different activist documents, exemplify these political actions.

Thirdly, it is possible to establish that the tense relationship with the LGT movement in Colombia in recent years had provided a sense of cohesion inside different bisexual groups, helping the creation of a strong sense of community in order to make a claim for recognition and respect for this sexual orientation in the public sphere. This is not unproblematic; one transgender Colombian interviewee reported that:

> Some bisexual activists have been using their sexual orientation as an excuse to obtain political power inside the LGBT movement and a lack of honesty about their real personal intentions have damaged our bisexual movement... they just sometimes said, 'hey! I am bisexual; we have to fight for our rights!' But, at the end of the day, it is just for political convenience and money. (Lorena)

It is impossible to verify the claim made in this quote. However, attempts to gain the resources associated with increasingly institutionalised rights claims may be common across the NGO sector.

Fourthly, the urgent need for a new set of public policies that respond to the needs and demands of bisexual people in the country emerged as a consequence of bisexual activism, providing an example of how this group is emerging as an active social and political actor in some Colombian urban areas.

Finally, the category of power has been crucial during developments in bisexual activism since 2006. This is because one of the main purposes of bisexual groups in Colombia is to empower bisexuals to exercise and demand rights in two ways: inside the LGBT movement in order to obtain recognition as an independent group (and not just to be a passive 'B' in this acronym) and outside the LGBT movement as an individual political and social actor concerned with the protection of the rights of bisexual people that live in particular situations of vulnerability, exclusion, or discrimination.

This section of the chapter has outlined the emergence and development of the bisexual activist movement in Colombia, from its inception as part of the LGBT movement around 2000, to the formation of an explicitly bisexual politics since 2006. It demonstrates the ways in which Colombian bisexual activists have acted strategically to engage with the media and the state, raising the visibility of bisexuality within frameworks and structures associated with participatory democracy. It also highlights some of the ambivalences found in this area of activism, around alliances and tensions with broader LGT movements, and the difficulties of having a bisexual-specific movement. The next section of the chapter addresses the UK situation in relation to bisexual activism. It starts with a brief contextualisation for bisexual activism, before outlining the development of the bisexual activist movement. The chapter section then draws out a number of key themes from the interviews with bisexual activists in the UK.

The UK

The UK comprises four different countries (England, Northern Ireland, Scotland, and Wales) and devolution of powers to Scotland, Wales, and Northern Ireland means that in each region, the situation for bisexuals is slightly different. Unlike Colombia, which is largely Catholic, the UK is secular and diverse in terms of faith, and where organised religions are involved in matters of sexual identity, their influence largely works against the rights of non-heterosexuals (see Richardson and Monro, 2012).

There is now 'an extensive set of legal mechanisms to promote the formal equality of lesbians, gay men and bisexuals' in the UK (Kollman and Waites, 2011, p.181; see also Monro and Richardson, 2014). This has been driven by wider cultural changes, LGB activism (see Kollman and Waites, 2011) and European directives. The legislative changes culminated in the Equality Act 2010, which replaced existing equalities legislation. This act includes people attracted to both the same and other sex, and it outlaws discrimination in the provision of goods, services, and facilities. The UK Equality Act (2010) sits within a much broader framework of EU legislation and frameworks. For example, the fundamental principle of equal treatment is expressed by Article 3 of the Treaty on European Union (TEU), brought together in the Preamble of the Charter of Fundamental Rights of the European Union (EU Charter), which provides for the protection of individual fundamental rights under EU law. The Preamble specifies that 'the Union is founded on the indivisible, universal values of human dignity, freedom, equality and solidarity'. Article 21 of the EU Charter prohibits 'any discrimination based on any ground such as sex [...] and sexual orientation'.

The lived experiences of UK bisexuals have been addressed throughout the book; as noted in Chapter 1, there are instances of hate crime, as well as active biphobia. The above equalities legislation provides a framework for tackling discrimination. Some of the UK bisexuality research contributors discussed this; for example, Elizabeth, when asked whether she thought that equalities legislation was making any difference to bisexual people 'in the real world' said:

> Yes, it definitely is! Without appropriate and effective equalities legislation, my workplace likely wouldn't care about LGBT equality at all. There's the whole 'business case' that Stonewall puts forward, but that wouldn't be listened to if some elements weren't being imposed at a legal level. (Elizabeth)

However, the majority of research contributors were either unaware of legislative frameworks, or were critical of their scope. For example, Lee commented on the way in which the term 'sexual orientation' in the Equality Act is interpreted as 'gay'; Pablo saw legislation generally as being largely ineffectual, and only useful as a recourse when bisexual people have suffered direct discrimination, whilst Andy noted the importance of legislation supporting same-sex marriage but that this legislation excludes non-monogamous bisexual people. Whilst these critiques concerned the remit and implementation of the legislation, other contributors, notably Grant, saw legislative frameworks themselves as problematic in relation to bisexuality; he preferred the voluntary adoption of values such as consent.

The above discussion provides a snapshot of the legal situation for bisexuals in the UK. It may be the case that the relatively benign legal landscape lends itself to a politically liberal and/or queer bisexual population. What is meant here is that in the UK, it appears that bisexual people (and others) may underestimate the importance of legal and state infrastructures that support human rights concerning homosexuality and bisexuality. At the same time, it is clear that there are limitations in the scope of the UK law in relation to bisexuality. The next section of the chapter outlines the development of bisexual activism in the UK.

Early stages of bisexual activism

Bisexual people were amongst the early campaigners for the decriminalisation and depathologisation of homosexuality in the UK. For example,

Keith Wigmore was part of a group in Cambridge that published the pioneering book *Towards a Quaker View of Sex* (1957) which included the statement 'An act which expresses true affection between two individuals and gives pleasure to them both, does not seem to us to be sinful by reason alone of the fact that it is homosexual' (Walker, 2014). By the 1960s and 1970s, the political agenda of the UK 'gay' liberation movement (which actually included bisexual and gender-diverse people) was to rid society of negative ideas about homosexuality, in particular that it was abnormal and unnatural (Weeks, 2008). This early movement fragmented to a degree soon after it was formed, so that by the early 1970s a shift towards autonomous lesbian organising took place (D'Emilio and Freedman, 1988). Both trans and bi people were increasingly excluded by lesbian feminist and gay movements, which had consequences for political organising (Ault, 1994). There were some later collaborations between gay men, lesbians, and bisexuals in the area of AIDS activism (Epstein, 1999). The bisexual and trans movements took different (although sometimes overlapping) trajectories, with the bi community developing as a grassroots-based community with an emphasis on lifestyle politics and political visibility (Hemmings, 2002).

Bisexual activism: 1985+

The first national bisexual conference in the UK, called BiCon, took place in 1985, and it was titled *The Politics of Bisexuality*; this conference heralded the start of the organised bisexual community in the UK. BiCons have subsequently been held annually http://bicon.org.uk/. In 2003, an online bisexual activist network was founded and workshops are held once or twice a year to support activism around bisexuality http://bicon.org.uk/. The magazine Bi Community News was first published in 2007 http://bicommunitynews.co.uk/resources/ providing reporting, networking, and resources. There are local groups and gatherings (BiFests) in several UK cities which also support some level of activism. Another organisation, Bisexual Index, provides further online resources http://www.bisexualindex.org.uk/.

Participant observation in the organised bisexual communities showed that there has been a step-change in UK bisexual politics in recent years, which may be linked with two new developments. The first BiReCon (Bisexual Research Convention) was organised in 2008; its aim was to 'bring together researchers and academics with activists, organisations and community members to develop, disseminate and discuss research and theory about bisexuality' (Barker *et al.*,

2011, p.157). BiReCon was followed by the formation of BiUK (http://www.biuk.org/) which actively engages with government and statutory sector bodies on a range of bisexuality-related issues. BiUK published *The Bisexuality Report: Bisexual Inclusion in LGBT Equality and Diversity* (Barker *et al.*) in 2012. This has been influential, reportedly being downloaded more than 70,000 times (personal communication with Meg John Barker, January 2015). At the same time, there has been more international networking than previously, including with European partners via the EuroBiNet online network https://groups.yahoo.com/neo/groups/EURO-BINET/info. More groups are also emerging around specific bisexual identities, for example the Bis of Colour group and an over 50s bisexuals network in London (as discussed in BiCon, 2014).

Historically, as noted above, there have been divergences between the bisexual communities and the lesbian and gay communities. The UK bisexuality research revealed that biphobia amongst lesbians and gay men is a major issue for bisexual people (see Chapter 1). There was also discussion of conflicts in aims, agendas, and activist style between established organisations that claim to represent gay, lesbian, and bisexual people but have historically overlooked bi people. For example, Lee reported that 'there are the LGBT organisations that say they are LGB but don't actually do anything for bi people'.

The commonalities between the lesbian and gay, and the bisexual communities run parallel to the divergences. Some UK contributors noted overlap with the lesbian and gay communities in terms of rights claims, and in some cases social and political alliances. One contributor (Lena) thought that 'Acceptance from the gay community has got to be the first thing, because they are our brothers and sisters; that has to be the first thing, because if we can't count on them we are lost'. Discussion of a need for collaboration was quite common. Some contributors reported bisexual people actively supporting gay and lesbian rights interventions. Some predominantly (to date) lesbian and gay organisations include bisexuals routinely in their work to an extent. For example, the Stonewall guide on the procurement of services from contractors provides mechanisms for including bisexual service users alongside lesbians and gay men (Ward, 2011). Participant observation in the bisexual communities in 2014 indicates that the influential LGB organisation Stonewall has become more actively engaged in supporting bisexual people's rights and equality and in challenging biphobia, for example including a bisexual role model in its national workplace conference, and producing publicity that tackles biphobia as well as homophobia.

It appears that this move is partly a result of activist pressure from the bisexual communities.

UK bisexual agendas and issues

There are a range of bisexual activist agendas in the UK. These include some that are relevant to both bisexuals and lesbians and gay men, such as same-sex partnership rights, and some that are specific to bisexuals, such as tackling biphobia. Bisexual activists tend to have a broad remit, for example research contributor Elizabeth said: 'I really think that the most important thing is to instil respect and acceptance of all sexualities and gender identities.' It is important to point out that not all of the contributors to the research supported bisexual activism; notably Lee failed to identify much need for it, seeing trans activism as more important, whilst Christian was critical of the focus on visibility and recognition that is so prominent in UK bisexual activism, and he preferred to support broader human rights campaigns (for example concerning reproductive rights).

The strongest theme coming out of the research with bisexual people in the UK is the lack of visibility about bisexuality, and the effects that this has on bisexual people. Almost all of the bisexual contributors mentioned the invisibility of bisexual people, as compared to lesbians, gay men, and heterosexuals. Some contributors also reported a need to challenge the stereotypes and stigmatisation facing bisexuals (see Chapter 2). For example, Kay thought that the main issue for bisexual activism is the amount of prejudice and misunderstandings that bisexual people face from both heterosexuals and gays and lesbians, such as being seen as 'greedy or loose'.

Alongside the direct prejudice faced by bisexual people, a few contributors mentioned awareness of a lack of knowledge about bisexual-specific issues. For example, Kate remarked that:

> the key thing is just getting people to understand what bisexuality is, and to understand what biphobia is, stuff like the thing in the [lesbian] magazine, the ignorance of people not even realising [that they are being biphobic], and saying something that is *wrong*, and whilst the people writing those things might not realise, the magazine should know they shouldn't be saying it.

Recognition of the specific issues faced by bisexual people has led some research contributors to consider the specific areas in which activism is needed.

Several of the research contributors discussed the issues faced by bisexuals in specific sectors, including housing, employment, education, healthcare, and asylum rights. This is demonstrated in the following two quotes:

> When I first talked to my GP and said I would like to have an HIV test they asked if I was gay, and I had to tell them I was bi, it didn't occur, so I think again it's just visibility and awareness, and not having to think twice that someone might be bi, having it there in your head. (Andy)

> there is a *huge, huge problem* in the asylum process for bisexuals, well for everybody it is a nightmare but for bisexuals, it is even, a legal invisibility... when you have the first interview... you [as a bisexual] are asked 'oh you are gay, how can you prove you are gay?' (Merina)

A few contributors raised the issue of whether bisexual people require special provision or not. For example, Pablo said that he could not see any areas of service provision where a bisexual person might need or desire a different type or level of provision, in comparison to a gay person. This assertion contradicts the arguments of the *Bisexuality Report* which emphasises bi-specific interventions (see Chapter 6). The levels of social erasure that bisexual people face, from both policy makers/practitioners and from the general population, can be seen to indicate a need for bi-specific interventions, as well as those that deal with discrimination against all people engaged in same-sex sexualities/desires. The requirement to not treat bisexual people differently to other people does in fact require some specific interventions, as demonstrated in the following quote:

> it [bisexuality] ought to be as part of the national [school] curriculum personal and social education – all alternative lifestyles should be included in that – not any more special treatment than anyone else, it should just be explained to people that these things exist, they are normal – in the same way that it is enshrined in education that you must learn about different religions, belief systems. (Pierrette)

A small number of the contributors took a more international slant to activism, and/or an approach that showed awareness of other equalities issues, beyond those relating to sexualities and gender diversity. Meg John suggested that intersectionality is crucial for bisexual activism and that there is a need to engage with, and learn more from, international bi communities. She noted a difference between local (UK) agendas such as bisexual representation in the media, and global agendas, and she discussed conflicts between people on international bisexual internet networks 'because the agendas are different in different countries'. Lawrence discussed his own engagement in international bisexual activist networks over many years. Nancy suggested:

> I think bi activists in liberal democracies like the UK have a responsibility to support and encourage research and literature on sexuality and to make resources available internationally where possible and exert as much influence as we can for change elsewhere.

Nancy's suggestion can be seen as problematic, given the colonial history of the UK, the difficulties with LGBT rights being framed as a 'Western import' in a wide range of Southern countries, and the fallibility of Western-originated sexual identity categories such as 'bisexuality' (see Chapter 1 and Richardson and Monro, 2012). At the same time, it appears that academic materials originating in the West may sometimes be useful to activists in Southern contexts, as mentioned in the section on Colombia, above. Of course, Southern experiences may also be useful to Western activists. For instance, understanding the importance of close liaison with LGT activists as a means of furthering bisexual activist agendas in Colombia could be important for a UK bisexual movement which has historically been alienated from – and marginalised by – the mainstream lesbian and gay movement.

This sub-section of the chapter has described UK bisexual agendas in relation to issues such as visibility, challenging prejudice and raising awareness, interventions targeted towards bisexuals, and international dimensions. The next part of the chapter analyses UK bisexual activist strategies. It focuses on individual bisexual people's views and experiences, reflecting the very wide range of activist identities and strategies found amongst the research contributors.

UK bisexual activist strategies

Overall, over the years, bisexual activism in the UK has taken place via a number of interconnected groups and organisations (see above). Participant observation shows that the bisexual activists associated with these organisations are fairly small in number, and often work across the different groups, almost always in a voluntary capacity. Of course, bisexual people outside of these networks may also engage in activism, but this is less easy to observe and document. As shown in Chapter 1, the UK bisexuality research sample included individuals who were involved in the organised bisexual networks and those who were not, but most of the material on activism comes from the former group.

The research contributors discussed a range of political activities and strategies. Only a very few contributors discussed the types of activism that might traditionally be seen as pertaining to the political sphere. For example:

> For me personally looking at bisexuality as sexual orientation and therefore pushing for change in terms of legislation which is based on sexual orientation... As a political tool based on identity politics it is very *strong*, because you can put that argument across for things like asylum, partnership rights. (Lawrence)

Most of the activist endeavours that contributors described were more wide-ranging. For example, Nancy listed the following:

- Community events of different sorts and with different aims, for example some family-friendly, some less so, some aimed at newcomers, some supporting existing community
- Academic work: research and publications and conferences
- Participation in events in the wider world: health events, Prides, and so on; and media appearances
- TV, radio, magazines, and blogging.

In terms of actual engagement in activism, it was noticeable that the research contributors quite often took strategic approaches. This could be in their personal lives, for example Andy challenged homophobia and biphobia in online discussion groups. Alternatively, it could take the form of public engagement, for example:

> you've got to think about how you can talk to the different audiences that you are talking to, and then you use different registers in different places... sometimes the strategy we need here is oppositional, sometimes its reformist. (Meg John)

Some activists focused on bisexuality-specific activism, for example the publication of the *Bisexuality Report* and activism via the groups and networks discussed above. A few contributors were active in specific sectors. For instance, Kay supported people facing discrimination at work via her union, and Elizabeth was active in her workplace's LGBT network (see Chapter 5). One contributor, Rosie, does her activism via the entertainment industry, specifically queer performance:

> In my performance I am basically out as – Rosie Lugosi is camp performance character, because I do believe that if you are trying to get over *really pretty* uncomfortable and challenging ideas, and my feeling is that I have had my most success doing that... if I can make people comfortable and more inclined to listen I am more likely to get my message over.

The overall picture provided by the research findings is that UK bisexuals are engaged in a range of activist endeavours but that these spread beyond the traditional spheres of political engagement. Whilst they increasingly include engagement in policy work (for example consultations, see below) and collaboration with predominantly lesbian and gay organisations (see above), they also include personal microactivisms such as challenging biphobia in everyday life and bisexual community-building. Bisexual activist trajectories are heterogeneous, and not without conflict, for example, between the more queer end of the bisexual agenda and the more assimilationist one (see Chapter 6). The next sub-section of the chapter focuses on activist involvement specifically with structures and institutions associated with the state.

Participatory democracy and engagement with state institutions

There has been a shift towards participatory democratic involvement by bisexual activists in the UK in recent years. This has involved a movement towards bisexual activist engagement with state institutions and a wide range of statutory and state-funded organisations. At the same time, a number of these bodies have conducted consultations and developed interventions in order to support bisexual people's rights. For example, contributor Camel described a piece of activism which led to biphobia being listed as a specific hate crime in a particular municipality:

> It was a long piece of work with... overall strategic type organisation which sponsored groups and one of those was a LGBT group... the Bi Report is incredibly important because when you are working with statutory providers and political organisations you *need* that – resources – and because at that point we had the Count Me In Too work [LGBT research project], which was at that point the only thing, or the only big thing, that separated out Bi. We had a forum with that

group, we had overall structures with an LGBT organisation that was broad, basically their job as a big umbrella organisation was to get big players at the table with small community groups, facilitate that meeting. And then we did a lot of work explaining biphobia.

Other forms of activism include those with national government departments that can then mainstream bisexual diversity awareness throughout their organisation. For example, in September 2012, following contacts made through the UK bisexuality research for this book, I was invited (as a volunteer) to deliver a training workshop to the Executive at the UK Department of Work and Pensions (who oversee more than 100,000 staff). The workshop subsequently fuelled (in 2013) the development of nation-wide training which focused on equality issues for bisexual employees. More generally, the network of activists and academics associated with BiCon, Bis of Colour, BiReCon, BiUK, and The Bisexual Index provide consultancy, trainings, and bisexual representation for statutory sector and other bodies on a regular, if ad hoc, basis. Engagement has until recently been largely on a voluntary basis, and there is an issue, reported by a few research contributors, with bisexual community representatives being expected to contribute for free, which can be exploitative and lead to exhaustion. There are other challenges with bisexual engagement in participative democracy. For example, contributor Grant talked about the difficulties that actors in statutory sector organisations have in understanding bisexual people's lives, and a general lack of consultation, especially with younger bisexual people.

Overall, whilst community-oriented, micro-level activisms continue to be important for UK bisexuals, there is also a trend towards the greater professionalisation of some sections of the bisexual activist community. Engagement in state machinery, for example consultation with government departments, forms a crucial part of this. This engagement is only possible because of the opportunities afforded by the UK government and state institutions which support LGBT equalities, and the broader, EU-based Equality Directives that underpin this support.

Analysis and discussion – Colombia and the UK

This chapter has begun to develop a comparative politics of bisexuality by looking at the Colombian and UK situations. It is recognised that the qualitative research samples are small (Colombia – six individuals; UK – 25) and that more research would be required before definitive statements could be made about bisexual activism in these countries.

However, it may be useful to provide some indicative analysis of the shared patterns, and divergences, across the two states.

As noted at the beginning of the chapter, there are some key differences between the states, which shape the development of bisexual activism. These include Southern/Western differences, large differences in per capita income, the fact that the UK was a colonising state and Colombia was colonised, and variations in ethnic makeup. The role of organised religion is also very different in the two localities; the strong Catholic Church in Colombia has at times been supportive of LGBT rights, whilst in the UK, Christian bodies have largely been oppositional. Lastly, a lengthy period of armed conflict has placed particular pressures on the Colombian population, including bisexuals, that are not present for UK bisexuals.

In the context of these major differences, it is perhaps surprising to notice so many similarities across the two states with respect to bisexual activism. Both sets of activists are centrally concerned with gaining visibility and legitimacy for bisexuality as a sexual identity. The lesbian and gay communities, as well as heterosexuals, in both locations demonstrate stigmatising attitudes toward bisexuals and hold discriminatory, stereotypical views. For Colombian and UK bisexuals, dealing with biphobia from both lesbians and gays, and heterosexuals, is a major challenge. In addition, both Colombian, and UK, activists recognise issues that are shared with lesbian and gay activists. A further commonality is that the organised movements in both states are striated in intersectional terms; the UK movement is largely middle class and located in urban areas, and in Colombia, it is described as mostly middle and upper class and restricted to large cities, despite the high levels of bisexuality amongst rural Colombians.

The Colombian bisexual activists have achieved a great deal, in terms of formal political participation, as well as related campaigns concerning visibility and awareness raising, despite their movement being much younger than the UK bisexual community. It is interesting to speculate about the reasons for this. One reason may be that the UK bisexual community was disenfranchised by lesbian and gay activists in the 1970s and 1980s and drifted into a grassroots oriented lifestyle politics, whilst the increasingly professionalised lesbian and gay organisations continued to marginalise them. In contrast, the more recently evolved Colombian LGBT movement included bisexuals (and transgender people) from the start, and some groups that were predominantly lesbian and gay actively supported emerging bisexual agendas. It is also possible that the state-sponsored human rights frameworks and interventions that developed post-1991 in Colombia provided a more fertile landscape for measures to support socially marginal groups such as bisexuals than has been the case in the UK.

Another reason for the advances in Colombian bisexual politics may be the way in which bisexual activist organisations formed in Colombia; they appear to have been more activist-oriented, professionalised, more assimilationist, more engaged with scholarship and research, and more knitted into the political opportunity structures and state institutions (see Tarrow, 1994) than their UK counterparts, at least in Bogotá. It is also clear that Colombian bisexuals have, at least at times, accessed state resources effectively and that they are part of the set of groups who vie for these resources. In contrast, the UK bisexual communities have been almost entirely unfunded, and until very recently have been mostly shut out of state funding structures. Another reason for the differences is that the UK bisexual communities may have more of a focus on mutual support, community-building, and micro-activisms carried out in an individualistic way, as opposed to the more traditionally political actions of the Colombians. Related to this is the lifestyle focus of the UK bisexuals and the extent to which they overlap with other groupings, such as those associated with kink and poly. These groups fall outside of UK equalities legislative remits, and links with them, plus connections with anarchist and queer politics, may have pulled UK bisexuals away from engaging with the state.

There are some themes that cut across both Colombia and the UK in addition to those discussed above. These can be addressed following the work of Christian Klesse (2014). In a presentation at BiCon 2014, Klesse provided analysis of Nancy Fraser and Axel Honneth's (2003) work on recognition and redistribution. He discussed the ways in which bisexual invisibility is a major theme for bisexual politics. As noted earlier, this assertion is supported by the research and literature from both Colombia and the UK. It appears that bisexual visibility and recognition is the single most prominent aim of bisexual activists. This may be because the social erasure of bisexuality causes minority stress which impacts negatively on bisexual people and others. As Klesse points out, 'the effects of homophobia and biphobia include socioeconomic degradation and class subordination' (2014, slide 6). In other words, if, for example, a bi person has mental health difficulties and cannot engage in paid employment due to the minority stress associated with experiences of biphobia, then issues of both recognition (social acceptance of bisexuality) and of redistribution (access to money) are at stake. For Klesse, there is a need to move beyond a politics of recognition, towards a politics which aims for redistribution, and the systemic transformation of society. The research findings suggested that, via participatory democratic engagement in a range of forms, this transformation is to a limited extent taking place in both Colombia and the UK.

There is a second reason for considering issues of recognition and redistribution in relation to bisexual activism. Some of the more institutional, systemic, or structural concerns, such as access to same-sex partnership rights, cover both bisexual and homosexual people. This dynamic seems to have been used for many years by non-bisexual people to deny the specific need for bisexual visibility and interventions. It is a problematic issue, as it seems that it is a case of adjusting existing social structures to include awareness of bisexuality and bisexual-positive policies. This makes the bisexual movement different from the lesbian and gay movement, which has sought greater structural change (for example marriage rights). Arguably, the lack of a bisexual-specific single issue beyond visibility plays out in such a way as to trivialise bisexual rights claims.

The research material from the UK counters a trivialisation of bisexual rights claims. It shows that there are a range of policy and political issues that require changes to be made to support the fundamental rights of bisexual people, including access to healthcare, asylum rights, education, and adoption and fostering rights. However, in structural terms, one major issue for some bisexual people concerns multiple partnership rights. Another key issue concerns rights for bisexual people who have multiple genders, or are non-gendered. Whilst some of the UK contributors to the research supported such rights, for others these seemed to fall beyond the 'logics of appropriateness'. For example, for UK activists generally, one of the current lines between 'possible' and 'not currently possible' is around monogamous versus multiple partnership forms. This trend is both assimilationist and strategic, and it is cross-cut by issues about the relationship between public and private (see Chapter 6). For example, there seems to be a trend for bisexual poly people, and behavioural bisexuals, to have primary heterosexual relationships and then other partners who may be of different sexes. Their heterosexual relationship may be the public relationship, and the one that matters most in structural terms (for example tax, pension, and benefit issues; welfare and housing issues). The other partner(s) remain, in structural terms, private and non-impactful. Bisexual people who are celibate, single, or asexual also remain unimportant in structural terms, because their civil status is the same as other single people. A similar pattern is apparent with non-binary gendered people; they are rendered invisible by current legal frameworks, but there is no prominent bisexual activist call to claim legal rights for this group. Therefore, in the UK, the more radical visions and claims of bisexual activists have remained largely within the fringe subcultures associated with BiCon and related organisations, meaning that structural change (change in legal, bureaucratic, and institutional frameworks and mechanisms) is not very likely beyond some adjustments being made to support the recognition of bisexual people. It is unclear from the available research how these themes play out in Colombia.

This chapter has provided an empirically oriented contribution to the emergent political science of bisexuality, focusing on bisexual activism, and the engagement of activists with the state via participative democratic mechanisms. In taking a broadly comparative approach using two states (Colombia and the UK) as case studies, it demonstrates similarities in the ways in which bisexual activisms have developed, and commonalities of agendas. The chapter also draws out some of the differences between the two activist movements, notably that the newer Colombian bisexual movement is more engaged with the state, more embedded in the LGBT movement within Colombia, and more effective in terms of certain actions such as raising awareness about bisexuality via state-funded campaigns. In contrast, the UK movement has until very recently been grassroots-based, lifestyle oriented, and excluded from the more professionalised lesbian and gay-dominated organisations; this is now changing and some sections of the UK bisexual activist community are increasingly engaged with the state. The chapter ends by examining the prominent bisexual claims for visibility and recognition, and it suggests that redistribution and recognition are both important for bisexual politics. Bisexual politics may suffer from a lack of viable rights claims that lead to redistribution; the most important claims which have structural implications concern, firstly, the multiple partnership rights that some bisexuals would benefit from, and, secondly, rights for non-binary gendered people. However, these are seen as outside of the realm of the 'possible' by most activists in the UK.

Summary

- Colombian bisexual activisms stemmed from broader LGBT activist communities that developed in the 1970s, with bisexual-specific groups developing from 2006 onwards.
- The UK bisexual movement dates back to the 1960s, but the exclusion of bisexuals from activism by lesbians and gay men meant that

the bisexual community developed outside of the lesbian and gay movement.
- The Colombian bisexual movement, in collaboration with state agencies and broader LGBT activists, has been highly successful in developing public awareness campaigns, sectoral work (for example in education), and media campaigns.
- The UK bisexual activist movement has for many years been fragmented and marginalised in political terms, but in recent years branches of it have become increasingly professionalised and have engaged with state institutions in a variety of successful ways, particularly in terms of awareness raising.
- The trends towards queer and sexual fringe type identities and politics that are found within the UK bisexual movement appear to pull it away from engagement in participatory democratic processes.
- Both Colombian and UK bisexuals have experienced stigmatisation from lesbian and gay-dominated groups, so that activist goals partly concern raising awareness within the lesbian and gay communities.
- For both Colombian and UK bisexuals, the emphasis on bisexual visibility and recognition is crucial, but this involves a primarily cultural shift (towards social support for bisexuals) rather than a structurally transformative one which could include, for example, legal changes to support multiple partnerships and to enable people of non-binary gender to gain full civil rights.

Bibliography

Adam, B., Duyvendak, J.W. and Krawel, A. (eds) (1999) *The Global Emergence of Gay and Lesbian Politics: National Imprints of a Worldwide Movement.* Philadelphia: Temple University Press.

Adkins, L. and Skeggs, B. (2004) *Feminism after Bourdieu.* Oxford and Malden, MA: Blackwell Publishing.

Ahmed, S. (2011) 'Problematic Proximities: Or Why Critiques of Gay Imperialism Matter', *Feminist Legal Studies*, 19: 119–132.

Altman, D. (1993) *Homosexual Oppression and Liberation* (2nd ed.). New York: New York University Press.

American Institute of Bisexuality (2014) American Institute of Bisexuality, available at: http://www.americaninstituteof bisexuality.org/home/html, accessed 28 November 2014.

Anderlini-D'Onofrio, S. (2009) *Gaia and the New Politics of Love: Notes for a Poly Planet.* Berkeley, CA: North Atlantic Books.

Anderson, E., McCormack, M. and Ripley, M. (2014) 'Sixth Form Girls and Bisexual Burden', *Journal of Gender Studies*, available at: http://www.tandfonline.com/doi/abs/10.1080/09589236.2013.877383#.VGJNbDSsVbE.

Andrijasevic, R. (2010) *Migration, Agency and Citizenship in Sex Trafficking.* Basingstoke: Palgrave Macmillan.

Angelides, S. (2001) *A History of Bisexuality.* Chicago: University of Chicago.

Anon (2012) 'Self Care at Bicon: Advice for First-Timers – and Old Hands', *BiCommunityNews*, 113(June Issue): unpaginated.

Anon (2014) 'Pakistan's Hidden Shame', available at: http://www.channel4.com/programmes/pakistans-hidden-shame, accessed 26 November 2014.

Anon (2014a) 'BiCon', available at: http://bicon.org.uk/, accessed 28 November 2014.

Anon (2014b) 'BCN', available at: http://bicommunitynews.co.uk/resources/, accessed 28 November 2014.

Anon (2014c) 'Bisexuality in the UK', available at: http://www.bisexualindex.org.uk/index.php/BiInTheUK, accessed 21 October 2014.

Apphia, K. (2009) 'Apphia K.', in R. Ochs and S. Rowley (eds) *Getting Bi: Voices of Bisexuals from Around the World.* Boston, MA: Bisexual Resource Centre.

Arden, K. (1996) 'Dwelling in the House of Tomorrow: Children, Young People, and their Bisexual Parents', in S. Rose, C. Stevens and the Off Pink Collective (eds) *Bisexual Horizons: Politics, Histories, Lives.* London: Lawrence and Wishart.

Ardila, R. (1998) *Homosexualidad y Psicología.* Bogotá: El Manual Moderno.

Atkins, D. (ed.) (2002) *Bisexual Women in the Twenty-First Century.* New York, London and Oxford: Harrington Park Press.

Ault, A. (1994) 'Hegemonic Discourse in an Oppositional Community: Lesbian Feminist Stigmatization of Bisexual Women', *Critical Sociology*, 20(3): 107–122.

Badgett, L., Lee, M.V. and Jefferson, F. (eds) (2007) *Sexual Orientation Discrimination: An International Perspective.* Oxon and New York: Routledge.

Bibliography

Balding, C. (2013) 'I Want to Make the World a Better Place…for Women, Mainly', *Guardian*, 12 January 2013.
Banerjee, P. (2009) 'Paramita Banerjee', in R. Ochs and S. Rowley (eds) *Getting Bi: Voices of Bisexuals from around the World*. Boston, MA: Bisexual Resource Centre.
Barker, M. (2004) 'Including the B-word: Reflections on the Place of Bisexuality within Lesbian and Gay Activism and Psychology', *Lesbian and Gay Psychology Review*, 5(3): 118–122.
Barker, M. (2007) 'Heteronormativity and the Exclusion of Bisexuality in Psychology', in V. Clarke and E. Peel (eds) *Out in Psychology: Lesbian, Gay, Bisexual, Trans, and Queer Perspectives*. Chichester: Wiley.
Barker, M. (2012) *Rewriting the Rules: An Integrative Guide to Love, Sex and Relationships*. London and New York: Routledge.
Barker, M. and Langdridge, D. (2008) 'II. Bisexuality: Working with a Silenced Sexuality', *Feminism and Psychology*, 18(3): 389–394.
Barker, M., Richards, C., Jones, R., Bowes-Catton, H. and Plowman, T. (2012) 'The Bisexuality Report: Bisexual Inclusion in LGBT Equality and Diversity'. Milton Keynes: Centre for Citizenship, Identity and Governance: Open University.
Barker, M., Richards, C., Jones, R. and Monro, S. (2011) 'BiReCon: An International Academic Conference on Bisexuality', *Journal of Bisexuality*, 11(2): 157–170.
Bauer, R. (2014) *Queer BDSM Intimacies: Critical Consent and Pushing Boundaries*. Basingstoke: Palgrave Macmillan.
Beemyn, B. and Eliason, M. (eds) (1996) *Queer Studies: A Lesbian, Gay, Bisexual, and Transgender Anthology*. New York: New York University Press.
Bell, D. and Binnie, J. (2000) *The Sexual Citizen: Queer Politics and Beyond*. Cambridge: Polity Press.
Bennett, K. (1992) 'Feminist Bisexuality: A Both/And Option for an Either/Or World', in E.R. Weise (ed.) *Closer to Home: Bisexuality and Feminism*. Seattle, WA: Seal Press.
Berlant, L. (1997) *The Queen of America Goes to Washington City: Essays on Sex and Citizenship*. Durham and London: Duke University Press.
Bi Academic Intervention (1997) *The Bisexual Imaginary: Representation, Identity and Desire*. London: Cassell.
Binnie, J. and Klesse, C. (2013) 'The Politics of Age, Temporality and Intergenerationality in Transnational Lesbian, Gay, Bisexual, Transgender and Queer Activist Networks', *Sociology*, 47(3): 580–595.
Bisexual Index (2014) UK Bisexual Community Outraged by Deportation, available at: http://www.bisexualindex.org.uk/index.php/OrashiaEdwards, accessed 15 October 2014.
Bishop, P. (1993) *Dreams of Power: Tibetan Buddhism and the Western Imagination*. London: The Athlone Press.
Blackwood, E. (2000) 'Culture and Women's Sexualities', *Journal of Social Issues*, 56(2): 223–238.
Blasius, M. and Phelan, S. (eds) (1997) *We Are Everywhere: A Historical Sourcebook of Gay and Lesbian Politics*. New York: Routledge.
Blumer, H. (1969) *Symbolic Interactionism: Perspective and Methods*. Englewood Cliffs, NJ: Prentice Hall.
Boone, J.A. (2010) 'Modernist Re-Orientations: Imagining Homoerotic Desire in the "Nearly" Middle East', *Modernism/Modernity*, 17(3): 561–605.

Boris, E., Gilmore, S. and Parreñas, R. (2010) 'Sexual Labors: Interdisciplinary Perspectives Toward Sex and Work', *Sexualities*, 13(2): 131–137.

Bouchard, J.W. (2010) 'India', in C. Stewart (ed.) *The Greenwood Encyclopedia of LGBT Issues Worldwide Volume 1*. Santa Barbara, CA, Denver, CO and Oxford: Greenwood Press.

Bourdieu, P. (1977) *Outline of a Theory of Practice*. London, New York and Melbourne: Cambridge University Press.

Bowes-Catton, H., Barker, M. and Richards, C. (2011) 'I didn't know that I could Feel this Relaxed in my Body: Using Visual Methods to Research Bisexual People's Embodied Experiences of Identity and Space,' in P. Reavey (ed.) *Visual Methods in Psychology: Using and Interpreting Images in Qualitative Research*. London: Routledge.

Brah, A. and Phoenix, A. (2004) 'Aint I a Woman? Revisiting Intersectionality' *Journal of International Women's Studies*, 5(3): 75–86.

Braun, V. and Clarke, V. (2006) 'Using Thematic Analysis in Psychology', *Qualitative Research in Psychology*, 3(2): 77–101.

Braziel, J.E. (2004) ' "Bye, Bye Baby": Race, Bisexuality and the Blues in the Music of Bessie Smith and Janis Joplin', *Popular Music and Society*, 27(1): 3–26.

Breno, A.L. and Galupo, M.P. (2008) 'Bias Toward Bisexual Women and Men in a Marriage-Matching Task', *Journal of Bisexuality*, 7: 217–235.

Brickell, C. (2006) 'The Sociological Construction of Gender and Sexuality', *The Sociological Review*, 54(1): 87–113.

Bristow, J. and Wilson, A. (1993) *Activating Theory: Lesbian, Gay, and Bisexual Politics*. London: Lawrence and Wishart.

Brown, K.M. (2009) 'Health Policy in the United States: Abstinence-Only and Comprehensive Sexuality Education Programs', 21st Annual National Conference on Social Work and HIV/AIDS, New Orleans.

Browne, K., Cull, M. and Hubbard, P. (2010) 'The Diverse Vulnerabilities of Lesbian, Gay, Bisexual and Transgender Sex Workers in the UK', in K. Hardy, S. Kingston and T. Sanders (eds) *New Sociologies of Sex Work*. Surrey and Burlington, VT: Ashgate Publishing Company.

Browne, K., Lim, J. and Brown, G. (2007) *Geographies of Sexualities*. Aldershot: Ashgate.

Bryant, K. and Vidal-Ortiz, S. (2012) 'Introduction to Retheorizing Homophobias', *Sexualities*, 11(4): 387–396.

Bryant, W. (1997) *Bisexual Characters in Film: From Anais to Zee*. New York: Harrington Park Press.

Butler, J. (1990) *Gender Trouble: Feminism and the Subversion of Identity*. London: Routledge.

Cahill, S. and Tobias, S. (2007) *Policy Issues Affecting Lesbian, Gay, Bisexual, and Transgender Families*. Ann Arbour: University of Michigan Press.

Caldwell, K. (2010) We Exist: 'Intersectional In/Visibility in Bisexuality and Disability', *Disability Studies Quarterly*, 30(3/4): available at: http://dsq-sds.org/article/view/1273/1303.

Callis, A.S. (2009) 'Playing with Butler and Foucault: Bisexuality and Queer Theory', *Journal of Bisexuality*, 9: 213–233.

Callis, A.S. (2013) 'The Black Sheep of the Pink Flock: Labels, Stigma, and Bisexual Identity', *Journal of Bisexuality*, 13: 82–105.

Cantarella, E. (1992) *Bisexuality in the Ancient World*. New Haven and London: Yale University Press.

Capiola, A., Griffith, J.D., Balotti, B., Turner, R. and Sharrah, M. (2014) 'Online Escorts: The Influence of Advertised Sexual Orientation', *Journal of Bisexuality*, 14(2): 222–235.
Carbado, D.W. (2013) 'Colorblind Intersectionality', *Signs*, 38(4): 811–845.
Casey, M.E. (2007) 'The Queer Unwanted and Their Undesirable Otherness', in K. Browne, J. Lim and G. Brown (eds) *Geographies of Sexualities*. Aldershot: Ashgate.
Cashmore, C. and Tuason, T.G. (2009) 'Negotiating the Binary: Identity and Social Justice for Bisexual and Transgender Individuals', *Journal of Gay and Lesbian Social Services*, 21: 374–401.
Cerny, J.A. and Janssen, E. (2011) 'Patterns of Sexual Arousal in Homosexual, Bisexual, and Heterosexual Me', *Archives of Sexual Behavior*, 40(4): 687–697.
Chakrapani, V., Kavi, A.R., Ramakrishnan, L.R., Gupta, R., Rappoport, C. and Raghavan, S.S. (2002) 'HIV Prevention and Men Who Have Sex with Men (MSM) in India: Review of Current Scenario and Recommendations', available at: http://indianlgbthealth.info/Authors/Downloads/MSM_HIV_IndiaFin.pdf.
Chakrapani, V. and Ramakrishnan, L.R. (2009) 'Venkateswan Chakrapani and L. Ramki Ramakrishnan', in R. Ochs and S. Rowley (eds) *Getting Bi: Voices of Bisexuals from around the World*. Boston, MA: Bisexual Resource Centre.
Chamberlain, B. (2009) *Bisexual People in the Workplace: Practical Advice for Employers. Stonewall Workplace Guides*. London: Stonewall.
Chapman, R., Watkins, R., Zappia, T., Nicol, P. and Shields, L. (2011) 'Nursing and Medical Students' Attitude, Knowledge and Beliefs Regarding Lesbian, Gay, Bisexual and Transgender Parents Seeking Health Care for their Children', *Journal of Clinical Nursing*, 21: 938–945.
Cho, S., Crenshaw, K.W. and McCall, L. (2013) 'Toward a Field of Intersectionality Studies: Theory, Applications, and Praxis', *Signs*, 38(4): 785–810.
Citizenship 21 (undated) *Profiles of Prejudice: The Nature of Prejudice in England: In-Depth Findings*. London: Stonewall.
Colgan, F., Creegan, C., McKearney, A. and Wright, T. (2007) 'Equality and Diversity Policies and Practices at Work: Lesbian, Gay and Bisexual Workers', *Equal Opportunities International*, 26(6): 590–609.
Colgan, F., Wright, T., Creegan, C. and McKearney, A. (2009) 'Equality and Diversity in the Public Services: Moving Forward on Lesbian, Gay and Bisexual Equality?', *Human Resource Management Journal*, 19(3): 280–301.
Collins, H. (2013) 'New Rules', *Guardian*, 13–19 July 2013.
Cook, J.A. (2000) 'Sexuality and People with Psychiatric Disabilities', *Sexuality and Disability*, 18(3): 195–206.
Cooper, D. (1994) *Sexing the City. Lesbian and Gay Politics Within the Activist State*. London: Rivers Oram Press.
Cooper, D. (2006) 'Active Citizenship and the Governmentality of Local Lesbian and Gay Politics', *Political Geography*, 25: 921–943.
Corrales, J. and Pecheney, M. (eds) (2010) *The Politics of Sexuality in Latin America: A Reader on Lesbian, Gay, Bisexual and Transgender Rights*. Pittsburgh: University of Pittsbugh Press.
Cossman, B. (2007) *Sexual Citizens. The Legal and Cultural Regulation of Sex and Belonging*. Stanford, CA: Stanford University Press.
Crenshaw, K.W. (1989) 'Demarginalizing the Intersection of Race and Sex: A Black Feminist Critique of Antidiscrimination Doctrine, Feminist Theory, and Antiracist Politics', *University of Chicago Legal Forum*, 1989: 139–167.

Crenshaw, K.W. (1991) 'Mapping the Margins: Intersectionality, Identity Politics, and Violence against Women of Colour', *Stanford Law Review*, 43(6): 1241–1299.

Crenshaw, K.W. (1997) 'Intersectionality and Identity Politics: Learning from Violence against Women of Colour', in M. Stanley and V. Naryan (eds) *Restructuring Feminist Political Theory: Feminist Perspectives*. Cambridge: Polity Press.

Cronin, A. and King, A. (2010) 'Power, Inequality and Identity: Exploring Diversity and Intersectionality Amongst Older LGB Adults', *Sociology*, 44(5): 876–892.

Currah, P., Juang, R.M. and Minter, S. (eds) (2006) *Transgender Rights*. Minneapolis: University of Minnesota Press.

D'Emilio, J. and Freedman, E. (1988) *Intimate Matters. A History of Sexuality in America*. New York: Harper and Row Publishers.

Davies, D. (2000) 'Sharing Our Stories, Empowering Our Lives: Don't Dis Me!', *Sexuality and Disability*, 18(3): 179–186.

Davis, K. (2009) 'Intersectionality as Buzzword: a Sociology of Science Perspective On What Makes a Feminist Theory Successful', *Feminist Theory*, 9(1): 67–85.

Delanty, G. (2000) *Citizenship in a Global Age: Society, Culture, Politics*. Buckingham: Open University Press.

Delphy, C. (1984) 'Rethinking Sex and Gender', *Woman's Studies International Forum*, 16(1): 1–9.

Dennis, A. and Martin, P.J. (2005) 'Symbolic Interactionism and the Concept of Power', *British Journal of Sociology*, 56(2): 191–213.

Doll, L.S. and Beeker, C. (1996) 'Male Bisexual Behaviour and HIV Risk in the United States: Synthesis of Research with Implications for Behavioural Interventions', *AIDS Education and Prevention*, 8(3): 205–225.

Downing, L. and Gillett, R. (eds) (2011) *Queer in Europe*. Surrey: Ashgate.

Du Plessis, M. (1996) 'Blatantly Bisexual', in D.E. Hall and M. Prammaggiore (eds) *RePresenting Bisexualities: Subjects and Cultures of Fluid Desire*. New York and London: New York University Press.

Dua, R. (2009) 'Rajiv Dua', in R. Ochs and S. Rowley (eds) *Getting Bi: Voices of Bisexuals from around the World*. Boston, MA: Bisexual Resource Centre.

Duggan, L. (2002) 'The New Homonormativity: The Sexual Politics of Neoliberalism', in R. Castronova and D.D. Nelson (eds) *Materializing Democracy: Toward a Revitalized Cultural Politics*. Durham, NC: Duke University Press.

Dugan, K.B. (2005) *The Struggle over Gay, Lesbian and Bisexual Rights: Facing Off in Cincinnati*. New York and London: Routledge.

Egan, J.E., Frye, V., Kurtz, S.P., Latkin, C., Minxing, C., Tobin, K., Yang, C. and Koblin, B.A. (2011) 'Migration, Neighbourhoods, and Networks: Approaches to Understanding How Urban Environmental Conditions Affect Syndemic Adverse Health Outcomes among Gay, Bisexual and other Men who have Sex with Men', *AIDS Behaviour*, 15: S35–S50.

Eisner, S. (2012) 'Love, Rage and the Occupation: Bisexual Politics in Israel/Palestine', *Journal of Bisexuality*, 12: 80–137.

Eisner, S. (2014) *Bi Notes for a Bisexual Revolution*. Berkeley, CA: Seal Press.

Ekins, R. (1997) *Male Femaling: A Grounded Theory Approach to Cross Dressing*. London: Routledge.

Elliott, R.D. (2005) 'International Lesbian and Gay Law Association', in H. Graupner and P. Tahminjis (eds) *Sexuality and Human Rights: A Global Overview*. New York, London, Victoria: Harrington Park Press.

Ellis, H.H. (1897) *Studies in the Psychology of Sex, Volume I: Sexual Inversion*. London: University Press.

Epprecht, M. (2006) '"Bisexuality" and the Politics of Normal in African Ethnography', *Anthropologica*, 48(2): 187–201.

Epprecht, M. (2008) *Heterosexual Africa: The History of an Idea from the Age of Exploration to the Age of AIDS*. Athens, USA: Ohio University Press.

Epstein, S. (1999) 'Gay and Lesbian Movements in the United States: Dilemmas of Identity, Diversity, and Political Strategy', in B.D. Adam, J.W. Duyvendak and A. Krouwel (eds) *The Global Emergence of Gay and Lesbian Politics: National Imprints of a Worldwide Movement*. Philadelphia: Temple University Press.

Erel, U. (2011) 'Reframing Migrant Mothers as Citizens', *Citizenship Studies*, 15(6–7): 695–709.

Evans, D. (1993) *Sexual Citizenship: The Material Construction of Sexualities*. London and New York: Routledge.

Faderman, L. (1981) *Surpassing the Love of Men: Romantic Friendships and Love between Women from the Renaissance to the Present*. London: Woman's Press.

Fahs, B. (2009) 'Compulsory Bisexuality? The Challenges of Modern Sexual Fluidity', *Journal of Bisexuality*, 9: 3–4.

Fajardo, L. (2006) *Legislación y derechos de lesbianas, gays, bisexuals y transgeneristas en Colombia*. Bogotá: Tercer Mundo Editores, Colombia Diversa.

Fausto-Sterling, A. (2000) *Sexing the Body*. New York: Basic Books.

Fee, A. (2010) 'Who put the "Hetero" in Sexuality?', in S. Hines and T. Sanger (eds) *Transforming Sociology: Towards a Social Analysis of Gender Diversity*. London and New York: Routledge.

Feinberg, L. (1996) *Transgender Warriors: Making History from Joan of Arc to Dennis Rodman*. Boston, MA: Beacon Press.

Firestein, B.A. (ed.) (1996) *Bisexuality: The Psychology and Politics of an Invisible Minority*. Thousand Oaks, CA, London and New Delhi: Sage Publications.

Foucault, M. (1977) *The History of Sexuality* (Vol. 1). New York: Pantheon Books.

Fox, R. (1996) in B.A. Firestein (ed.) *Bisexuality: The Psychology and Politics of an Invisible Minority*. Thousand Oaks, CA: Sage.

Fox, R.C. (1998) 'Bisexuality in Perspective: A Review of the Theory and Research', in B. Firestein (ed.) *Bisexuality: The Psychology and Politics of an Invisible Minority*. London: Sage Publications.

Fraser, N. and Honneth, A. (2003) *Redistribution or Recognition? A Political-Philosophical Exchange*. London and New York: Verso.

Fundamental Rights Agency (2013) EU LGBT survey – European Union Lesbian, Gay, Bisexual and Transgender Survey – Main Results. Vienna, Fundamental Rights Agency.

Gagnon, J. (1977) *Human Sexualities*. Dallas: Scott, Foreman and Co.

Gagnon, J. and Simon, W. (1967) *Sexual Deviance*. New York, Evanston and London: Harper and Row.

Gagnon, J. and Simon, W. (1969) 'Sex Education and Human Development', in P. Fink and V. Hammett (eds) *Sexual Function and Dysfunction*. Philadelphia: F.A. Davis.

Gagnon, J. and Simon, W. (1973) *Sexual Conduct: the Social Sources of Human Sexuality*. Chicago: Aldine.

Ganesh, M. (2009) 'Maya Ganesh', in R. Ochs and S. Rowley (eds) *Getting Bi: Voices of Bisexuals from around the World*. Boston, MA: Bisexual Resource Centre.

Garber, M. (1995) *Vice Versa: Bisexuality and the Eroticism of Everyday Life*. New York: Simon and Schuster.

Garcia, O. (2006) 'Bisexualidad: De la Tercería a la Ruptura de Dicotomías', in M. Viveros (ed.) *Saberes, culturas y desenos sexuales en Colombia*. Bogotá: Universidad Nacional de Colombia.Tercer Mundo.

Garfinkel, H. (1967) *Studies in Ethnomethodology*. Englewood Cliffs, NJ: Prentice Hall.

Gelder, K. and Thornton, S. (1997) *The Subcultures Reader*. London and New York: Routledge.

George, S. (2002) 'British Bisexual Women: A New Century', in D. Atkins (ed.) *Bisexual Women in the Twenty-First Century*. New York, London and Oxford: Harrington Park Press.

Gibbs, G.R. (2007) *Analyzing Qualitative Data*. London: Sage Publications.

Giddens, A. (1992) *The Transformation of Intimacy: Sexuality, Love and Eroticism in Modern Societies*. Stanford: Stanford University Press.

Gosine, A. (2006) '"Race", Culture, Power, Sex, Desire, Love: Writing In "Men who have Sex with Men"', *IDS Bulletin*, 37(5): 1–9.

Green, H.B., Payne, N.R. and Green, J. (2011) 'Working Bi: Preliminary Findings from a Survey on Workplace Experiences of Bisexual People', *Journal of Bisexuality*, 11(2–3): 300–316.

Greene, B. (2000) 'African American Lesbian and Bisexual Women', *Journal of Social Issues*, 56(2): 239–249.

Halberstam, J. (2002) 'An Introduction to Female Masculinity: Masculinity without men', in R. Adams and D. Savran (eds) *The Masculinity Studies Reader*. Malden, Massachusetts and Oxford: Blackwell Publishers.

Hall, D.E. (1996) 'Graphic Sexuality and the Erasure of a Polymorphous Perversity', in D.E. Hall and M. Prammaggiore (eds) *RePresenting Bisexualities: Subjects and Cultures of Fluid Desire*. New York and London: New York University Press.

Hall, D.E. (1996a) 'BI-Introduction II: Epistemologies of the Fence', in D.E. Hall and M. Prammaggiore (eds) *RePresenting Bisexualities: Subjects and Cultures of Fluid Desire*. New York and London: New York University Press.

Hall, D.E. (2003) *Queer Theories*. London: Palgrave Macmillan.

Hardy, K., Kingston, S. and Sanders, T. (eds) (2010) *New Sociologies of Sex Work*. Surrey and Burlington, VT: Ashgate Publishing Company.

Hartman-Linck, J.E. (2014) 'Keeping Bisexuality Alive: Maintaining Bisexual Visibility in Monogamous Relationships', *Journal of Bisexuality*, 14:2: 177–193.

Head, S. and Milton, M. (2014) 'Filling the Silence: Exploring the Bisexual Experience of Intimate Partner Abuse', *Journal of Bisexuality*, 14(2): 277–299.

Hearn, J. (1992) *Men in the Public Eye: The Construction and Deconstruction of Public Men and Private Patriarchies*. London and New York: Routledge.

Hearn, J., Oleksy, E.H. and Golanska, D. (2011) 'Introduction: The Limits of Gendered Citizenship', in E.H. Oleksy, J. Hearn and D. Golanska (eds) *The Limits of Gendered Citizenship: Contexts and Complexities*. New York and London: Routledge.

Hearn, J. and Parkin, W. (2001) *Gender, Sexuality and Violence in Organizations*. London: Sage Publications.
Heath, J. and Goggin, K. (2009) 'Attitudes towards Male Homosexuality, Bisexuality, and the Down Low Lifestyle: Demographic Differences and HIV Implications', *Journal of Bisexuality*, 9: 17–31.
Heckert, J. and Cleminson, R. (2011) (eds) *Anarchism and Sexuality: Ethics, Relationships, and Power*. Oxon and New York: Routledge.
Hemmings, C. (2002) *Bisexual Spaces: A Geography of Sexuality and Gender*. New York and London: Routledge.
Hemmings, C. (2007) 'What's in a Name? Bisexuality, Transnational Sexuality Studies and Western Colonial Legacies', *The International Journal of Human Rights*, 11(1–2): 13–32.
Herdt, G.H. (1984) 'A Comment of Cultural Attributes and Fluidity of Bisexuality', *Journal of Homosexuality*, 10(3/4): 53–61.
Highleyman, L.A. (1995) 'Identity and Ideas: Strategies for Bisexuals', in N. Tucker (ed.) *Bisexual Politics: Theories, Queries and Visions*. New York and London: Harrington Park Press.
Hines, S. (2007) *TransForming Gender: Transgender Practices of Identity, Intimacy and Care*. Bristol: The Policy Press.
Hines, S. (2010) 'Introduction', in S. Hines and T. Sanger (eds) *Transforming Sociology: Towards a Social Analysis of Gender Diversity*. London and New York: Routledge.
Hines, S. and Sanger, T. (eds) (2010) *Transforming Sociology: Towards a Social Analysis of Gender Diversity*. London and New York: Routledge.
Hird, M. (2006) 'Animal Trans', *Australian Feminist Studies*, 21(49): 35–48.
Hooks, B. (2000) *Feminist Theory: From Margin to Centre* (2nd ed.). London: Pluto Press.
Horncastle, J. (2008) 'Queer Bisexuality: Perceptions of Bisexual Existence, Distinctions, and Challenges', *Journal of Bisexuality*, 8(1–2): 25–49.
Hudson, J.H. (2013) 'Comprehensive Literature Review Pertaining to Married Men Who Have Sex With Men (MMSM)', *Journal of Bisexuality*, 13(4): 417–601.
Hurtado, A. and Sinha, M. (2008) 'More than Men: Latino Feminist Masculinities and Intersectionality', *Sex Roles*, 59: 337–349.
Hutchins, L. (1996) 'Bisexuality: Politics and Community', in B.A. Firestein (ed.) *Bisexuality: The Psychology and Politics of an Invisible Minority*. Thousand Oaks, CA, London and New Delhi: Sage Publications.
Hutchins, L. (2002) 'Bisexual Women as Emblematic Sexual Healers and the Problematics of the Embodied Sacred Whore', in D. Atkins (ed.) *Bisexual Women in the Twenty-First Century*. New York, London and Oxford: Harrington Park Press.
Hutchins, L. (2011) 'Rethinking the Sacred Ho', *Journal of Bisexuality*, 11: 574–581.
Hutchins, L. and Kaahamanu, L. (1991) *Bi Any Other Name: Bisexual People Speak Out*. Boston, MA: Alyson Publications Inc.
Itaborahy, L.P. and Zhu, J. (2014) 'State-Sponsored Homophobia. A World Survey of Laws: Criminalisation, Protection, and Recognition of Same-Sex Love'. International Lesbian, Gay, Bisexual, Transgender and Intersex Association, available at: www.ilga.org.
Jackson, S. and Scott, S. (eds) (1996) *Feminism and Sexuality: A Reader*. Edinburgh: Edinburgh University Press.

Jackson, S. and Scott, S. (2010) 'Rehabilitating Interactionism for a Feminist Sociology of Sexuality', *Sociology*, 44: 811–826.

James, C. (1996) 'Denying Complexity: The Dismissal and Appropriation of Bisexuality in Queer, Lesbian, and Gay Theory', in B. Beemyn and M. Eliason (eds) *Queer Studies: Lesbian, Gay, Bisexual and Transgender Anthology*. New York and London: New York University Press.

Jeffries, W.L. and Dodge, B. (2007) 'Male Bisexuality and Condom Use at Last Sexual Encounter: Results from a National Survey', *Journal of Sex Research*, 3: 278–289.

Jenkins, R. (1992) *Key Sociologists: Pierre Bourdieu*. London and New York: Routledge.

Jeppesen, S. (2010) 'Queer Anarchist Autonomous Zones and Publics: Direct Action Vomiting against Homonormative Consumerism', *Sexualities*, 13(4): 463–478.

Jivraj, S. and de Jong, A. (2011) 'The Dutch Homo-Emancipation Policy and its Silencing Effects on Queer Muslims', *Feminist Legal Studies*, 19: 143–158.

Jones, T. and Hiller, L. (2014) 'The Erasure of Bisexual Students in Australian Education Policy and Practice', *Journal of Bisexuality*, 14(1): 53–74.

Jules (2012) 'Bi Media Watch', *BCN*, December 2012: 5.

Keeble, S.E., Viney, D. and Wood, G.W. (2011) *Out and About: Mapping LGBT Lives in Birmingham*. Birmingham: Birmingham LGBT.

Kessler, S. and McKenna, W. (1978) *Gender: An Ethnomethodological Approach*. New York: Wiley.

Khan, S. (2004) MSM and HIV/AIDS in India. Naz Foundation International.

Kinsey, A.C., Pomeroy, W.B. and Martin, C.E. (1948) *Sexual Behaviour in the Human Male*. Philadelphia: W.B. Saunders.

Kinsey, A.C., Pomeroy, W.B., Martin, C.E., and Gebhard, P. (1953) *Sexual Behavior in the Human Female*. Philadelphia: Saunders.

Klein, F. (1978) *The Bisexual Option* (2nd ed.). New York: Harrington Park.

Klesse, C. (2005) 'Bisexual Women, Non-Monogamy and Differentiated Anti-Promiscuity Discourses', *Sexualities*, 8(4): 445–464.

Klesse, C. (2007) *The Spectre of Promiscuity: Gay Male and Bisexual Non-Monogamies and Polyamories*. Aldershot: Ashgate.

Klesse, C. (2014) 'Bisexual Rights? On Bisexuality, Rights Discourse and Sexual Politics' *Paper Presented at the BiReCon Conference*, 31 July 2014, Leeds Trinity University, Leeds, UK.

Köllen, T. (2013) 'Bisexuality and Diversity Management: Addressing the B in LGBT as a Relevant "Sexual Orientation" in the Workplace', *Journal of Bisexuality*, 13(1): 122–137.

Kollman, K. and Waites, M. (2009) 'The Global Politics of Lesbian, Gay, Bisexual and Transgender Human Rights: an Introduction', *Contemporary Politics*, 15(1): 1–17.

Kollman, K. and Waites, M. (2011) 'United Kingdom: Changing Political Opportunity Structures, Policy Successes and Continuing Challenges for Lesbian, Gay and Bisexual Movements', in M.D. Tremblay, D. Paternotte and C. Johnson (eds) *The Lesbian and Gay Movement and the State: Comparative Insights into a Transformed Relationship*. Surrey and Burlington, VT: Ashgate Publishing.

Landers, S., Pickett, J., Rennie, L. and Wakefield, S. (2011) 'Community Perspectives on Developing a Sexual Health Agenda for Gay and Bisexual Men', *AIDS Behaviour*, 15: 101–106.

Lano, K. (1996) 'Bisexual History: Fighting Invisibility', in: S. Rose, C. Stevens and the Off Pink Collective (eds) *Bisexual Horizons: Politics, Histories, Lives*. London: Lawrence and Wishart.

Lee, J.C.H. (2011) *Policing Sexuality: Sex, Society and the State*. London and New York: Zed Books.

Lister, R. (1997) *Citizenship: Feminist Perspectives*. London: Palgrave Macmillan.

Lister, R. (2003) *Citizenship: Feminist Perspectives* (2nd ed.). London: Palgrave Macmillan.

Lister, R. (2011) 'From the Intimate to the Global: Reflections on Gendered Citizenship', in E.H. Oleksy, J. Hearn and D. Golanska (eds) *The Limits of Gendered Citizenship: Contexts and Complexities*. New York and London: Routledge.

Lofgren-Martenson, L. (2009) 'The Invisibility of Young Homosexual Women and Men with Intellectual Disabilities', *Sexuality and Disability*, 27: 21–26.

Lombardo, E. and Meier, P. (2011) 'EU Gender Equality Policy: Citizen's Rights and Women's Duties', in E.H. Oleksy, J. Hearn and D. Golanska (eds) *The Limits of Gendered Citizenship: Contexts and Complexities*. New York and London: Routledge.

Lorber, J. (1994) *Paradoxes of Gender*. New Haven: Yale University Press.

Lustiger-Thaler, H., Nederveen-Pietevse, J. and Roseneill, S. (eds) (2011) *Beyond Citizenship: Feminism and the Transformation of Belonging*. Basingstoke: Palgrave Macmillan.

MacDowell, L. (2009) 'Historicising Contemporary Bisexuality', *Journal of Bisexuality*, 9(1): 3–15.

Marshall, T.H. (1950) *Citizenship and Social Class*. Cambridge: Cambridge University Press.

Matteson, D.R. (1996) 'Counselling and Psychotherapy with Bisexual and Exploring Clients', in B. Firestein (ed.) *Bisexuality: The Psychology and Politics of an Invisible Minority*. Thousand Oaks, CA, London and New Delhi: Sage Publications.

McCaghy, C.H. and Skipper, J.K. Jr. (2000) 'Lesbian Behavior as an Adaption to the Occupation of Stripping', in P.C. Rust (ed.) *Bisexuality in the United States: A Social Sciences Reader*. New York: Columbia University Press.

McCall, L. (2005) 'The Complexity of Intersectionality', *Signs*, 30(3): 1771–1800.

McCormack, M., Anderson, E. and Adams, A. (2014) 'Cohort Effect on the Coming Out Experiences of Bisexual Men', Sociology Online First, available at: http://soc.sagepub.com/content/early/2014/02/17/0038038513518851.

McDermott, E. (2011) 'The World Some Have Won: Sexuality, Class and Inequality', *Sexualities*, 4(63): 63–78.

McGrath, S. (2013) 'World Pride Power List 2013', *Guardian*, 29 June 2013.

McIntosh, M. (1998 [1968]) 'The Homosexual Role', in P. Nardi and B. Schneider (eds) *Social Perspectives in Lesbian and Gay Studies*. London: Routledge.

McLean, K. (2008) 'Inside, Outside, Nowhere: Bisexual Men and Women in the Gay and Lesbian Community', *Journal of Bisexuality*, 8: 63–80.

McLelland, M. and Suganama, K. (2010) 'Sexual Minorities and Human Rights in Japan: An Historical Perspective', *The International Journal of Human Rights*, 13(2–3): 329–343.

Mead, G.H. (1934) *Mind, Self and Society*. Chicago: University of Chicago Press.

Mead, M. (1975) *Bisexuality: What's it all About?* Redbook, January: 29–31.

Mishra, A.K. and Sharma, A.K. (2007) 'Redefining Vulnerabilities: A Study of Men Having Sex with Men in the Wake of the HIV Epidemic in Mumbai,

India', Paper Presented at the Annual Meeting of the Population Association of America, 29–31 March, New York.
Mitchell, M., Howarth, C., Kotecha, M. and Creegan, C. (2008) *Sexual Orientation Research Review 2008*. Manchester: Equality and Human Rights Commission.
Monro, S. (2003) 'Transgender Politics in the UK', *Critical Social Policy*, 23(4): 433–452.
Monro, S. (2005) *Gender Politics: Citizenship, Activism and Sexual Diversity*. London: Pluto Press.
Monro, S. (2007) 'New Institutionalism and Sexuality at Work in Local Government', *Gender, Work, and Organisation*, 14(1): 1–19.
Monro, S. (2010) 'Gender Diversity: The Indian and UK Cases', in S. Hines and T. Sanger (eds) *Transforming Sociology: Towards a Social Analysis of Gender Diversity*. London and New York: Routledge.
Monro, S. (2010a) 'Sexuality, Space and Intersectionality: The Case of Lesbian, Gay, and Bisexual Equalities Initiatives in UK Local Government', *Sociology*, 44(5): 1–15.
Monro, S. and Richardson, D. (2014) 'Lesbian, Gay and Bisexual Populations: The Role of English Local Government', *Local Government Studies*, 40(6): 869–887.
Monro, S. and Warren, L. (2004) 'Transgendering Citizenship', *Sexualities*, 7: 345–362.
Morrow, K.M. and Allsworth, J.E. (2000) 'Sexual Risk in Lesbians and Bisexual Women', *Journal of the Gay and Lesbian Medical Association*, 4(4): 159–165.
Mulick, P.S. and Wright, L.W. (2002) 'Examining the Existence of Biphobia in the Heterosexual and Homosexual Populations', *Journal of Bisexuality*, 2(4): 45–64.
Mulick, P.S. and Wright, L.W. (2011) 'The Biphobia Scale a Decade Later: Reflections and Additions', *Journal of Bisexuality*, 11: 453–457.
Murray, S. and Roscoe, W. (eds) (1998) *Boy-Wives and Female Husbands: Studies of African Homosexualities*. New York: St. Martin's Press.
Nandi, D.N. (1980) 'The Concept of Bisexuality and Psychiatry', *Indian Journal of Psychiatry*, 22: 3–18.
Nilan, P. and Feixa, C. (2006) 'Introduction: Youth Hybridity and Plural Worlds', in P. Nilan and C. Feixa (eds) *Global Youth? Hybrid Identities, Plural Worlds*. London and New York: Routledge.
Noel, M.J. (2006) 'Progressive Polyamory: Considering Issues of Diversity', *Sexualities*, 9: 602–620.
Ochs, R. (1996) 'Biphobia: It Goes more than Two Ways', in B.A. Firestein (ed.) *Bisexuality: The Psychology and Politics of an Invisible Minority*. Thousand Oaks, CA: Sage Publications.
Ochs, R. and Rowley, S.E. (eds) (2009) *Getting Bi: Voices of Bisexuals Around the World*. Boston, MA: Bisexual Resource Centre.
Oleksy, E.H. (ed.) (2009) *Intimate Citizenships: Gender, Sexualities, Politics*. London: Routledge.
Oleksy, E.H., Hearn, J. and Golanska, D. (eds) (2011) *The Limits of Gendered Citizenship: Contexts and Complexities*. New York and London: Routledge.
Owen, M. (2011) 'Still Sitting on Fences: Reflections on "Overstepping the Bounds: Bisexuality, Gender and Sociology"', *Journal of Bisexuality*, 11(4): 493–497.
Pateman, C. (1988) *The Sexual Contract*. Palo Alto, CA: Stanford University Press.

Peterson, L.W. (2011) 'The Married Man Online: Ten Years Later', *Journal of Bisexuality*, 11(4): 394–398.

Pettaway, L., Bryant, L., Keane, F. and Craig, S. (2014) 'Becoming Down Low: A Review of the Literature on Black Men Who Have Sex With Men and Women', *Journal of Bisexuality*, 14(2): 209–221.

Peumans, W. (2014) 'Queer Muslim Migrants in Belgium: A Research Note on Same-Sex Sexualities and Lived Religion', *Sexualities*, 5/6: 618–631.

Phelan, S. (2001) *Sexual Strangers: Gays, Lesbians and Dilemmas of Citizenship*. Philadelphia: Temple University Press.

Phillips, A. (2006) *Which Equalities Matter?* Cambridge: Polity Press.

Phillips, A.E., Lowndes, C.M., Boily, M.C., Garnett, G.P., Ramesh, B.M., Anthony, J., Moses, S. and Alary, M. (2010) 'Men who have Sex with Men and Women in Bangalore, South India, and Potential Impact on the HIV Epidemic', *Sexually Transmitted Infections*, 86(3): 1–18.

Planeta Paz (2002) *Documentos de cacarterización sectorial*. Sector LGBT. Bogotá: Ediciones Antroopos.

Plummer, K. (1975) *Sexual Stigma: An Interactionist Account*. London and Boston, MA: Routledge and Kegan Paul.

Plummer, K. (ed.) (1992) *Modern Homosexualities: Fragments of Lesbian and Gay Experience*. London and New York: Routledge.

Plummer, K. (1995) *Telling Sexual Stories: Power, Change and Social Worlds*. London and New York: Routledge.

Plummer, K. (2001) 'The Square of Intimate Citizenship: Some Preliminary Proposals', *Citizenship Studies*, 5(3): 237–253.

Plummer, K. (2002 [1982]) 'Symbolic Interactionism and Sexual Conduct: An Emerging Perspective', in C. Williams and A. Stein (eds) *Gender and Sexuality*. Malden: Blackwell.

Plummer, K. (2003) *Intimate Citizenship. Private Decisions and Public Dialogues*. Seattle, WA and London: University of Washington Press.

Plummer, K. (2006) 'Intimate Citizenship in an Unjust World', in M. Romero and E. Margolis (eds) *The Blackwell Companion to Social Inequalities*. Oxford: Wiley Blackwell.

Pramaggiore, M. (1996) 'BI-Introduction I: Epistemologies of the Fence', in M. Prammagiore and D.E. Hall (eds) *Representing Bisexualities: Subjects and Cultures of Fluid Desire*. New York: New York University Press.

Prideaux, S. (2005) *Not so New Labour: A Sociological Critique of New Labour's Policy and Practice*. Cambridge: Polity Press.

Prieto, C. (2011) *Sexualidad en Colombia, Mitos y Verdades*. Bogotá: SNM editors.

Puar, J.K. (2007) *Terrorist Assemblages: Homonationalism in Queer Times*. Durham, NC: Duke University Press.

Puar, J.K. (2011) 'Citation and Censorship: The Politics of Talking about the Sexual Politics of Israel', *Feminist Legal Studies*, 19: 133–142.

PUCL-K (2003) 'Human Rights Violations against the Transgender Community: A Study of Kothi and Hijra Sex Workers in Bangalore, India. Karnataka: PUCL-K', available at: http://ai.eecs.umich.edu/people/conway/TS/PUCL/PUCL%20Report.html.

Putnam, R. (1993) *Making Democracy Work: Civic Traditions in Modern Italy*. Princetown, NJ: Princetown University Press.

Ramakrishnan, R. (2009) 'Bisexual politics for Lesbians and Gay Men', in R. Ochs and S. Rowley (eds) *Getting Bi: Voices of Bisexuals from around the World*. Boston, MA: Bisexual Resource Centre.
Ramasubban, R. (undated) 'Culture, Politics, and Discourses on Sexuality: A History of Resistance to the Anti-Sodomy Law in India', available at: www.sxpolitics.org/frontlines/book/pdf/capitulos3_india.pdf.
Ravikumar, A.V. and Kumar, K.A. (2011) 'Sexual Behaviour and its Determinants among Homosexual and Bisexual Men in Mumbia, India', *The Journal of Family Welfare*, 57(2): 2–22.
Reddy, G. (2006) *With Respect to Sex: Negotiating Hijra Identity in South India*. New Delhi: Yoda Press.
Reddy, V. (2009) 'Queer Marriage: Sexualising Citizenship and the Development of Freedoms in South Africa', in M. Steyn and M. Van Zyl (eds) *The Prize and the Price: Shaping Sexualities in South Africa*. Cape Town: HSRC Press.
Reddy, V., Sandfort, T., Baumann, L., Matebeni, Z., and Southey-Swartz, I. (2012) 'Forced Sexual Experiences as Risk Factor for Self-Reported HIV Infection among Southern African Lesbian and Bisexual Women', *PLOS One*, 8(1).
Rembis, M.A. (2010) 'Beyond the Binary: Rethinking the Social Model of Disabled Sexuality', *Sexuality and Disability*, 28: 51–60.
Republic of Colombia (1991) *Colombian Political Constitution*. Bogotá: National Press Office.
Richardson, D. (1996) 'Heterosexuality and Social Theory', in D. Richardson (ed.) *Theorising Heterosexuality*. Buckingham: Open University Press.
Richardson, D. (1998) 'Sexuality and Citizenship', *Sociology*, 32(1): 83–100.
Richardson, D. (2000) 'Constructing Sexual Citizenship: Theorizing Sexual Rights', *Critical Social Policy*, 20(1): 105–135.
Richardson, D. (2000a) 'Claiming Citizenship? Sexuality, Citizenship and Lesbian/Feminist Theory', *Sexualities*, 3(2): 255–272.
Richardson, D., McLaughlin, J. and Casey, M.E. (eds) (2006) *Intersections Between Feminist and Queer Theory*. Basingstoke: Palgrave Macmillan.
Richardson, D. and Monro, S. (2012) *Sexuality, Equality and Diversity*. Basingstoke: Palgrave Macmillan.
Richardson, D. and Monro, S. (2013) 'Public Duty and Private Prejudice: Sexualities Equalities and Local Government', *Sociological Review*, 61(1): 131–152.
Richardson, D. and Robinson, V. (eds) (2008) *Introducing Gender and Women's Studies*. Basingstoke: Palgrave Macmillan.
Richardson, D. and Seidman, S. (2002) *Handbook of Lesbian and Gay Studies*. London: Sage Publications.
Riggle, E.D.B. and Tadlock, B.L (eds) (1999) *Gays and Lesbians in the Democratic Process: Public Policy, Public Opinion, and Political Representation*. New York and Chichester: Columbia University Press.
Robinson, M. (2014) '"A Hope to Lift Both My Spirits": Preventing Bisexual Erasure in Aboriginal Schools', *Journal of Bisexuality*, 14(1): 18–35.
Rose, S., Stevens, C. and the Off Pink Collective (eds) (1996) *Bisexual Horizons: Politics, Histories, Lives*. London: Lawrence and Wishart.
Roseniel, S. (ed.) (2013) *Beyond Citizenship? Feminism and the Transformation of Belonging*. Basingstoke: Palgrave Macmillan.

Rouhani, F. (2007) 'Religion, Identity and Activism: Queer Muslim Diasphoric Identities', in K. Browne, J. Lim and G. Brown (eds) *Geographies of Sexualities*. Aldershot: Ashgate.

Roy, A. (2012) *The Desire of the Soul: Negotiating the Politics of Sexuality, the Body and HIV/AIDS Discourse in Mumbai, India*. Doctoral thesis, University of Sussex.

Ruspini, E. (2013) *Diversity in Family Life: Gender, Relationships and Social Change*. Bristol: Policy Press.

Rust, P.C. (2000) *Bisexuality in the United States: A Social Sciences Reader*. New York: Columbia University Press.

Rust, P.C. (2000a) 'Bisexuality: A Contemporary Paradox for Women', *Journal of Social Issues*, 56(2): 205–221.

Safra (2003) *Initial Findings*. London: Safra project.

Safra (2013) 'About Us', available at: http://www.safraproject.org/aboutus.htm, accessed 6 July 2014.

Salazar, L. (2009) 'Notas Para un Movimiento en Construcción en Colombia. El Caso de la Bisexualidad. Mujeres al borde', available at: http://www.mujeresalborde.org/spip.php?article48.

Salazar, L. (2009a) 'La Bisexualidad Organizada. Dimensión Bi', available at: http://dimensionbi.blogspot.com/.

Salazar, L. and Galvis, J. (2008) Aportes Desde la Bisexualidad al Movimiento de Personas LGBT en Colombia. Un Texto Desde el Activismo Social. Ponencia Seminario Internacional 'Derechos Humanos, Diversidad Sexual y Políticas de Estado'. Bogotá: Dimensión Bi.

Salazar, L. and Galvis, J. (2009) Apuntes Sobre el Trabajo, Necesidades y Retos del Movimiento de Personas Bisexuales en Colombia. Atrevidas Magazine. Bogotá: Revista de la Red de Mujeres Enredadas LBTI.

San Francisco Human Rights Commission LGBT Advisory Committee (undated) Bisexual Invisibility: Impacts and Recommendations. San Francisco: San Francisco Human Rights Commission LGBT Advisory Committee.

Sanabria, F. (2006) 'Derechos y Políticas Sexuales. Derechos, Legislación y Ciudadanía. De Reivindicaciones Homogéneas al Derecho a la Indiferencia', in M. Viveros (ed.) *Saberes, Culturas y Derechos Sexuales en Colombia*. Bogotá: Universidad Nacional de Colombia: Tercer Mundo.

Sandbrook, R., Edelman, M., Heller, P. and Teichman, J. (2007) *Social Democracy in the Global Periphery: Origins, Challenges, Prospects*. Cambridge: Cambridge University Press.

Sanders, E. (2010) 'Situating the Female Gaze: Understanding (Sex) Tourism Practices in Thailand', in K. Hardy, S. Kingston and T. Sanders (eds) *New Sociologies of Sex Work*. Surrey and Burlington, VT: Ashgate Publishing Company.

Sandfort, T., Baumann, L., Matebeni, Z., Reddy, V. and Southey-Swartz, I. (2012) 'Forced Sexual Experiences as Risk Factor for Self-Reported HIV Infection among Southern African Lesbian and Bisexual Women', *PLOS One*, 8(1), available at: http://www.plosone.org/article/info%3Adoi%2F10.1371%2Fjournal.pone.0053552#pone-0053552-t003.

Sandfort, T. and Dodge, B. (2008) '…And Then There was the Down Low: Introduction to Black and Latino Male Bisexualities', *Archives of Sex Behavior*, 37: 675–682.

Seabrook, J. (1997) 'Not "Straight", Not Gay', The Pioneer, 30 September 1997.

Sedgewick, E.K. (1991) *Epistemology of the Closet*. Hemel Hempsted: Harvester Wheatsheaf.
Seidman, S. (1996) *Queer Theory/Sociology*. Oxford: Blackwell.
Seidman, S. (1997) *Difference Troubles: Queering Social Theory and Sexual Politics*. Cambridge: Cambridge University Press.
Serrano, F. (2003) *Body and Conflict in Colombia: Reflections in a Political Practice*. Bogotá: Central University and University of Bradford.
Serrano, F. (2010) 'Colombia', in C. Stewart (ed.) *The Greenwood Encyclopedia of LGBT Issues Worldwide, Volume 1*. Santa Barbara, CA, Denver, CO and Oxford: Greenwood Press.
Shakespeare, T., Gillespie-Sells, K. and Davies, D. (1996) *The Sexual Politics of Disability: Untold Desires*. London: Cassell.
Shyamantha, A. (2013) 'India's Supreme Court Turns the Clock Back with Gay Sex Ban', available at: Reuters http://uk.reuters.com/article/2013/12/11/us-india-rights-gay-idUKBRE9BA05620131211.
Smith, M. (2008) *Political Institutions and Lesbian and Gay Rights in the United States and Canada*. New York and Oxon: Routledge.
Sprinkle, A. (1991) 'Beyond Bisexual', in L. Hutchins and L. Kaahumanu (eds) *Bi Any Other Name: Bisexual People Speak Out*. Boston, MA: Alyson Publications.
Steinman, E. (2011) 'Revisiting the Invisibility of (Male) Bisexuality: Grounding (Queer) Theory, Centering Bisexual Absences and Examining Masculinities', *Journal of Bisexuality*, 11(4): 399–411.
Stekel, W. (1950 [1922]) *Bi-Sexual Love*, trans. J.S. van Tenslaar. New York: Emerson Books.
Storr, M. (1999) *Bisexuality: A Critical Reader*. London and New York: Routledge.
Storr, M. (1999a) 'Postmodern Bisexuality', *Sexualities*, 2: 309–325.
Strachey, J. (ed.) (1953) *The Standard Edition of the Complete Psychological Works of Sigmund Freud* (Vol. 7), trans. J. Strachey. London: Hogarth Press.
Sulkunen, I., Nevala-Nurmi, S., and Markkola, P. (2009) (eds) *Suffrage, Gender and Citizenship: International Perpectives on Parliamentary Reforms*. Newcastle-upon-Tyne: Cambridge Scholars Publishing.
Tarrow, S. (1994) *Power in Movement: Social Movements, Collective Action and Politics*. Cambridge: Cambridge University Press.
Taylor, Y. (2007) *Working Class Lesbian Life: Classed Outsiders*. Basingstoke: Palgrave Macmillan.
Taylor, Y. (2009) *Lesbian and Gay Parenting: Securing Social and Educational Capital*. Basingstoke: Palgrave Macmillan.
Teppo, A. (2009) 'A Decent Place? Space and Morality in a Former "Poor White" Suburb', in M. Steyn and M. van Zyl (eds) *The Prize and the Price: Shaping Sexualities in South Africa*. Cape Town: HSRC Press.
Teunis, N. (2001) 'Same-Sex Sexuality in Africa: A Case Study from Senegal', *AIDS and Behaviour*, 5(2): 173–182.
Thomas, B., Mimiaga, M.J., Kumar, S., Swaminathan, S., Safren, S.A. and Mayer, K.H. (2011) 'HIV in Indian MSM: Reasons for a Concentrated Epidemic and Strategies for Prevention', *Indian Journal of Medical Research*, 134: 920–929.
Toft, A. (2014) 'RE-Imagining Bisexuality and Christianity: The Negotiation of Christianity in the Lives of Bisexual Women and Men', *Sexualities*: 5/6: 546–564.
Towle, C. (2011) 'Highlighting the B in LGBT: The Experiences of One U.K. Trade Union', *Journal of Bisexuality*, 11: 317–319.

Tremblay, M., Johnson, C. and Paternotte, D. (2011) *The Lesbian and Gay Movement and the State: Comparative Insights into a Transformed Relationship*. Surrey: Ashgate.

UNICEF (2009) *Progress for Children: A Report on Child Protection*. Number 8. New York: UNICEF.

Vanita, R. and Kidwai, S. (eds) (2001) *Same-Sex Love in India: Readings from Literature and History*. New York: Palgrave, St Martins Press.

Viveros, M. (2006) *Saberes, Culturas, y Derechos Sexuales en Colombia*. Bogotá: National University of Colombia.

Waites, M. (2009) 'Critique of "Sexual Orientation" and "Gender Identity" in Human Rights Discourse: Global Queer Politics beyond the Yogyakarta Principles', *Contemporary Politics*, 15(1): 137–156.

Waites, M. (2009a) 'Lesbian, Gay and Bisexual NGOs in Britain: Past, Present and Future', in N. Crowson, M. Hilton and J. McKay (eds) *NGOs in Contemporary Britain: Non-State Actors in Society and Politics Since 1945*. Basingstoke: Palgrave Macmillan.

Waites, M. (2010) 'Human Rights, Sexual Orientation and the Generation of Childhoods: Analysing the Partial Decriminalisation of "Unnatural Offenses" in India', *The International Journal of Human Rights*, 14(6): 971–993.

Walker, A. (2014) ' "Our Little Secret": How Publicly Heterosexual Women Make Meaning From Their "Undercover" Same-Sex Sexual Experiences', *Journal of Bisexuality*, 14(2): 194–208.

Walker, P. (2014) 'How Quakers were 50 years Ahead of Time on Gay Rights', *Guardian*, 14 September 2014.

Ward, J. (2008) 'Dude-Sex: White Masculinities and "Authentic" Heterosexuality Among Dudes Who Have Sex With Dudes', *Sexualities*, (11): 414.

Ward, L. (2011) *Procurement: Embedding Lesbian, Gay, and Bisexual Equality in the Supply Chain*. London: Stonewall, available at: www.stonewall.org.uk/workplace.

Warner, M. (ed.) (1993) *Fear of a Queer Planet: Queer Politics and Social Theory*. Minneapolis: University of Minnesota Press.

Webb, J., Schirato, T. and Danaher, G. (2002) *Understanding Bourdieu*. London, Thousand Oaks, CA and New Delhi: Sage Publications Ltd.

Weeks, J. (1968) *Sexuality*. London: Routledge.

Weeks, J. (1977) *Coming Out: Homosexual Politics in Britain from the Nineteenth Century to the Present*. London: Quartet Press.

Weeks, J. (1985) *Sexuality and its Discontents: Meanings, Myths and Modern Sexualities*. London: Routledge Kegan Paul.

Weeks, J. (1998) 'The Sexual Citizen', *Theory, Culture and Society*, 15(3–4): 35–52.

Weeks, J. (2008) *The World We Have Won: The Remaking of Erotic and Intimate Life*. London: Routledge.

Weeks, J. (2009) 'Regulation, Resistance, Recognition', *Sexualities*, 11(6): 787–792.

Weinberg, G. (1972) *Society and the Healthy Homosexual*. New York: St. Martin's.

Weinberg, M.S., Williams, C.J. and Pryor, D.W. (1994) *Dual Attraction: Understanding Bisexuality*. New York and Oxford: Oxford University Press.

Weinrich, J.D. and Klein, F. (2002) 'Bi-Gay, Bi-Straight, and Bi-Bi: Three Bisexual Subgroups Identified using Cluster Analysis of the Klein Sexual Orientation Grid', *Journal of Bisexuality*, 2(4): 109–139.

Weise, E.R. (1992) *Closer to Home: Bisexuality and Feminism*. Seattle, WA: Seal Press.

Welzer-Lang, D. (2008) 'Speaking Out Loud About Bisexuality: Biphobia in the Gay and Lesbian Community', *Journal of Bisexuality*, 8(1–2): 81–95.

Werum, R. and Winders, B. (2001) 'Who's "In" and Who's "Out": State Fragmentation and the Struggle over Gay Rights, 1974–1999', *Social Problems*, 48(3): 386–410.

Whittle, S. (2006) 'Foreword', in S. Stryker and S. Whittle (eds) *The Transgender Studies Reader*. New York and Abingdon: Routledge.

Whittle, S., Turner, L. and Al-Alami, M. (2007) *Engendered Penalties: Transgender and Transsexual People's Experiences of Inequality and Discrimination*. London: The Equalities Review.

Wilchins, R.A. (1997) *Read My Lips: Sexual Subversion and the End of Gender*. Ann Arbor, MI: Firebrand Books.

Williams, H.H.S. (2008) 'A Bisex-Queer Critique of Same-Sex Marriage Advocacy', *Journal of Bisexuality*, 7(3–4): 313–318.

Williams, P. and Chrisman, L. (eds) (1993) *Colonial Discourse and Post-Colonial Theory*. Harlow: Longman.

Williams, Z. (2014) 'Beyond Muesli', *Guardian*, 1 November: 39–45.

Wilson, A.R. (2000) *Below the Belt: Sexuality, Religion and the American South*. London: Cassell.

Wilson, A.R. (2009) 'The "Neat Concept" of Sexual Citizenship: a Cautionary Tale for Human Rights Discourse', *Contemporary Politics*, 15(1): 73–85.

Wilson, F.M. (2003) *Organizational Behaviour and Gender* (2nd ed.). Aldershot: Ashgate Publishing Ltd.

Wolff, C. (1979) *Bisexuality: A Study*. London: Quartet.

Wright, L.W., Bonita, A.G. and Mulick, P.S. (2011) 'An Update and Reflections on Fear of and Discrimination against Bisexuals, Homosexuals, and Individuals with AIDS', *Journal of Bisexuality*, 11: 458–464.

Yip, AK-T. (2010) 'Coming Home from the Wilderness: An Overview of Recent Scholarly Research on LGBTQI Religiosity/Spirituality in the West', in K. Browne, S.R. Munt and AK-T. Yip (eds) *Queer Spiritual Spaces: Sexuality and Sacred Places*. Surrey: Ashgate.

Yockney, J. (2013) 'The BiCon 2013 Survey Report', available at: http://www.biphoria.org.uk/bicon_survey_report_2013.pdf.

Yun, K., Xu, J.J., Reilly, K.H., Zhang, J., Jiang, Y.J., Wang, N. and Shang, H. (2012) 'Prevalence of Bisexual Behaviour among Bridge Population of Men who have Sex with Men in China: A Meta-Analysis of Observational Studies', *Sexually Transmitted Infections*, 87: 567–570.

Yuval-Davis, N. (2006) 'Intersectionality and Feminist Politics', *European Journal of Women's Studies*, 13(3): 193–210.

Zahiruddin, Q.S., Gaidhane, A.M., Shanbhag, S. and Zodpey, S.P. (2011) 'High Risk Sexual Partnerships and Condom use among Truckers entering Mumbia City', *International Journal of Biological and Medical Research*, 2(4): 938–941.

Zea, M.C., Reisen, C.A., Bianchi, F.T., Gonzales, F.A., Betancourt, F., Aguilar M. and Poppen, P.J. (2013) 'Armed Conflict, Homonegativity and Forced Internal Displacement: Implications for HIV among Colombian Gay, Bisexual and Transgender Individuals', *Culture, Health & Sexuality: An International Journal for Research, Intervention and Care*, 15(7): 788–803.

Index

Adam, B., 143
Adkins, L., 85
African, 10, 60, 80
   American, 20, 25
Ahmed, S., 51, 77
AIDS activism, 43, 167
Al-Fatiha, 76
Allsworth, J. E., 17
Altman, D., 17
anarchism
   bisexual activism, 148, 176
   citizenship framework, 146–8, 154
   counter-publics, 44, 111
Anderlini-D'Onofrio, S., 98
Anderson, E., 16, 23, 27
Andrijasevic, R., 136
Angelides, S., 3, 12, 13, 14, 43, 44, 45
Anon, 63, 90
anticategorical approaches (intersectionality theory), 61–2, 77–8, 82–3
anti-commercialism, 95
anti-hierarchy, 95
Apphia, K., 68, 71
Arden, K., 90
Ardila, R., 158, 159
asexuality/asexual, 7, 86, 97, 102, 121–2, 141, 143–4, 177
assimilationism
   citizenship framework, 135, 147–8
   in Colombia, 176
   feminism vs., 143
   lesbian and gay activism, 143
   reformist politics, 143–4
   trends, 29, 120, 177
asylum seeker, 65, 78, 82
Atkins, D., 16, 39
Ault, A., 167
autobiographical material, 8, 39, 70–2
autonomy, 140, 167

Badgett, L., 51
Balding, C., 21
Banerjee, P., 70, 71, 72
Barker, M., 6, 16, 21, 22, 23, 26, 27, 50, 60, 90, 106, 112, 113, 115, 118, 127, 149, 167, 168
Bauer, R., 18, 91
BDSM, *see* bondage, domination, submission, and masochism (BDSM)
Beeker, C., 17
Beemyn, B., 18
Bell, D., 57, 140, 141, 142
Bennett, K., 23, 27
Berlant, L., 140
Bi Academic Intervention, 16
biphobia/biphobic, 5–6, 13, 23–7, 31, 37, 40–2, 52–5, 64, 76, 80–1, 89, 94, 103–4, 112–13, 115–17, 122, 124, 131–2, 149, 153–4, 166, 168–9, 172–6
Bi Community News, 90, 167
BiCon (bisexual conference)
   activists and academics, 174
   alternative families, 91–2
   BDSM environment, 102–3, 106
   behaviours characteristic, 96
   class issues, 74
   denial of asylum, 65
   diversity awareness, 73
   first national conference, 167
   group identity, 97
   habitus type, 95–6
   monthly meeting, 94
   pluralist approach, 156
   public/private dynamics, 138–9
   racism, 78–80, 82
   safer sex culture, 91
   sexual rights agendas, 93
   subcultures, 178
   themes in 2014, 176
   universalism, 151
   volunteer counselling, 90

Index

BiFest, 78–9, 95–7, 167
Binnie, J., 57, 58, 140, 141, 142
BiReCon (Bisexual Research Convention), 167–8, 174
Bis of Colour, 79–80, 82, 168, 174
bisexual activism, 29–30, 37, 138, 146, 148, 154, 157–60, 162, 164–7, 169–71, 174–5, 177–8
bisexual communities
  alternative definitions, 102
  Anglophone, 18
  care culture, 90–3
  Catholicism, 76
  citizenship discourse, 29, 145
  class structure, 74
  in Colombia, 161–2
  cultural norms and values, 84, 86, 100
  divergences issues, 103, 105–6, 168–9
  erotic communities, 98–100
  faith-related prejudices, 74
  gender variance, 100–2
  habitus, 96, 98, 103
  identity politics, 78
  literature on, 17
  middle and upper class women, 69
  1998–2014, 6
  organised, 6
  public/private divide, 139
  queer activism, 44–5
  racism, 75, 78–83
  safer sex practices, 91
  set of fields, 93–5, 108
  sexual identities and expressions, 106–7
  shared identity issues, 95
  UK organisations, 57, 59, 62, 85, 111, 134–5, 138, 144, 162, 176
  in the USA, 85
  whiteness, 78–83
Bisexuales Unidos (Bisexuals United), 160–1
Bisexualidad: De la Tercería a la Ruptura de Dicotomías (García), 155
Bisexual Index, 112, 167, 174
bisexuality
  academic marginalisation, 2
  biphobia, 23–7
  citizenship, 29
  commodification, 7, 28–9
  cross-cultural context, 9–11
  definition, 18–23
  early theories, 14–16
  intersectionality, 28
  key literatures, 16–18
  kinship and community, 28
  origin of the term, 11–14
  political science of, 29–30
  prejudices against, 5
  qualitative interviews (UK research), 6
  social theory and, 27–8
  stigmatisation, 1
  subgroups ('Bi-Gay,' 'Bi-Straight,' and 'Bi-Bi'), 15
  temporality, 3–4
  in workplace organisation, 28–9
  see also queer theory
The Bisexuality Report: Bisexual Inclusion in LGBT Equality and Diversity (Barker), 168
Bisexuality: A Study (Wolff), 15
Bisexuality: What's It All About? (Mead), 15
Bisexual Media Watch, 127
Bishop, P., 4
BiUK, 168, 174
black and minority ethnic (BME) people
  at BiCon, 79–80
  class intersection, 81
  intersectional marginalisation, 81, 116
  intracategorical theory, 63
  UK convention, 75–8, 82
  in Western countries, 65
  whiteness and, 59
Blackwood, E., 2, 10, 16
Blumer, H., 32, 33
body, first territory of peace, The (Paz), 160
Bogotá City Council, 162
Bogotá LGBT pride parade, 162
bondage, domination, submission, and masochism (BDSM), 5, 7–9, 18, 80, 84, 87, 91–2, 97–103, 106–8, 129, 139

Index 199

Boone, J. A., 10
Boris, E., 98, 128
Bouchard, J. W., 66
Bourdieu, P., 3, 85, 94, 95
Bowes-Catton, H., 16
Brah, A., 58
Braun, V., 7
Braziel, J. E., 16
Breno, A. L., 89
Brickell, C., 32, 33, 34, 39, 51
Brown, K. M., 57, 111, 128, 140
Browne, K., 57, 128
Bryant, K., 24
Bryant, W., 16
Butler, J., 32, 43

Cahill, S., 90
Caldwell, K., 57, 58
Callis, A. S., 32, 44
Cantarella, E., 14
Capiola, A., 109
capitalism, 12, 28, 109, 111
Carbado, D. W., 58
Casey, M. E., 51, 105
Cashmore, C., 27
celibacy/celibate, 86, 122, 141, 177
Cerny, J. A., 16
Chakrapani, V., 66, 67, 68, 69, 70
Chamberlain, B., 112, 113, 118
Chapman, R., 90
Charter of Fundamental Rights of the European Union (EU Charter), 165–6
Chinese, 7, 76–7, 119
Cho, S., 58
Chrisman, L., 13
cisgender/cis, 9–10, 22, 69, 139, 144
citizenship
  bisexual issues, 29, 133, 135–6
  concept, 152
  definition, 133
  disability and elder, bisexuals, 152
  dominant models, 138
  existing literature, 153
  feminist approaches, 136–7, 139
  heteronormativity models, 142–6
  homonationalism, 65
  intimate issues, 138, 140–2
  liberal approaches, 135
  lived experiences, 85
  neoliberalism, 120
  particularist approaches, 149–50, 152–3
  public and private sphere, 137–9
  queer, 146–7
  radical *vs.* assimilationist politics, 148
  sexual, 140–3, 149–51, 153–4
  traditional models, 134, 137, 154
  transgender, 139–40
  universalist approaches, 148–51
Clarke, V., 7
Colgan, F., 109, 111
Collins, H., 27, 127
Colombia
  bisexual activism, 29, 157–60, 171
  bisexual groups and organisations, 161–2
  bisexuality analysis, 163–5, 174–9
  context-specific bisexualities, 66, 149
  first specific study, 155
  intersectional construction of sexuality, 60
  legal measures (LGBT people)-9, 158
  LGB or LGBT acronyms, 156, 160
  LGBT movement, 161
  LGT community in, 25
  participants characteristics, 8
  political actions, 163
  radio shows, 162
  sexual identity roots, 158
commercialism, 105–6
commodification, 7, 29, 109, 120–1, 123–7, 131
constructionism, 34–6
  see also social constructionism
Cook, J. A., 57
Cooper, D., 18, 140
Corrales, J., 17, 155
Cossman, B., 142
Craig, S., 127
Crenshaw, K. W., 58
Cronin, A., 58

cross-cultural context, bisexuality
  egalitarian same-sex relationships, 10
  gender role variance, 9–10
  initiatory relationships, 10
Currah, P., 155

Davies, D., 57
Davis, K., 58
de Jong, A., 65
Delanty, G., 134
Delphy, C., 51
D'Emilio, J., 167
Dennis, A., 43
desexualisation, 110, 120
Dimensión Bi, 162
DIY sexualities, 125, 130
Doble Vía (Two ways), 162
Dodge, B., 17, 20, 91, 99
Doll, L. S., 17
domesticisation, 107, 110, 120
Downing, L., 44
Dua, R., 71
Dugan, K. B., 17
Du Plessis, M., 3
Duyvendak, J. W., 143

Egan, J. E., 58
Eisner, S., 3, 37, 59
Ekins, R., 48
Eliason, M., 18
Ellis, H. H., 14
employment
  agendas and rights, 131, 149
  bisexual people's experiences, 52, 109–11, 117–19
  capitalist imperatives, 120
  gender roles, 12, 50–1
  precariousness, 115–16
  workplace biphobias, 113, 176
Epprecht, M., 9, 10, 12, 19
Epstein, S., 167
equalities-positive countries, 1
  see also UK (United Kingdom)
Equality Act 2010, 165–6
Erel, U., 136
erotophobia/erotophobic, 24

essentialism, 14, 33–6, 61
ethnicity, 13, 19, 28, 57, 59–60, 72, 74–5, 77, 79, 82, 152
Evans, D., 51, 110, 135, 141

Faderman, L., 18
Fahs, B., 120, 125, 126
faith, 75–7, 79, 81–3, 165
Fajardo, L., 159
Fausto-Sterling, A., 49
Fee, A., 48
Feinberg, L., 64, 103
Feixa, C., 58
feminism
  anti-essentialist thinking, 51
  assimilationists, 143
  black thinking, 58, 82
  Butler's notion of performativity, 32
  cisgender females, 139
  grassroot activists, 71
  on intersectionality, 58
  LGBT issues, 155–6
  literature about new forms of family, 84
  materialist framework, 110, 125
  political organising, 167
  on sexual citizenship, 29, 134–7, 142, 153–4
fetish club organisers, 9, 111
Firestein, B. A., 16, 94
Foucault, M., 12
Fox, R. C., 9, 10, 16, 64
Fraser, N., 176
Freedman, E., 167

Gagnon, J., 32, 33, 34, 39, 41
Galupo, M. P., 89
Galvis, J., 156, 161, 162
Ganesh, M., 71, 72
Garcia, O., 155, 160
Garfinkel, H., 33
gay men
  AIDS activism, 167
  biphobia, 23, 25, 27, 131, 168–9
  bisexuality *vs.*, 51
  bisexual movement (UK), 178–9
  citizenship rights, 143
  commercialism, 105
  formal equality, 165

inclusion by networks, 104
in India, 71
kinship and care, 90
mononormative element, 106
'out' partnered, 92
safer sex practices, 91, 104
sex workers, 128
static identities, 3, 26
stigmatisation, 1, 18, 118, 160
trans studies, 48
UK acronym, 112, 149, 155
Gelder, K., 81, 96, 97
genderqueer, 7, 48–9
George, S., 16
Getting Bi: Voices of Bisexuals Around the World (Ochs and Rowley), 70
Gibbs, G. R., 6
Giddens, A., 126
Gillett, R., 44
Girls Gone Wild (films), 127
Goggin, K., 20, 99
Gosine, A., 20
Green, H. B., 37, 114, 118
Greene, B., 25

Hall, D. E., 12, 43, 44
Hardy, K., 128
Head, S., 85
Hearn, J., 109, 140, 141, 149, 152
Hemmings, C., 3, 16, 26, 27, 51, 167
Herdt, G. H., 11, 16
heterosexism, 16, 52, 64, 81, 94, 110, 129
Highleyman, L. A., 16, 17
Hines, S., 43, 48, 51, 84, 90, 91, 110
Hird, M., 51
homophobia/homophobic, 13, 24, 27, 54, 64–5, 67, 76, 116–17, 168, 172, 176
homosexuality
  anti-LGBT countries, 134
  biphobia, 26–7, 116
  bisexuality *vs.*, 19, 24–5, 65, 139, 150
  in Christianity, 77
  class identity and, 117
  empirical research, 15
  European systems, 5
  Gender pluralist theory, 50
  hierarchical structures, 15–16
  historical contextualisation, 9–11
  human right concerns, 166
  in India, 67, 71
  Islamic faith, 63
  19th century categorisation, 13–14
  passive partnership, 10
  punitive laws, 1
  Queer theory, 44–5
  recognition issues, 177
  social construction, 12
  typology, 18
  in UK, 166–7
Honneth, A., 176
Hooks, B., 51
Horncastle, J., 45
Hudson, J. H., 21
Hurtado, A., 58
Hutchins, L., 16, 39, 85, 93, 98
hypersexuality/hypersexual, 28–9, 42, 52, 110, 120–2, 124–5, 127, 129–32
hypersexualisation, 29, 42, 52, 110, 121–2, 127, 131–2

India
  alternative sexualities, 68–9
  biphobic laws, 64
  bisexualities, 57, 66–8, 70–2
  case study, 83
  female bisexuals, 69
  gender role variance, 10, 66–7
  hijra, 20
  Hindu cultural norms, 68
  identity-based male bisexuality, 69
  intersectionality theory, 82
  Kothis and panthis, 70
  MSM in, 67–8
  non-heterosexual sexualities, 66
  particularist approach, 149
  post-structural approaches, 4
  research methods, 5
  sex/gender categorisation, 13, 66, 150
  sexual variance, 71
  socioeconomic class, 69–70
  themes, research, 8
  web analysis, sexualities, 6

Index

The Institute for Participation and Community Action (IDPAC), 162
interactionist theory
  anticategorical approaches vs., 61
  anti-essentialist position, 34
  construction of bisexual identities, 27
  on cultural and social practices, 95
  intercategorical complexity, 62
  negative social effects, 42
  on physiological realities, 36
  social discomfort, 41
  social labels, 46
  social strands, 31–2
  structural approach, 52, 56
  thought, varieties, 33
  workplace bisexualities, 111
intercategorical approaches (intersectionality theory), 61–3, 66, 72–3, 82–3
intersex, 7, 48, 66–7, 69
intimate citizenship, 29, 85, 134, 138, 140–2, 146, 153–4
intracategorical approaches (intersectionality theory), 61–3, 66, 72, 76, 81–3
intrapsychic processes, 31, 34, 39–40
invisibility, 42, 46–7, 59, 115, 127, 154, 169–70, 176
Itaborahy, L. P., 1, 55, 134

Jackson, S., 17, 32
James, C., 26, 27
Janssen, E., 16
Jefferson, F., 51
Jeffries, W. L., 91
Jenkins, R., 3, 24, 85, 94
Jeppesen, S., 43, 44, 111
Jivraj, S., 65
Jones, T., 16
Juang, R. M., 119
Jules, 127

Kaahamanu, L., 93
Keeble, S. E., 112
Kessler, S., 33
Khan, S., 66, 68, 69, 70
Kidwai, S., 4
King, A., 58
Kinsey, A. C., 15
Klein, F., 15
Klein Sexual Orientation Grid (KSOG), 15, 19
Klesse, C., 6, 18, 22, 24, 45, 57, 58, 176
Köllen, T., 114
Kollman, K., 17, 143, 150, 151, 156, 165
Krawel, A., 143
Kumar, K. A., 66

Landers, S., 91
Langdridge, D., 16, 26
Lano, K., 17
Lee, J. C. H., 157
Lee, M. V., 51
lesbian, gay, bisexual, and transgender (LGBT)
  acronym, 18, 23, 112, 138, 144, 156
  affinity-based group, 118
  assimilationism, 143
  biphobia, 24
  in Christianity, 76, 175
  citizenship rights, 134
  in Colombia, 158–65, 171
  Colombian movement, 29–30, 178–9
  colonial prejudices, 64–5
  forms of discrimination, 53
  homonationalism issues, 65
  in India, 71
  international context, 1–2
  issues in the USA and Canada, 155
  Latin American politics, 17
  online communities and resources, 49
  organisations in UK, 168
  problematic terminology, 20
  sex workers, 128
  social context, 18, 150
  in UK, 77, 82, 103
  umbrella term, 45
  universalist approach, 148–9, 151
  workplace activisms, 114, 116, 118–19
  workplace network, 172–4

lesbians
  acronym, 156
  African American, 25
  agendas and issues (UK), 169
  AIDS activism, 167
  biphobia, 23, 27, 104, 124, 168
  care and intimacy, 90
  in Christianity, 76
  citizenship rights, 143, 150
  Colombian activism, 160–1, 175, 179
  commercialism, 105
  domesticisation, 107
  equality issues, 112, 165
  in India, 69, 71
  international context, 25
  lifestyle politics, 167
  materialist analysis, 51
  parents, 92
  patriarchal dominance, 123
  safer sex packs, 104
  sex workers, 128
  social category, 48
  social exclusion, 53
  socio-economic class, 131
  specific identities and concerns, 155
  static identities, 3
  stigmatisation, 1, 18, 118
  UK policy, 26
LGBH identities, 101
LGBT activism, 160, 163
Lister, R., 137, 149, 150, 152
Lofgren-Martenson, L., 57
Lombardo, E., 136
Lorber, J., 48
Lustiger-Thaler, H., 143

MacDowell, L., 5, 11
Married Men who have Sex with Men (MMSM), 21
Marshall, T. H., 133
Martin, P. J., 43
Matteson, D. R., 111
McCaghy, C. H., 128
McCall, L., 57, 58, 61, 62, 63, 82, 83
McCormack, M., 16, 58

McGrath, S., 127
McIntosh, M., 33
McKenna, W., 33
McLaughlin, J., 51
McLean, K., 23
McLelland, M., 17
Mead, G. H., 32
Mead, M., 15
media
  bisexual erasure, 26
  bisexual role models, 37
  commodification of bisexuality, 109, 124–5
  hypersexualised bisexualities, 120–1
  lesbian terminology, 122
  portrayal of bisexuality, 126–8
  social, 76
  stigmatisation, 117
  workplace contexts, 111
Meier, P., 136
Men who have Sex with Men (MSM), 17, 20–1, 24, 58, 67–8, 85, 98–9
Men who have Sex with Men and Women (MSMW), 21, 24, 67–8, 85
Milton, M., 85
Mishra, A. K., 66, 68
Mitchell, M., 19, 20
monogamous/monogamy, 40, 42, 49, 65, 68, 86, 92, 97, 102, 122, 136, 138, 142, 144–5, 166, 177
mononormativity, 27, 42, 45, 52, 94, 105–7, 110, 142, 146
monosexism, 27
monosexual/monosexuality, 6, 15, 61, 136
Monro, S., 1, 4, 8, 16, 17, 24, 26, 32, 35, 46, 48, 50, 51, 57, 64, 69, 72, 85, 103, 107, 109, 110, 111, 112, 118, 133, 136, 137, 138, 139, 140, 141, 142, 143, 145, 156, 157, 165, 171
Morrow, K. M., 17
Mujeres al Borde (Women on the Border), 160
Mulick, P. S., 16, 24
multiple sexualities, 53
Murray, S., 10

Nandi, D. N., 67
National University of Colombia, 162
Nilan, P., 58
Noel, M. J., 58
nonheterosexualities, 5, 9, 53

Ochs, R., 8, 23, 70, 89
Organisational Change, Resistance and Democracy (project), 112
Organisations, *see* workplace organisations
Owen, M., 24

pansexual/pansexuality, 21, 101, 127
Parkin, W., 109
participatory democracy, 165, 173–4
Pateman, C., 137
patriarchy, 64, 122–3
Pecheney, M., 17, 155
Pettaway, L., 19
Peumans, W., 58, 65, 76
Phelan, S., 9, 140
Phillips, A. E., 68, 150
Phoenix, A., 58
Planeta Paz, 159, 160
Plummer, K., 17, 18, 32, 33, 36, 40, 44, 52, 84, 85, 134, 137, 140, 141
Politics of Bisexuality, The (BiCon Conference), 167
polyamory/polyamorous, 38, 49
pornography, 29, 38, 41, 121, 126, 128–31
Pramaggiore, M., 44
Prideaux, S., 84
Prieto, C., 158
Profiles of Prejudice: The Nature of Prejudice in England: In-Depth Analysis of Findings (UK policy-related literature), 26
promiscuity/promiscuous, 23, 87, 106, 110, 122, 127, 130, 132
psychiatrists, 135
psychologists, 135
psychosexual hermaphroditism, 14
Puar, J. K., 65
PUCL-K., 67, 69
Putnam, R., 86

queer politics, 22, 43, 147, 176
queer theory
  criticisms, 47
  deconstruction of identities, 44, 46, 56
  degendering approach, 62
  identity categories, 18, 31
  interactionism, 32
  multiplicity and complexity of identities, 43
  origin of the term 'queer', 46
  polymorphic analytic category, 45
  structural discrimination, 55
  symbolic emphasis, 52
  transgression, 50
  vanguard nature, 46–7

racism, 25, 51, 59, 72, 74–5, 78–83, 98
Radio Diversia, 162
Ramakrishnan, L. R., 66, 68, 70, 71
Ramasubban, R., 67, 68, 69
Ravikumar, A. V., 66
Reddy, G., 68
Reddy, V., 140
Rembis, M. A., 57
Republic of Colombia, 158
Revenge (show), 127
Richardson, D., 1, 16, 17, 19, 26, 51, 64, 72, 85, 103, 107, 109, 110, 111, 112, 118, 133, 136, 137, 138, 140, 141, 142, 143, 145, 146, 156, 157, 165, 171
Riggle, E. D. B., 17, 156
Robinson, M., 16
Robinson, V., 19
Roscoe, W., 10
Rose, S., 16
Rouhani, F., 64, 76
Rowley, S. E., 8, 70
Roy, Ahonaa, 8, 69, 70, 72
Ruspini, E., 84, 91
Rust, P. C., 12, 16, 19, 85

Safra, 64, 82
Salazar, L., 64, 156, 160, 161, 162
same-sex sexualities, 1, 9, 11, 64, 67–8, 86, 118, 125, 127, 150–1, 153, 170
see also homosexuality

Sanabria, F., 155, 160
Sandbrook, R., 157
Sanders, E., 123
Sandfort, T., 17, 20, 99
San Francisco Human Rights Commission LGBT Advisory Committee, 20, 21, 24–5
Sanger, T., 43, 48
Scott, S., 17, 32
Seabrook, J., 67
Sedgewick, E. K., 17, 43, 44
Seidman, S., 17, 43, 51, 103
Sentido Bisexual, 161–2
Serrano, F., 2, 156, 157, 158, 159, 160
sex industry, 110–11, 129
sexism, 25, 27, 51, 131, 146
sexologists, 13–14, 16, 31, 135
sexual citizenship, 140–3, 149–51, 153–4
sexual desires, 3, 26, 32, 141
sexual identities
  'fixing and naming,' 1
  Klein Sexual Orientation Grid (KSOG), 15, 19
  primitive races, 14
  social context, 4
  Victorian times, 12
sexual orientations, 2, 9, 159, 163
sexual services, 86, 120, 124, 128–32
Shakespeare, T., 57
Sharma, A. K., 66, 68
Shyamantha, A., 68
Simon, W., 32, 33, 34, 39
Sinha, M., 58
Skeggs, B., 85
Skipper, J. K. Jr., 128
Smith, M., 17, 155
social constructionism, 31, 33
social exclusion, 53
social marginalisation, 46, 54, 62, 71, 125
social scientists, 3, 135
social theory
  bisexuality, 27–8
  constructionism, 34–6
  essentialism, 34–6
  identity process, 39–40
  interactionism, 32–4
  interpersonal construction of identities, 36–8
  sexual desire, 38–9
  social erasure, 42–3
  unintelligibility, 41–2
Sprinkle, A., 98
Steinman, E., 16, 44, 46, 51, 52
Stekel, W., 15
Storr, M., 3, 11, 12, 14, 15, 17, 19
Strachey, J., 14
Suganama, K., 17

Tadlock, B. L., 17, 156
Tarrow, S., 176
Taylor, Y., 51, 57, 85, 105
Thomas, B., 13, 67, 68, 114
Thornton, S., 81, 96, 97
Tobias, S., 90
Toft, A., 74, 76
Towards a Quaker View of Sex (Wigmore), 167
Towle, C., 113, 114
transgender
  care and intimacy, 90
  citizenship, 139–40, 153
  in Colombia, 162–4, 175
  commodification, 124
  destabilisation of gender binaries, 47–51
  movement, 156, 160
  queer politics, 22
  social institutions, 143
  social theory, 27
  visibility, 21
transvestites (TVs), 101
Treaty on European Union (TEU), 165
Tremblay, M., 18, 156
Triangulo Negro (Black Triangle), 160
Tuason, T. G., 27

UK (United Kingdom)
  activism, 171–3
  affirmative approach, bisexuality, 16
  agendas and issues, 169–71

UK (United Kingdom) – *continued*
  BiCon (Bisexual conference in 2014), 65
  biphobia, 27, 54, 116–17
  bisexuality, 28–9, 39
  commodification, 120–6
  definitions of bisexuality, 18
  equalities-positive countries, 1, 55
  faith communities, 75–6
  gender rules, 33
  hypersexualisation, 121–4
  intersectionality approaches, 28, 72–3
  key literature, 16
  lesbian and gay movement, 29
  LGBT categories, 71, 77
  master identity, 77
  organised bisexual communities, 57, 59, 62
  participants characteristics, 7, 35, 48–9, 52
  qualitative study, 27, 32, 53
  queer identities, 18, 45–6
  race categories, 75
  research methods and findings, 5–6, 19–22, 25, 34, 42, 44, 47
  sexual diversity, 36, 38
  sexual rights, 103–4
  themes, research, 8
  unintelligibility (social awkwardness), 41
  white-domination, 60
  workplace experience, 111–16
UK Department of Work and Pensions, 174
UNICEF, 63
UNISON (trade union), 113–15
USA
  bisexual communities, 85
  bisexuals life experiences, 28
  black feminists, 82
  discrimination, 131
  'Down Low' (DL) lifestyle, 19–20, 99
  expanded model of sexuality, 98
  gender rules, 33
  Human Potential Movement, 98
  key literatures, 16
  LGBT categories (colonial period), 64
  LGBT issues, 155
  neoliberalism, 130
  queer Muslim group, 76
  race categories, 75
  research methods, 5
  rights of sexual minorities, 16
  safer sex practices, 91
  types of sexual identity, 108
  workplace context, 111, 117–19

Vanita, R., 4
Vidal-Ortiz, S., 24
Viveros, M., 155, 160

Waites, M., 17, 64, 68, 143, 150, 156, 165
Walker, A., 86
Walker, P., 167
Ward, J., 20
Ward, L., 168
Warner, M., 17, 18, 43
Warren, L., 139
Webb, J., 24, 86, 95
Weeks, J., 14, 17, 33, 115, 140, 167
Weinberg, G., 24
Weinberg, M. S., 16, 117, 118
Weinrich, J. D., 15
Weise, E. R., 16
Welzer-Lang, D., 23
Werum, R., 155
whiteness, 58–9, 72, 75, 78–83
  see also racism
Whittle, S., 46, 50, 51
Wilchins, R. A., 51
Williams, H. H. S., 107
Williams, P., 13
Williams, Z., 129
Wilson, A. R., 57, 76, 140
Wilson, F. M., 109, 110
Winders, B., 155
Wolff, C., 15
Women who have Sex with Men and Women (WSMW), 21, 67

Women who have Sex with
  Women (WSW),
  21, 67
workplace activisms, 113–15
workplace organisations, 3,
  28, 109–10, 116–17,
  130
Wright, L. W., 16, 24

Yip, AK-T., 65
Yockney, J., 73, 94, 111
Yun, K., 17, 85
Yuval-Davis, N., 58

Zahiruddin, Q. S., 68, 70
Zea, M. C., 157, 159
Zhu, J., 1, 55, 134